GRIEVING REPRODUCTIVE LOSS: THE HEALING PROCESS

Kathleen Gray
Founder and President
Centre for Reproductive Loss

Anne Lassance
Co-Founder and Vice-President
Centre for Reproductive Loss

D1522012

Death, Value and Meaning Series
Series Editor: John D. Morgan

Baywood Publishing Company, Inc.
AMITYVILLE, NEW YORK

Baywood Publishing Company, Inc.
26 Austin Ave.
Amityville, NY 11701
(800) 638-7819
E-mail: baywood@baywood.com
Web site://baywood.com

Library of Congress Catalog Number: 2002035622
ISBN: 0-89503-227-9 (cloth)

Library of Congress Cataloging-in-Publication Data

Gray, Kathleen, 1940-
    Grieving reproductive loss : the healing process / Kathleen Gray, Anne Lassance.
        p. cm. -- (Death, value, and meaning series)
    Includes bibliographical references and index.
    ISBN 0-89503-227-9 (cloth : alk. paper)
        1. Perinatal death--Psychological aspects. 2. Miscarriage--Psychological aspects. 3. Abortion--Psychological aspects. 4. Infertility--Psychological aspects. 5. Grief therapy. 6. Bereavement--Psychological aspects. 7. Loss (Psychology) I. Lassance, Anne, 1930- II. Title. III. Series

RG631 .G735 2002
618.3'92'019--dc21   2002035622

Many citations were taken from J. W. Worden, *Grief Counseling & Grief Therapy*, Springer, New York, 1991. Springer Publishing Company, Inc., New York, 10012, used by permission.

Dedication

To all who grieve the loss of a child

To those bereaved individuals who gave us the honor and privilege of sharing in their grief and who have taught us so much

To their precious babies who are gone but not forgotten

Table of Contents

CHAPTER 10

Foreword

One in four pregnancies ends in miscarriage; stillbirth, one in eighty pregnancies. As many as one out of six couples experience problems of infertility. In the United States over one million elective abortions are performed each year, and more than one hundred thousand in Canada.

The grief associated with such reproductive losses is often minimized, denied, and considered to be outside the normal "grieving rules" of society. Yet individuals who have suffered these losses can experience profound grief and emotional pain. Their grief needs to be acknowledged not only by themselves but by others as well.

Grieving Reproductive Loss: The Healing Process acknowledges the devastating impact these losses can have. Written in "plain language," the book attempts to bring about a greater understanding of the grief associated with reproductive loss and, through the Healing Process Model$^{\copyright}$, offers a holistic approach for constructive healthy grieving and healing of body, mind, and spirit.

The Healing Process Model$^{\copyright}$ is especially helpful for individuals who have suffered a reproductive loss because it is derived from their experiences of loss and grief, which differs from some existing models of grief developed in studies of widows and widowers. Bereaved parents present a special challenge due to the uniqueness of parental grief: not only have they experienced a reproductive loss and the tragic death of a child, but also the loss of part of themselves, the loss of a future life with that child, and the loss of hopes and dreams. The guidelines of the Healing Process Model$^{\copyright}$ can be used for recognizing, acknowledging and intervening in reproductive loss by the bereaved themselves, by friends and family of the bereaved, as well as by health care providers whether or not trained in grief care.

Preface

This book is a labor of love and a response to the urgings of clients, colleagues, and friends. We were encouraged especially by bereaved clients who wanted us to tell their stories of grief in order to bring about a greater understanding of the impact of reproductive loss. Such devastating losses include miscarriage, stillbirth, abortion, giving up a child for adoption, SIDS (sudden infant death syndrome), infertility, sterility, or life situations which precluded having children. In our ten years of clinical practice providing counseling and grief care education through the Centre for Reproductive Loss, bereaved individuals have taught us much, sharing their thoughts, tears, and feelings, as we walked with them on their grieving/healing journey. In using examples from their stories, dynamics, and healing interventions, clinical integrity has been preserved, sometimes by changing details to protect identity or by constructing a representative picture with components from several different situations.

Recognizing the need to respond to the pain and suffering of individuals who had experienced reproductive loss, as health care practitioners we felt obligated to address this issue. Hence, through the collaborative brainstorming efforts of Kathleen Gray, Anne Lassance, and colleague Nancy Paré, the Centre for Reproductive Loss was founded in 1992 in Montreal, Quebec, Canada, as a charitable, non-denominational organization. It was a project whose time had come. Health care providers, especially nurses and social workers having direct contact with and responsibility for women and for families dealing with these losses, referred clients to the Centre and requested workshops for colleagues to broaden their understanding of grief and reproductive loss. In response to their requests, the Centre offered workshops and seminars which were enthusiastically received. The format of the seminars became the basis for the book and for the development of the Healing Process Model$^{©}$.

The book is written in "plain language" to make it readily understandable especially for those who are grieving a loss. It is not a "how to" book of rigid rules, but rather one which provides guidelines not only for the layperson, in particular friends and families of the bereaved, but also for those health care providers not trained in grief care education. Bereaved individuals wanting to read about grief have often said that they can do so only in small doses. Keeping this in mind, the chapters were written in such a way that, while they are related, many of them can also stand alone in order to facilitate use by parents exhausted in grieving. This format also facilitates reading by the busy health care provider seeking some specific information without having to read sequentially from beginning to end. Repetition will be found in the text. This was purposefully done to elaborate on a concept or to show the application of the concept in a variety of clinical situations. While the authors shared ideas, offered suggestions and critiques throughout the writing of the book, the individual chapters were written independently. Kathleen Gray wrote Chapters 1, 2, 3, 4, 5, 6, and 10; Anne Lassance wrote Chapters 7, 8, and 9.

Finally a word about the uniqueness of parental grief and the Healing Process Model© described in Chapter 3. Parents who have suffered the tragic death of a child have not only experienced the loss of the child but also the loss of part of themselves, the loss of a future life with that child, the loss of hopes and dreams, as well as the collapse of their assumptive world. Dennis Klass, in his book *Parental Grief: Solace and Resolution,* has wisely pointed out that bereaved parents present a special challenge because "parental bereavement has more intense symptoms and different expectable problems" [1, p. 176]. This challenge to the clinician or researcher is most evident when models of grief which were developed in studies of widows and widowers are applied to parents who have experienced the death of a child. He further explains that "the time tables and expectable problems which are current in the field are based on conjugal bereavement" [1, p. 176]. Therese A. Rando has also recognized that same challenge of parental grief and wrote about it in the book *Parental Loss of a Child*: "Bereaved parents often will be construed as having failed to appropriately complete their grief work according to the general model of mourning currently utilized" [2, p. 56].

It should be noted that the Healing Process Model© is not based upon those existing models of grief that were developed in studies of widows and widowers. Rather, the Healing Process Model© is derived from our clinical observations of the actual experiences of bereaved parents who have lost a child and from bereaved individuals who have struggled with other reproductive losses. This model not only provides guidelines for the bereaved (Chapter 3), for the grief counselor (Chapter 4), and for the caregiver (Chapter 10), but also it can be used as an evaluation tool (Chapter 4).

REFERENCES

1. D. Klass, *Parental Grief: Solace and Resolution,* Springer, New York, 1988.
2. T. Rando, *Parental Loss of a Child,* Research Press, Champaign, Illinois, 1986.

Kathleen Gray, R.N., M.Sc., M.Ed.
Anne Lassance, R.N., M.Ed.

Acknowledgments

An undertaking such as this book could only be completed with the encouragement and assistance of a number of people. First of all thanks to our friends and colleagues, who urged us to write the book and sustained their interest throughout the entire project. A heartfelt thank you goes to our families for their confidence in us and in the project.

Evelyn Adam, an established author in her own right and fellow health professional, greatly assisted us through careful reading of the manuscript, offering many valuable and useful suggestions for clarification; for these we are most grateful. Thanks go to Dawn Cruchet, bereavement educator, for her support and particularly for the material she provided on children and grief. Deborah Rankin was very helpful in providing information and resources through library research as well as proofreading.

Our Baywood editor, John D. Morgan, who encouraged us several years ago to write a book on this subject for publication, has shown much patience in answering our numerous questions as we worked to bring this project to completion—Thanks Jack! We also thank Baywood for their helpful and courteous staff, and Baywood's anonymous peer reviewers who carefully read the manuscript and provided thoughtful critiques and recommendations.

Many thanks are extended to Genevieve Gray Boyer who put her desktop publishing skills at our disposal and typed draft after draft of the manuscript. It is impossible to list the many ways in which Christopher Gray contributed to this work. He has spent hours typing, editing, proofreading, enabling us to find resources, and dealing with the nervous concerns of two rookie authors. Without his support this book could not have been written.

The persons mentioned above contributed directly to our work in writing this book. However, mention must be made of others who have contributed significantly if indirectly. This project grew out of the work of Kathleen Gray and Anne Lassance through the Centre for Reproductive Loss. A number of exceptional people contributed to the "care and maintenance" of the Centre, in its mission to address the grief of individuals, couples and families experiencing reproductive loss, to promote healing and health through counseling and other interventions, and to educate caregivers and the public on these grief issues.

We remember funeral director Gary Fetterly who left this life, his family, friends, and community much too soon. Gary understood the grief of parents who lost their babies and responded to their needs in many tangible and compassionate ways. He was ahead of his time in responding to this grief. Gary supported the work of the Centre fully and generously. He was, until his death, Chairman of the Board of the Centre.

As one of the co-founders of the Centre, Nancy Paré brought her sensitivity, insight, intelligence, and creativity to the work of the Centre. While Nancy has moved back to her original field of work in special education, she has left her mark at the Centre. Sheila Woodhouse has been with us right from the start, sharing her business skills, donating computer materials and skills for the Centre's benefit, and providing wise, kind advice. Suzy Fréchette-Piperni, nurse in the area of reproductive loss, encouraged us and provided a liaison to the French-speaking community in Montreal.

Mary Pat Hébert, social worker, is a colleague excellent in her field and enthusiastically supportive of our work, generous in cooperation, in helpful advice, and in material assistance. Mary Savor was one of the first donors and encouragers of the Centre. Alana Ronald continues to use her writing talents to advance the work of assisting grieving parents. Cathy Fagan, Elizabeth Stewart, Loretta O'Keefe, and Clare Soulis have always been there as friends and supporters. The outstanding generosity of David Fitzpatrick, Montreal pastor, still amazes us.

The EJLB Foundation and the Gustav Levinschi Foundation have contributed financial assistance to the Centre and this publication. The Pillars Trust Fund continues to support us, for which we are most grateful. Unfortunately, we cannot mention all of the many other generous people and groups who foster our work. But, even unacknowledged by name, they made a difference, and indirectly have helped lift the burden of grief from the brokenhearted and to educate the public as to this important need. A heartfelt thank you!

Last but certainly not least, we especially want to thank Pascale Archambault for giving us permission to use for the cover of our book, a photograph of the sculpture that she created for the children's memorial garden located in Montreal's Mt. Royal Cemetery. Her dedication reflects the essence of her creation: "I create this work for the people left behind, a peaceful reminder of the children who are no longer with us in body but whose love remains."

Kathleen Gray
Anne Lassance

CHAPTER 1

Grief: The Body, Mind, Spirit Connection

> When we honestly ask ourselves which persons in our lives mean the most to us, we often find that it is those who, instead of giving much advice, solutions, or cures, have chosen rather to share our pain and touch our wounds with a gentle and tender hand. The friend who can be silent with us in a moment of despair or confusion, who can stay with us in an hour of grief and bereavement, who can tolerate not knowing, not-curing, not-healing and face with us the reality of our powerlessness, that is the friend who cares.
>
> Henri J. M. Nouwen [1, p. 34]

"Bloody awful!" exclaimed the actor Sir Anthony Hopkins in the film *Shadowlands*, in which he portrayed C. S. Lewis who was describing the pain of his grief after the death of his wife.

This description of grief as being "bloody awful" is an emotive expression of the painful reality of what the experience of grief is, namely, "keen mental suffering or distress over affliction or loss; sharp sorrow; painful regret; anguish, heartache, woe, misery, sadness, melancholy, moroseness" [2, p. 622]. In addition to this dictionary definition, there are various ways to conceptualize grief and mourning as they appear in the grief literature. Some of these descriptions take the form of tasks, phases, stages, steps, and even symptoms. Some grief experts have argued that grief is an illness or a disease, while others oppose that theory. Some definitions have even changed over time. Dr. Glen Davidson spoke about such a change in his presentation at the October 1997 National SHARE Conference on Perinatal Bereavement in St. Louis, Missouri. He indicated that the DSM, *The Diagnostic and Statistical Manual of Mental Disorders* [3] which is the standard guide for psychiatry and mental health definitions, in its Second Edition (1968), listed characteristics of mourning as chronic displacement, delusional, or psychotic. In DSM-III and subsequent revisions, mourning is treated as a normal and necessary process. This change in the definition of mourning did not come about easily. This shift from pathology to normal process represented a great deal of professional struggle; Dr. Davidson was part of that struggle. It was largely

1

through his efforts and others like him, who also believed that mourning was a normal and necessary process, that this change finally came about.

It is not the intention of this chapter to compare, contrast, or critique various theories or descriptions of grief. That has been done elsewhere by many writers in the grief literature. While the debate continues over what grief is or is not, bereaved individuals might feel a sense of confusion when faced with numerous descriptions of grief. Would they wonder about such questions as, "Which stage am I in now?" or "This model has only four stages, but this other one has five, which one is right for me?" Perhaps the most helpful approach would be to acknowledge that each of these conceptualizations presents various perspectives on the grief experience which the bereaved can take or leave as they choose and decide for themselves what offers them help, healing, and comfort. To illustrate that point, I would like to mention briefly three examples of the stage model of grief which have appeared in the grief literature. Even though these stages are somewhat different, each of them can help explain the grief experience.

The first of these was named by John Bowlby and Colin Murray Parkes as Four Stages of Grief:

1. Shock and numbness
2. Searching and yearning
3. Disorganization
4. Reorganization [4]

In the second example, Robert Kavanaugh discussed seven stages of the grieving process in his book *Facing Death*. The seven stages are 1) shock, 2) disorganization, 3) volatile emotions, 4) guilt, 5) loss and loneliness, 6) relief, and 7) reestablishment [5, p. 107].

The third stage model of grief is based upon Dr. Elisabeth Kübler-Ross' stages of dying. These stages include denial, anger, bargaining, depression, and acceptance [6]. Over the course of time, Kübler-Ross' stages of dying have become mis-cast as stages of grief. At one of the seminars on grief and reproductive loss that Anne Lassance and I were giving for health professionals, one of the participants, a psychologist, shared her story of what she went through in her grief over being infertile.

She told how she had experienced denial, anger, bargaining, depression, and acceptance in her struggle with infertility, and thus, she could relate to what Kübler-Ross had named originally as stages of dying, but within the context of grief and loss of fertility. Any negative critique of the grief model at that time could have invalidated or minimized her source of comprehension and understanding in dealing with her loss. Fortunately, the telling of her story prevented me from doing that. All of us can learn from this example; despite differences in one model of grief over another, grieving individuals can find comfort, consolation, or common sense in many different theories or models of grief since the bereaved need all the help they can get in order to make sense out of devastating events that seem to make no sense at all.

MOURNING, GRIEVING, BEREAVEMENT

Bereavement comes from an ancient word meaning to be robbed. Bereave means to deprive or make desolate, especially by death.

The words to mourn and to grieve both mean to feel sorrow. Grieving is the stronger word, implying deep mental suffering. Mourning usually refers to manifesting sorrow outwardly, either with or without sincerity; to mourn publicly and wear black [2, p. 622].

Grieving is "neither a simple nor an uncomplicated phenomenon," states J. William Worden in his book *Grief Counseling & Grief Therapy* [7, p. 4]. Not only is grieving complex, but some would say that grieving is always complicated. Yet, in the interest of simplicity and hopefully without being simplistic, there is a working definition of grief and another of grieving that we use to help describe grief to bereaved parents and health care professionals alike. Those working definitions are as follows :

Grief is a reaction (or response) to loss. It is natural, necessary, and normal. This reaction affects and encompasses the whole person in body, mind, and spirit.

Grieving is a healing process consisting of those essential components which are needed in order to comfort, restore, and renew the body, mind, and spirit of those who grieve and mourn. The process is an uneven one, much like the zig-zag pattern of a lightening bolt, with peaks and valleys. It has been described in terms of riding an emotional roller coaster or of taking three steps forward and two steps back. (See Chapter 3, "The Healing Process Model©".)

Losses are either death-related or non death-related. A death-related loss can be that of a parent, spouse, child, other family members, friends; reproductive loss such as miscarriage, stillbirth, and abortion; and even the many "little deaths" including death of a pet. Non death-related losses include changes, transitions, trauma, natural disasters, divorce, job loss, moving, amputation, and organ transplants, to name only a few. Many life transitions, even happy ones, such as marriage and graduation, are also touched by grief and loss, as people move on, leaving friends and perhaps family members behind.

NORMAL GRIEF MANIFESTATIONS

While the terms characteristic, manifestation, response, and reaction can be used interchangeably when speaking of grief, the word manifestation is preferable because it conveys a sense of something that shows itself clearly and plainly, is visible, evident, and observable by both the bereaved and the clinician; also it will decrease pathologizing. Bereaved parents may not always understand what is happening to them, especially in regard to their reporting of the feeling, "I feel like I'm going crazy." The clinician, upon hearing this reported, can then normalize their experience by explaining that such a feeling is often expressed by many parents after they have lost a baby.

Early writings on characteristics of normal and pathological grief classified some behaviors as pathological that today would be considered normal. Today what constitutes normal grief reactions cover a broader spectrum of behavior and it is important for the bereaved, their families and friends, as well as health professionals to understand that the characteristics or manifestations of normal grief represent a wide range and variety of thoughts, feelings, and behaviors associated with loss. As Worden explains :

> Obviously, not all these behaviors will be experienced by one person. However, it is important for bereavement counselors to understand the wide range of behaviors covered under normal grief so they will not pathologize behavior that should be recognized as normal. Having this understanding will also enable counselors to give reassurance to people experiencing such behavior as disturbing, especially in the case of a first significant loss [7, p. 30].

Over the years, many clinicians and grief educators have categorized and classified characteristics or manifestations of grieving patterns based upon their observations of recently bereaved individuals. Erich Lindemann, for example, writing in the *American Journal of Psychiatry* in 1944, observed the following characteristics :

1. Somatic or bodily distress of some type
2. Preoccupation with the image of the deceased
3. Guilt relating to the deceased or circumstances of the death
4. Hostile reactions
5. The inability to function as one had before the loss [8, pp. 147-148].

J. William Worden placed normal grief behaviors under four general categories :

1. Feelings
2. Physical sensations
3. Cognitions
4. Behaviors [7, pp. 22-30].

More recently, Thomas Attig, in his 1996 book *How We Grieve,* views grieving as relearning the world through a variety of challenges the bereaved must face, namely, psychological, behavioral, physical, social, intellectual, and spiritual [9, p. 23].

THE BODY, MIND, SPIRIT CONNECTION

In helping bereaved individuals understand what it is they are going through, the characteristics or manifestations of normal grief are explained to them in terms of a body, mind, spirit connection. This compilation of normal grief manifestations is intended to be a broad conceptualization of how grief affects the individual.

Some of these characteristics may not appear to fall neatly or accurately into a specific category of body, mind, or spirit. For example, while the feeling or emotion of anger is located under the category "spirit," it could be placed under the "mind" and "body" category as well, since emotions and feelings permeate body, mind, and spirit. The objective of this listing of manifestations is not to write in stone or to pinpoint accurately where these thoughts, feelings, and behaviors occur or originate. All of these manifestations affect the person's body, mind, and spirit in a holistic manner, with a great deal of overlap, as they interact and interface with one another. Despite the artificial separation into body, mind, spirit categories, we have found this compilation to be very helpful to bereaved parents; they find it easy to understand; they relate to the specific manifestations of grief, and they sometimes add some from their own experience.

Almost every time examples are offered from this listing, our bereaved clients will confirm those manifestations and the counselor, in turn, is able to normalize those experiences which they report. Everyone who goes through a grief experience puts his or her own stamp of individuality on it by virtue of the different life circumstances, specific coping abilities, and the numerous other details of that particular person's path; each bereavement and grieving is therefore unique. Sharing commonalities of the grief experience does not necessarily take away respect for one's individuality; Attig states, "Respect for us as individuals does not come with seeing how we are like everyone else in our grieving" [9, p. 57]. There is comfort for bereaved parents in knowing that others are experiencing similar manifestations, albeit in their own unique way, and that "sorrow shared is sorrow diminished."

The manifestations listed are not all inclusive, and it must not be assumed that others which are excluded are less valid simply because they are not mentioned. This compilation of grief manifestations is drawn largely from our clinical observations over the course of ten years of counseling hundreds of bereaved parents who have experienced reproductive loss as well as from the observations of other clinicians. Many of these grief manifestations are similar to observations made by those clinicians and researchers previously mentioned, namely, Kübler-Ross, Bowlby and Parkes, Kavanaugh, Worden, Lindemann, and Attig. Other writers have compiled features of the grief response and referred to them as "grief symptoms." (See Appendix A.) These grief reactions or manifestations are similar to reactions seen in other bereaved individuals who had experienced different losses, since losses whether they be death-related or non death-related can evoke similar manifestations of grief. In other words, they are not necessarily peculiar to reproductive loss, although some may be. As such there is a great deal of similarity between the body, mind, spirit connection and the stages, characteristics, and normal grief behaviors observed and documented by other clinicians and writers.

THE BODY, MIND, SPIRIT CONNECTION

Body

- tightness in chest, throat
- aching, empty arms
- breathlessness; short of breath
- helplessness
- sighing
- overactivity or social withdrawal
- isolation
- appetite affected (by undereating more than overeating)
- change in libido (more common in reproductive loss)
- muscle weakness
- lack of energy, fatigue
- numbness, shock
- hollow, emptiness
- yearning, searching
- crying
- sleep disturbances

Mind

- "going crazy syndrome"
- thought process affected
- memory loss, slowed thinking
- inability to concentrate, forgetful
- impaired judgment and comprehension
- confusion
- sense of vulnerability
- sense of deceased baby's presence
- intrusive thoughts, nightmares
- preoccupation with thoughts of deceased
- shock, denial
- absent minded
- impaired decision-making ability
- feeling loss of control, powerless

Spirit

- loss of faith/return of faith
- questioning "Why?", "Why me?"
- anger and blame directed at God, self, spouse, etc.
- guilt, anxiety, fear
- looking for meaning of the loss itself
- encounter with the mystery of healing through grieving
- collapse of one's assumptive world
- deepening of spirituality
- depression, sadness, shame
- world view affected
- looking for meaning and purpose of life, death, and suffering

TIMETABLE

Grieving parents who are experiencing these normal but painful manifestations of grief often ask, "How long will this take?", "How long before I'll feel normal again?", "When will the hurting end?" Unfortunately, there is no easy answer, nor is there one answer to these questions because the process of grieving takes time. It is understandable that anyone who is bereaved wants to "get over grief" as quickly as possible. It has been said that the only way to "get over" grief is to go through it, not under it, not over it, not around it. One has to face the pain and feel the hurt. There is no one timetable for grief because everyone's timeframe for grieving is unique. For example, one woman said that she was so confused and absent minded that she "bounced" sixteen checks in the first six months following her stillborn baby boy's death. Another mother found that every spring for five years she went into a depression because this was the time of year her baby had died. For yet another woman, Tuesdays and Wednesdays were days she dreaded. She was filled with anxiety as she recalled the devastating loss of her miscarried baby on a Tuesday and a subsequent D & C on a Wednesday which she described as an additional trauma. This anxiety lasted several weeks following her miscarriage.

While the grieving process timetable can span weeks, months, or even years, for most parents the initial intense pain gradually diminishes. Some bereaved parents say that their grieving only began at three months after the loss, because up to that point they were in shock and felt numb. Just when parents may be needing ongoing support after three months, that support unfortunately stops. No one calls anymore, people stop bringing food, or they may even avoid altogether the grieving parents. Family and friends believe that it's over and now is the time to "get on with your life." This vacuum of support leaves parents feeling abandoned, bewildered, isolated, and generally feeling as if they are going crazy.

CRITICAL TIME PERIODS

For parents who have suffered a reproductive loss, there are many other time- and date-related reminders within the overall timeframe of the grieving process besides the actual date of the death. Sometimes even a particular day of the week or a season of the year may bring painful memories of when the death occurred. Anniversaries (especially the first birth date, death date, due date, and in some cases, date of conception) are sad reminders of the times that parents need to prepare for and anticipate. I have often telephoned parents on those dates only to find that they were indeed feeling sad and depressed but usually without being aware of the significance of that date. Worden refers to these dates as "critical time periods."

> I have found that certain points in time are particularly difficult and I encourage those who are doing grief counseling to recognize these critical time periods and get in touch with the person if there is no regular ongoing contact. Three months is one such point [7, p. 49].

SHADOW GRIEF

In addition to these "critical time periods," there is another remembrance factor, an indescribable "something" that remains. It is called "shadow grief," a term which was named by Peppers and Knapp in their book *Motherhood & Mourning* [10]. "Shadow grief" can occur not only with reproductive losses but also with other losses—parents, spouse, child—as well. It may be of some historical interest to know that Sigmund Freud used a similar phrase, "something else," to convey a sense of lingering mourning; in a letter to his friend Binswanger, whose son had died, he wrote:

> We find a place for what we lose. Although we know that after such a loss the acute stage of mourning will subside, we also know that we shall remain inconsolable and will never find a substitute. No matter what may fill the gap, even if it be filled completely, it nevertheless remains something else [11, p. 386].

Peppers and Knapp consider "shadow grief" to be a "common charac-teristic of the postmourning response" [10, p. 48]. They explain "shadow grief" as follows:

> Shadow grief does not manifest itself overtly; it does not debilitate the individual. No effort is required to cope with it. In fact, a fairly established normal existence is usually resumed. On the surface, most observers say that the grief has been resolved and the individual has resumed a normal life.
>
> How then is shadow grief experienced? For one thing, it has a tendency to pop up insidiously on special occasions, such as birthdays, or deathdays. It

can occur at times when the mother is forced to recall her loss, such as during our interview sessions. Shadow grief reveals itself through the form of a dull, unresponsive ache or an emotional dullness in which the person is unable to respond fully and completely to outer stimulation. She can laugh and appear to enjoy life, but there is always that dull ache in the background that remains constant and, under certain circumstances, surfaces. Frequently, it's in the form of tears, but it is always accompanied by a mild feeling of sadness and, sometimes, even a sense of anxiety. Shadow grief can vary in intensity depending upon the person and the unique factors involved. It is more emotional for some than for others [10, pp. 47-48].

TRIGGERS

Closely connected with "critical time periods" and "shadow grief" is something called a "trigger." Any event, holiday, anniversary, special occasion, births, deaths, sights, sounds, smells, songs, or places which remind the mother of her loss are referred to as "triggers." Some triggers may reactivate the mourning response and thus release the shadow grief which in turn can lead her to re-grieve her loss, although usually in a less intense manner than she did initially. There are exceptions to this, however. At a perinatal bereavement conference, one woman told of her suicide attempt at the one year anniversary of the death of her baby. While suicide attempts are rare and infrequent among parents who have experienced reproductive loss, families, grief counselors, and other health professionals need to be aware that there may be the remote possibility of such an occurrence. Parents have often said, "I just want to be with my baby"; yet they quickly add that they have no intention of harming themselves.

Those triggers which are most often reported are the sight of pregnant women, of a baby carriage or stroller similar to the one that had been purchased but never used, of babies in television commercials, and attendance at baby showers or christenings. Such triggers are painful reminders of loss, especially for the mothers. One young mother who had lost premature twins did not want to leave her house because she feared seeing pregnant women, as this was distressing to her.

Encountering a trigger may feel like a step backward in the healing process. This may lead the bereaved to believe she has lost ground in her grief recovery. Others may look upon her re-grieving as "prolonged grief" or failure "to get over it" and "get on with your life" and, thus, disenfranchising her grief.

Friends, relatives, and health professionals must make every effort to be supportive and understanding toward bereaved mothers and fathers at such times. They can learn how to help the bereaved cope with these trigger situations when they arise by becoming aware of the close connections among "critical time periods," "shadow grief," and "triggers."

USE OF MEDICATIONS

Parents who have experienced the death of a baby feel sadness, sorrow, and even depression as part of the natural and normal grief response to their loss. In addition to this intense feeling of sadness, they may experience anxiety, sleeplessness, fatigue, lack of energy, muscle tenseness and tightening, a general sense of malaise—many of the manifestations mentioned previously in the body, mind, spirit connection. Their initial suffering may be so acute as to warrant some kind of medical intervention such as the prescribing of medications. Regarding the use of medications, Worden states the following :

> The general consensus is that medications ought to be used sparingly and focused on giving relief from anxiety or from insomnia as opposed to providing relief from depressive symptoms [7, p. 54].

Contrary to this admonition given by Worden, many of the bereaved individuals I have seen report that they had been given antidepressants as the first and only medication and usually for long periods of time. Such bereaved parents, especially the mothers, complained that these medications were prescribed as a substitute for listening to them talk about their grief experience which is what they had most wanted. Visits to their physicians, some said, were mostly used to evaluate and adjust medication, leaving only a few minutes for talking, if even that.

It is understandable that most physicians would not have sufficient time to listen to the bereaved tell their story, as they must do to heal. Even for those physicians who want to spend the time listening to the bereaved, it may not be feasible due to their heavy caseload of patients. When physicians make appropriate referrals to grief counselors for their bereaved patients, it is not only helpful for them but also for the bereaved who will then have the necessary time to tell their story and process their grief. In fact, this has been happening quite frequently in the last few years, as physicians are beginning to make more referrals for grief counseling for their bereaved patients.

It is important not to overlook those bereaved people who already are taking medication for an underlying or pre-existing condition such as depression, anxiety, or panic disorder. For those individuals, taking their medication may be needed to survive and to grieve their loss. Thus, their overall care requires that grief counseling be interwoven with the appropriate treatment of any other underlying or concurrent condition.

There seems to be some evidence that the prolonged use of medications can interfere with the grieving process. "Heavy use of drugs or alcohol can intensify the experience of grief and depression and impair the bereavement process," states Worden [7, p. 51].

Medications, especially antidepressants, could mask or even bury the normal, natural, and necessary grief response for the duration of treatment; at some point, the bereaved individual still has to deal with the underlying grief. Worden claims:

> . . . it is usually inadvisable to give antidepressant medications to people undergoing an acute grief reaction. These antidepressants take a long time to work, they rarely relieve normal grief symptoms, and they could pave the way for an abnormal grief response . . . I believe that drugs might be beneficial at the time of the loss when some sedation or help managing anxiety is useful. However, such administrations are usually of short duration and unnecessary in most cases [7, p. 54].

Marie-Rose, a bereaved mother, said that while she was on Prozac, she had no spiritual life. Since grief affects body, mind, and spirit, she could not address the spiritual aspect of her loss during that time she was taking Prozac.

Sandra, the mother of a child who died of Sudden Infant Death Syndrome (SIDS) suggests that medication may have delayed her progression through the grieving process:

> It was one year, almost to the day, after Billy's death before I truly became aware of what had really happened to us. I maintained myself on tranquilizers for one year, living in what I now believe to be a constant state of shock and denial [10, p. 33].

Commenting on this, the authors Peppers and Knapp explain: ". . . the bereavement process itself, characterized by an outpouring of grief, does not begin until the shock has abated and the individual has progressed to the next stage" [10, p. 33].[1]

Medications which relieve anxiety and promote sleep and relaxation may be necessary in cases of traumatic bereavement arising from those reproductive losses which are particularly devastating and tragic events which threaten one's sense of safety and security such as the aftermath of the September 11, 2001 terrorist attacks on the United States. Therese A. Rando underscored this view in her presentation on "Clinical Considerations in Understanding and Responding to Traumatic Bereavement: It's More Than Merely Trauma Added to Grief," which was given at a conference in May 2002 at King's College, London, Ontario.

It is strongly recommended that bereaved individuals consult with their physician rather than try any remedy on their own due to the interaction of drugs and possible harmful side effects. While some bereaved parents are reluctant to take any medication, in particular sleeping pills, because they worry about becoming addicted, others find substitutes for sleeping pills. Patricia, a nurse, felt she needed something for sleep following her miscarriage and found that anti-nausea pills helped. Others have used medications such as muscle relaxants

---

[1] Reprinted with permission of Greenwood Publishing Group, Inc., Westport, Connecticut.

and even anti-histamines to induce sleep. Dreams are also affected by medications. Several of our bereaved parents have reported that they dream less or not at all while taking certain medications. This is unfortunate since dreams can be very healing in the processing of any loss, in particular reproductive loss.

Some mothers have told us that they were fine while on antidepressant medication but once off it, they were right back where they were when they started. Taking such medications may even give a false sense of security that no other intervention is needed. Medications may "buy time" but they do not necessarily heal the grief. Then again, it may beneficial to "buy time," to delay having to face the pain until the bereaved are able and ready. Readiness is an important factor in entering into the work of grieving. Our haste to help them may be another "quick fix" which might possibly postpone the healing.

OTHER SOURCES OF DEPRESSION
AND DISTRESS

A careful assessment of what is a normal grief behavior must be made for each bereaved individual since "many of the normal grief behaviors may seem like manifestations of depression" [7, p. 30]. Physicians who prescribe antidepressants for the bereaved face the difficult task of differentiating grief and depression [12] because "it is true that grief looks like depression and it is also true that grieving may develop into a full blown depression" [7, p. 30]. This task of differentiating grief and depression is made less difficult when health professionals care for the bereaved in a holistic manner instead of treating them for grief and only grief. This holistic approach also makes it easier to distinguish between feelings of upset or distress that are related to the loss itself and those that are related to other factors. The latter have an additional impact on the grief experience and they must be teased out and treated directly. The bereaved need to be gently reminded that not everything that happens to them is necessarily related to the loss and that some of their distress may be due to other factors. Depression which has many contributing factors other than, and in addition to, the grief experience is a prime example. Feelings of depression may also be associated with certain medications, allergies, sleep disturbances, inadequate nutrition, and irritability resulting from simple dehydration, to mention a few.

During the normal course of grieving, the bereaved experience not only stress but also distress. Distress includes such feelings as "anxiety, discomfort, misery, pain, sorrow, suffering and worry" [13, p. 70]. They often report this experience of stress and distress as depression. They usually say to their physician, "I am depressed," not "I am distressed." Based upon their use of the word depression alone, and even the manner in which the bereaved report feelings of depression, they have frequently been given antidepressants as a matter of course. In order to help clarify what they mean by depression, bereaved individuals can be asked to replace the word depression with other words or analogies that mean depression for them. Asking them to describe a typical day or a particular incident that brought about this feeling of depression or distress is helpful. The bereaved are encouraged to assist in their diagnosis by being their own detective, as it were, to identify those "critical time periods" or "triggers" that they may have encountered. For example, the depression, the distress that accompanies the first menstrual cycle following a reproductive loss is a very real source of emotional suffering and anguish because it is a painful reminder of the loss of the baby; women who are having difficulty conceiving may also experience similar anguish and distress due to the menstrual cycle. Emotional support and understanding may be more helpful than antidepressants at this time because of the self-limiting nature of this particular trigger experience.

Insomnia is another very real source of distress for the bereaved. While they feel they are distressed because they cannot sleep, at the same time they may report this as depression, and consequently are given an antidepressant for their insomnia. Ironically enough, some antidepressants have been found to have a negative effect on sleep [14]. "Insomnia, which was once seen as a manifestation of depression to be fought with antidepressants, is now treated with drugs that adjust neurotransmitters" [15, p. 59]. Suggesting ways to overcome sleep disturbances would seem more helpful before and even in addition to prescribing medications when needed. Such simple things as drinking hot milk, taking a warm bath, reducing work activities or television viewing or "surfing the net," especially prior to bedtime; using meditation and relaxation techniques, deep breathing and mild exercising such as going for a walk in the early evening; eliminating caffeine consumption of coffee, tea, and cola drinks; taking calcium supplements or natural herbal remedies ("valerian root has proven sedative qualities") [15, p. 64]; keeping a "grateful" journal or other journal writing and simply turning off the lights can promote relaxation and induce sleep. During the ice storm of January 1998 that hit Montreal and other parts of Canada and the United States, when we were suddenly deprived for several days of our wired existence, namely electricity, we discovered a natural tendency to want to sleep early and long in the cold and the dark. Perhaps by becoming "unplugged," we may have found a cure for insomnia.

Certain medications themselves have been linked to depression. One example is cited by Dr. Allen Douma who reports that oral contraceptives may cause depression [16]. This fact has also been reported by several of my clients.

Underlying conditions already present in the bereaved is another factor which needs to be teased out and evaluated. For example, it is not uncommon for some women to develop allergies after they have been pregnant. Allergies can cause loss of sleep and irritability [17]. People experiencing this might understandably report that they are depressed, while the underlying problem, the allergies, may be overlooked. Such an example is that of one woman who had experienced a miscarriage and was treated for depression and headaches. The antidepressants she had been taking for over a year did not relieve her symptoms. She reported that these symptoms began around the time that she acquired a new pet animal to which she was unknowingly allergic. This fact had not been taken into account in her initial diagnostic assessment by her physician. Anyone taking medications would do well to heed the advice of Dr. Allen Douma who cautions: "It is a good idea to evaluate every drug taken for a long period of time. And certainly, stopping a medication can give valuable clues about how much benefit it provides" [16]. Needless to say, this should only be done in consultation with one's appropriate health care provider, nurse practitioners and nurse midwives not excluded.

Not eating properly or not getting enough fluid intake is another factor which can make the bereaved feel miserable and further distressed. Low blood sugar levels (hypoglycemia) reduce the supply of glucose to the brain, resulting in diminished mental function. "Hypoglycemia is a health problem that affects all aspects of the person. There are physical symptoms like fatigue, drops in energy levels, difficulties with sleep and concentration, headaches and sometimes even blackouts. Then there are the psychological symptoms which may include irritability, anxiety, depression and mood swings" [18]. A young pregnant mother, Rosalie (not her real name), with whom I was doing grief work for a previous reproductive loss, telephoned me one day in a state of panic and anxiety because she was feeling miserable and discouraged that she might have taken a step back in the grieving process. This puzzled me since I had seen her just two days before and she was fine, felt peaceful, and generally was doing well. After listening to her for several minutes, I asked about her day including everything she had eaten. The conclusion was that her nutritional intake that day was inadequate, heavy on "junk" food and consequently led her to feel irritable and fatigued. I advised her to have something nutritious to eat, such as milk, yogurt, and fruit, and to telephone me in an hour. When Rosalie called back, she reported that she felt much better. Another factor which apparently led this woman to feel distressed was the fact that she was not taking her pre-natal vitamins. Knowing the importance of pre-natal vitamins during pregnancy, I asked her why she was not taking them. Rosalie replied that her physician believed she did not need them as long as she was eating a balanced diet! After a few weeks of feeling fatigued, distressed, and depressed, a blood test revealed that she was anemic. She was immediately put on a vitamin and mineral supplement by her physician, after which her mood and general well being improved. Due to her pregnancy, she was unable to take antidepressants; otherwise they might have been prescribed for her and nutritional factors would not have been examined as a possible source of her depression and distress.

Symptoms of depression can be the result of hormonal imbalance. Hypothyroidism, as just one example, includes the symptoms lethargy, apathy, and depressed mood which could easily be mistaken for true depression. Conditions such as these must be ruled out when making a diagnostic assessment for depression.

GRIEVING, STRESS, AND THE IMMUNE SYSTEM

The impact of loss and grief can depress the immune system [19]. While trying to cope emotionally and psychologically with the death of a baby, bereaved parents face yet another stress factor, that of a depressed immune system. This can decrease their resistance, making them more susceptible to colds, flu, other illnesses, and physical symptoms such as fatigue and lack of energy. Coincidentally enough, two women in one of our support groups reported that they both developed pneumonia following their miscarriages. Although not everyone will become ill following a loss, health care providers and the bereaved themselves, nevertheless, should bear in mind the possible consequences of a depressed immune system, and take pro-active, preventative measures to build up the immune system during the grieving process. Health care providers can assist the bereaved to take an overall common sense approach to health care, especially in the area of nutrition. Following a loss, many mothers report that they were not eating well, felt fatigued, and had very little energy. Doing even simple tasks that they had previously accomplished quickly and easily now required a great deal of effort. If they are not getting sufficient vitamins and minerals through their food intake, they may need to take vitamin and nutritional supplements. For example, vitamin C has long been regarded as the anti-stress vitamin and more recently has been found to enhance immune system functioning. The B complex vitamins have also been used in combating depression [20]. Even though these vitamins are known to be helpful, bereaved parents are not always encouraged to take them by their health care providers; some clients reported being told by them, "I don't believe in vitamins." As a nurse clinician and counselor, I have heard this said by a few health care providers quite often over the years. With some exceptions (e.g., nutritionists, dieticians, nurses), it should be noted that the study of nutrition had not always been part of medical education and related health sciences curricula until recently. It is unfortunate that this area of physical health care in general, particularly nutrition and the use of vitamin supplements, seems to be overlooked in caring for the bereaved. Not only do I hear this from the bereaved, but I find that the topic had sometimes been neglected by those who want to help them. Unlike those articles and books on grief written today which take a more holistic view of bereavement, in some earlier ones that I have seen, there was very little or no mention of nutrition, vitamins, or care of the general physical health of the bereaved. This interface between emotional and physical health must not be overlooked for it plays a vital role in the grieving process and the healing of body, mind, and spirit.

HEALING TEARS

"Tears, by and large, are uniquely human. We differ from animals in our ability to cry and tear," states Dr. Arthur Janov [21, p. 318]. The experience of crying or weeping, of when to cry, of how much, how often, and where is made even more unique by the influence of social and family values and conditioning which can either foster or inhibit the release of tears. Janov believes that "the way a society treats tears is indicative of its degree of humanity" [21, p. 323]. Some individuals and families in certain cultures are able to cry easily, openly, and without shame. There are others who only cry privately and others still who seem to consider it a badge of honor never to cry at all. "You will never see us cry in this family," they vigorously vow. Such social and cultural conditioning to repress tears seems to go against the natural tendency for humans to cry, weep, wail, and lament in times of loss and grief, thus turning a heart-felt expression of sorrow into a head-felt decision: to weep or not to weep.

Despite society's approval or non-approval of crying, research suggests that there may be a potential healing value to tears. It has been shown that emotionally-triggered tears have a different chemical composition than tears which resulted from breathing onion fumes. Dr. Janov, one of the researchers, explains why tears are a biological necessity:

> There is little doubt that crying releases stress, since stress hormones are found in tears. In our own research on tears, together with Dr. William Frey of St. Paul Ramsey Medical Center in Minnesota, we found the release of ACTH, a stress hormone triggered by the pituitary gland in the brain. These same tears also release the endorphins. They help remove the biochemical aspect of stress and are therefore a biological necessity [21, p. 321].

It is commonly known that stress causes a physiological imbalance in the body. Because loss and grief act as stressors in those who are bereaved, this biochemical reduction of stress through tears has great significance in grief work and the body, mind, spirit connection. Not only is "crying a biological necessity," it is "an attempt at healing, an effort to restabilize the organism and restore an essential natural function" [21, p. 317].

While the experience of crying or weeping may appear to be unpleasant or even painful, most people who have had a "good cry" usually feel better afterward. One of the commonly experienced benefits of weeping is its calming effect. Through clinical observation, Janov has noted this manifestation of the calming effect of weeping in subjective reports of patients. Furthermore, he believes that "patients who weep need progressively less [sic] tranquilizers" [21, p. 324].

Some of our bereaved parents were hesitant to allow their tears to surface because they feared they would never stop. Janov does not believe this can happen:

> The amount of tranquilizers necessary in adult life will depend, by and large, on the amount of crying "not done." The optimistic part of all this is that the amount of crying needing to be done is "finite," so that after you cry for a certain amount of time you feel good again, because you have done something that the body needed to do [21, p. 319].

Not only are tears healing, but I believe they are also a gift, a gift of healing tears. Bereaved parents who seek help need reassurance that they will be allowed, but never forced, to cry if they wish; that they will be supported through their tears and not abandoned; that they do not need to apologize for their tears. The grief counselor or other helping person can convey that reassurance through a simple touch on the hand; by being present totally to them even during moments of compassionate silence; by encouraging them to take whatever time they need for their tears. Even the presence of a box of facial tissues in the counselor's office sends a message that tears are allowed here. Bereaved parents also appreciate it when the health care providers are not afraid to show some indication that they have been touched by the parents' loss. It is much more acceptable today than it was in previous years for professional caregivers to show their humanity through tears. Today, caregivers may cry with their clients/patients as long as they do not cry *more* than those bereaved individuals who are in their care.

SUMMARY

Grief as a reaction to loss affects and encompasses the whole person in body, mind, and spirit. The characteristics or manifestations of normal grief represent a wide range and variety of thoughts, feelings, and behaviors associated with loss. There are many pathways to healing the grief associated with reproductive loss, two of which will be explored in the following chapters on "Tasks of Mourning" and "The Healing Process Model©."

REFERENCES

1. H. J. M. Nouwen, *Out of Solitude,* Ave Maria Press, Notre Dame, Indiana, 1974.
2. *The Random House Dictionary of the English Language,* J. Stein (ed.), Random House, Inc., New York, 1966.
3. *Diagnostic and Statistical Manual of Mental Disorders, Second Edition*–Revised, American Psychiatric Association, Washington, D.C., 1968.
4. J. Bowlby and C.M. Parkes, *The Child in His Family,* E. J. Anthony and C. Koupernik (eds.), Wiley, New York, 1978.
5. R. Kavanaugh, *Facing Death,* Penguin Books, Baltimore, 1974.
6. E. Kübler-Ross, *On Death and Dying,* Macmillan, New York, 1969.
7. J. W. Worden, *Grief Counseling & Grief Therapy* (2nd Edition), Springer, New York, 1991.
8. E. Lindemann, Symptomatology and Management of Acute Grief, *American Journal of Psychiatry, 101,* pp. 147-148, 1944.
9. T. Attig, *How We Grieve: Relearning the World,* Oxford University Press, New York, 1996.
10. L. G. Peppers and R. J. Knapp, *Motherhood & Mourning: Perinatal Death,* Praeger, New York, 1980.
11. E. L. Freud (ed.), *Letters of Sigmund Freud,* Basic, New York, 1961.

12. P. J. Robinson and S. Fleming, Differentiating Grief and Depression, *Hospice Journal 5*, pp. 77-88, 1989.
13. *Webster's Thesaurus,* PMC, New York, 1992.
14. Y. Zacharias, "Happy Pills" Cause Sad Sex: Study, *The Gazette,* Montreal, p. A3, October 22, 1997.
15. R. Sullivan, Sleepless in America, *Life,* Time Inc., New York, pp. 56-66, February, 1998.
16. A. Douma, Oral Contraceptives May Cause Depression, *The Gazette,* Montreal, November 27, 1997.
17. A. Douma, Perennial Allergies, *The Gazette,* Montreal, December 12, 1997.
18. T. Mintz, Hypoglycemia Affects the Brain, *The Gazette,* Montreal, p. F12/WE, December 11, 1997.
19. S. J. Schleifer, S. E. Keller, M. Camerio, J. C. Thornton, and M. Stein, Suppression of Lymphocyte Stimulation Following Bereavement, *Journal of the American Medical Association, 250,* pp. 374-377, 1983.
20. J. F. Balch and P. A. Balch, *Prescription for Nutritional Healing* (2nd Edition), Avery, Garden City Park, New York, 1997.
21. A. Janov, *The New Primal Scream,* Enterprise, Wilmington, Delaware, 1991.

CHAPTER 2

Tasks of Mourning

... grief is healed when we are able to courageously stand in it and not run. When we are able to name it and start to know its comings and goings. When we are able to slow down our pace and find a place to experience our pain within. When we are able to be in our body. When we are able to accept it as a temporary visitor and not think that we are that grief. When we are able to make an agreement with the part of ourselves that is the mask self, in order to access our pain. And when we can discriminate between the pain of grief and the pain of pain.

Thomas R. Golden [1, p. 52]

The Four Tasks of Mourning defined by J. W. Worden in his book *Grief Counseling & Grief Therapy* are the following:

TASK I: To accept the reality of the loss.
TASK II: To work through to the pain of grief.
TASK III: To adjust to an environment in which the deceased is missing.
TASK IV: To emotionally relocate the deceased and move on with life [2, pp. 10-18].

Worden believes that the Tasks of Mourning concept presents as valid an understanding of the mourning process as do other schema of mourning and is useful for the clinician as well. Tasks "imply that the mourner needs to take action and can do something" [2, p. 35]. The task approach, because it is more active oriented rather than passive, offers some hope to mourners "that something can be done and that there is an end point. This can be a powerful antidote to the feelings of helplessness that most mourners experience" [2, p. 35]. I have included Worden's Tasks of Mourning here because I believe that these tasks have an important application to reproductive loss; they contribute significantly to a fuller understanding of the mourning mosaic; they are compatible with the Healing Process Model© which was developed for the Centre's seminars; they serve as a bridge to the following Chapter on the Healing Process Model©.

TASK I:
TO ACCEPT THE REALITY OF THE LOSS

Accepting the reality of the loss can be especially difficult in reproductive loss. Parents often experience a sense of unreality associated with the death of a baby either through miscarriage, stillbirth, or other reproductive loss. "Did this really happen?", "Was I dreaming this?", "Was I ever really pregnant at all?", are frequently heard as expressions of their shock and disbelief. The unmet parental expectation that "Babies aren't supposed to die" plunges them deeper into this sense of unreality when a reproductive loss causes them to experience the collapse of their assumptive world and shatters their dreams.

There is a high shock value inherent in most reproductive losses due to the impact of the suddenness of the death that occurs without warning and the traumatic experience of "giving birth at the same time as death" both of which foster the sense of disbelief, thus making it more difficult to accept the reality of the loss. "A sudden death will usually leave the survivor with a sense of unreality about the loss," notes Worden [2, p. 98].

Although reproductive loss is usually not cited as an example of sudden death, nevertheless I have seen several of those survivor characteristics in the aftermath of sudden death as manifested by parents following a miscarriage, abortion, or stillbirth. These characteristics are similar to Worden's descriptions:

> It is not unusual for the survivor to feel numb and to walk around in a daze following such a loss. It is not unusual for the survivor to experience nightmares and intrusive images after a sudden loss, even though they were not present at the time of the death. Appropriate counseling intervention can help the survivor deal with this manifestation of sudden death and heighten the reality of the event [2, p. 98].

In fact, Worden believes that the principles of "crisis intervention" are appropriate here and are helpful after a sudden death [2, p. 100].

There is still the expectation in our society today (although decreasingly so) that parents who have lost a baby need to get over this quickly and have another child to replace the one who died. Because the grief experienced from reproductive loss (in particular miscarriage and abortion) is often minimized, dismissed as unimportant, and thus disenfranchised, grieving parents may find it difficult to acknowledge, even to themselves, the meaning of the loss or to sense the full impact of the reality of that loss prior to its acceptance.

While the task of accepting the reality of the loss is intended for the bereaved, I believe this task should also apply to those health professionals caring for parents who have suffered a reproductive loss. In some instances, health professionals themselves were the ones who did not accept the reality of the loss by their minimizing of the loss, especially miscarriage and abortion.

One of my clients, whom I shall call Joanne, made a special effort to communicate to her obstetrician-gynecologist how grief counseling had helped her deal with her miscarriage. She went back to him hoping this information would be well received and used to help other women with reproductive losses. When Joanne gave him one of our brochures describing the purpose and services of the Centre for Reproductive Loss, he promptly gave it back to her after giving it a brief glance, and said, "You're making a big deal out of this. Most women don't react like you. Why don't you go home and get pregnant again so you won't be so emotionally involved." Joanne felt that his words and actions minimized her loss by his failure to acknowledge her pain and grief. Joanne also reported that this physician came from a culture and ethnicity which did not acknowledge such losses. Instead of responding to her in terms of his ethnic background, as a clinician he should have observed and responded to her need for "emotional attention," a term she used to describe what she failed to receive from him after her miscarriage. Regardless of one's ethnicity, *a clinician first and foremost must be a "keen observer" and respond to what the clients'/patients' manifested behavior indicates what those needs are*. There is an added ironic twist to this story. Shortly before Joanne's miscarriage occurred, the hospital at which the doctor was a staff member held a day-long conference on responding to patients' needs in family practice. One of the physicians speaking at this conference stressed how important it was for patients to communicate their needs to their physicians and make them aware of what they want, something which Joanne had tried to do. Joanne was certain her physician had not attended that conference. Grieving individuals who want to receive "emotional attention," just as Joanne did, would be well-advised to seek help from health care providers knowledgeable about grief and loss, such as bereavement or pastoral counselors.

Recalling memories of the deceased helps the bereaved to process the grief and to accept the reality of the loss following the death of a loved one. Unfortunately, for many parents who have suffered a reproductive loss, memories may be few or even non-existent. Without tangible memories such as photographs, a funeral (in miscarriage, there is often no visible body), a memorial service, or some kind of ritual of remembrance which offers comfort and closure, the sense of unreality is re-enforced. Creating memories surrounding the loss and finding "a place to remember" help parents to accept the reality of their loss.

Writing letters, stories, prose, or poetry about the reproductive loss experience provides a concrete, tangible tool for acknowledging the reality of the loss and for finding "a place to remember." Many parents who have never before written poetry have been inspired to do so after the death of their child; they find that writing can be a source of catharsis, consolation, and comfort for them (see Appendix B).

TASK II:
TO WORK THROUGH TO THE PAIN OF GRIEF

Closely related to the first task, accepting the reality of the loss, is the second task, working through to the pain of grief. It is nearly impossible for anyone who has suffered a reproductive loss not to experience some degree of physical, emotional, mental, or spiritual pain, albeit with varying levels of intensity and duration. Once the reality of the loss sets in (the completion of Task I), the pain "hits you like an emotional Mack truck," as one parent described it. This pain can either be faced and felt or avoided and denied. Avoiding and burying the pain of loss brings with it the consequences of slowing down the grieving/healing process. Based upon his research and studies, Parkes has stated:

> If it is necessary for the bereaved person to go through the pain of grief in order to get the grief work done, then anything that continually allows the person to avoid or suppress this pain can be expected to prolong the course of mourning [3, p. 173].

Janov affirms this when he says, "When repression sets in, it also blocks the healing processes. The wound becomes hidden" [4, p. 324].

When bereaved individuals do not face the pain and feel the hurt, they are at risk for suffering the consequences of dealing with the pain in unhealthy ways, or "grief substitutes," some of which can be harmful, through the use of drugs and alcohol, through overwork, aggressive behavior, and even violent acting out. Many bereaved women had reported that after a miscarriage or other reproductive loss, they had noticed a change in their partner's behavior even though their partners appeared not to experience any pain from the loss per se; some expressed verbal aggression toward their wives; alcohol consumption had increased for some; while others began putting in longer hours at work. "Not to feel" the pain negates this second task, of working through the pain, states Worden:

> People can short-circuit Task II in any number of ways, the most obvious being to cut off their feelings and deny the pain that is present. Sometimes people hinder the process by avoiding painful thoughts [2, pp. 13-14].

Our society, too, sends a message about not feeling the pain of grief. Most people feel very uncomfortable with death from a reproductive loss (miscarriage, abortion, stillbirth) and may behave in subtle ways (or sometimes *not* so subtle ways) as to provide some sort of distraction or rationale for the loss, often by resorting to such clichés as, "You can have other children. You're still young." Geoffrey Gorer summarizes the rationale for society's discomfort with mourners:

> Giving way to grief is stigmatized as morbid, unhealthy, demoralizing. The proper action of a friend and well-wisher is felt to be distraction of a mourner from his or her grief [5, p. 130].

Although this rationale in our society of the third millennium may be changing to one of greater acceptance of grief as natural, normal, and necessary, it is understandable how such an attitude toward grief, as described by Gorer, can hinder the completion of Task II.

Worden stresses the necessity of working on this second task at the time of the loss, rather than later on:

> One of the aims of grief counseling is to help facilitate people through this difficult second task so they don't carry the pain with them throughout their life. If Task II is not adequately completed, therapy may be needed later on, at which point it can be more difficult for the person to go back and work through the pain he or she has been avoiding. This is very often a more complex and difficult experience than dealing with it at the time of the loss. Also, it can be complicated by having a less supportive social system than would have been available at the time of the original loss [2, p. 14].

Janov, too, recognizes the importance of experiencing pain and of dealing with it as it happens:

> The question is, "Why does healing only take place with weeping and feeling?" The answer is because active "suffering" and "healing" occur simultaneously. The reason that we did not heal in the first place is because we did not feel the totality of an early series of traumas. If one could have felt one's early traumas originally, there would be no biological motive to re-experience them [4, p. 324].

A renowned authority on grief and loss, psychiatrist John Bowlby said it well when he wrote: "Sooner or later, some of those who avoid all conscious grieving, break down—usually with some form of depression" [6, p. 158].

This second task of mourning, working through to the pain of grief as a way to find healing, sounds very much like a paradox, as does the expression "In the grieving is the healing," a term which was coined by the Centre for Reproductive Loss. Janov recognized the paradox that healing comes through suffering:

> When a person is cut off from the experience of suffering, he is stripped of the necessary condition for healing and prepared instead for disease. Just as pain and repression form a dialectic unity, so do active suffering and healing [4, p. 325].

Caregivers, families, and friends of those individuals who have suffered a reproductive loss can facilitate this second task of mourning by recognizing their pain and not minimizing or dismissing it; by providing comfort and support not only initially but at other critical time periods as well; by honoring their pain and allowing them to face it instead of talking them out of it; by reassuring them that they do not have to be alone in their suffering and affliction; by walking with them on the grieving/healing journey.

TASK III:
TO ADJUST TO AN ENVIRONMENT IN WHICH THE DECEASED IS MISSING

The primary focus of the third task is role related—the role of the deceased and the impact that role has upon the survivors. As Worden states, "Adjusting to a new environment means different things to different people, depending on what the relationship was with the deceased and the various roles the deceased played" [2, p. 14].

In the case of reproductive loss, there are roles that are anticipated but never actualized. The role of the deceased baby in reproductive loss is not, for the most part, played out over time. The anticipation of that future role, nevertheless, has a powerful effect upon the survivors—parents, siblings, grandparents, other relatives, and even friends. Some couples expecting their first child may have made major occupational decisions or purchased a house in anticipation of their role as parents, only to have the playing out of their parental role tragically altered by the death of their baby. Others have had to adjust to coming home with empty arms to the lovingly prepared nursery, replete with its baby furniture, crib, carriage, rocking chair, toys, clothing, and numerous other reminders of an anticipated joyful event. One mother was terribly distressed when well meaning relatives took everything out of the nursery before she came home from the hospital in order to help her adjust to the environment without the baby. Unfortunately, the good intentions of her family did not help this mother adjust. Instead, it only compounded her loss. Parents should be allowed to decide for themselves what it is that they want to do about all the baby things in the nursery. They will have to decide if and when to "put things away for a while" or to "keep everything in place." Among the clients we have seen, the woman usually wants to keep everything intact for a longer time than the man. Some parents have regretted that they had hastily dismantled the nursery in their attempt to adjust.

Siblings are also affected by the expectation of a baby brother or sister and subsequent death of that baby. Their adjustment, in part, depends upon their level of understanding about death, how effectively parents communicate with them and reassure them that the death was not their fault, especially when they may not have welcomed a new baby in the first place. Children have difficulty coping with the mother's sadness, often thinking they are to blame for making "Mommy feel bad." In general, it is better to tell children about the death, in terms they can understand, rather than not telling them and thereby creating family secrets which can even have an impact later on in life.

Grandparents may be inconsolable over the death of their grandchild, especially if it is the first. Having their own grief to deal with, they may be unable to offer their own children, the bereaved parents, the support they may need. Caregivers should not automatically assume that social support is adequate simply because there are grandparents available to help out. A woman from one of our support groups, Linda, told how she resented a health professional advising her she did not need additional social support since her mother was there to help her. Linda did not want to burden her mother who was having a hard enough time dealing with her own grief in losing a grandchild.

Other role relationships within the family are affected by the death of a baby. Family members who were looking forward to becoming aunts or uncles suddenly are deprived or robbed of that anticipated role. Due to the more distant role relationship with the deceased, their grief might be overlooked. The measure of the intensity of one's relationship to the deceased should not be determined solely on the basis of the proximity to or distance from that role. A special relationship with a "distant cousin," for example, could have a greater impact on one's grief experience than the role relationship would seem to suggest.

Sisters and friends who are pregnant at the same time face a difficult adjustment in their role relationship with one another when one of them loses a baby due to miscarriage or stillbirth while the other one's pregnancy successfully carries to term. It is not unusual for them to stop seeing each other or, indeed, even speaking to one another after such a tragic event. The bereaved sister does not want to be reminded of what she lost; the other sister may feel so guilty about having a baby that she does not want her sister to see her.

Renée wanted to share the joy of her baby's birth with her sister Denise who had been pregnant at the same time as Renée, but unfortunately had miscarried. Renée thought that sending in her letters pictures of her baby, Denise's nephew, would help to console Denise. Instead of having that desired effect, Denise resented this and felt intense anger and hostility for a long time after toward her well meaning sister; Renée intended no harm but unknowingly was the cause of hurting her sister.

Just as with role relationships of family members, in a similar manner when friends have been pregnant at the same time, those relationships are affected and also require adjustment after one of the friends has lost a baby. They, too, may stop speaking or even avoid having to see each other. These behaviors of avoidance and non-communication severely test friendships and may contribute to dissolving those long-term, supportive, and caring relationships, adding yet another loss to grieve. Since friends' interactions help us know who we are, the bereaved could also experience a loss of identity upon the loss of a friendship. The kind of adjustment that friends and family require for this task of mourning within the environment of roles and relationships, is one of reconciliation and healing through the release of anger and through the act of forgiveness which is an essential therapeutic component of the spiritual dimension within the body, mind, spirit connection.

Worden identifies another challenge the bereaved face:

> Not only do the bereaved have to adjust to the loss of roles previously played by the deceased, but death also confronts them with the challenge of adjusting to their own sense of self [2, p. 15].

Because the parental role is so special in that it is defined through the relationship with the child, there is also the loss of a sense of self and subsequent lowered self-esteem with the death of a baby. Bereaved parents have often reported that they felt as if they had lost a part of themselves after the death of their child.

In addition to adjusting to the loss of roles, adjusting to their own sense of self and sense of identity, the bereaved are further challenged by having to adjust to their sense of the world, their values and beliefs about life and meaning. Worden explains:

> Loss through death can challenge one's fundamental life values and philosophical beliefs—beliefs that are influenced by our families, peers, education, and religion as well as life experiences. It is not unusual for the bereaved to feel that they have lost direction in life. The bereaved person searches for meaning in the loss and its attendant life changes in order to make sense of it and regain some control of his or her life. This is especially true when there are sudden and untimely deaths. For many there is no clear answer [2, pp. 15-16].

The third task emphasizes the spiritual aspect of the body, mind, spirit connection. The bereaved parents I have counseled have taught me that these babies did not come into their lives, however brief the time, without bringing some gift, perhaps of courage, some message or lesson to be learned about the meaning of life, loss, and grief, along with an increase in their capacity for compassion and empathy. The matter of timing and pacing the bereaved are critically important when inviting bereaved parents to look for the gift, even through their grief and their tears; this can help them to adjust to an environment in which their baby is gone but not forgotten. There is perhaps no better way to summarize this task than through the poetry of bereaved parents themselves (see Appendix B and D).

TASK IV:
TO EMOTIONALLY RELOCATE THE DECEASED AND MOVE ON WITH LIFE

Worden explains what the counselor can do to facilitate this fourth task:

> The counselor's task then becomes not to help the bereaved give up their relationship with the deceased, but to help them find an appropriate place for the dead in their emotional lives—a place that will enable them to go on living effectively in the world [2, p. 17].

Finding a "place to remember" is an important therapeutic component in the grieving/healing process. Parents who have suffered a reproductive loss find much comfort in locating or placing their deceased babies on their family tree. They want to remember and not forget that "significant relationship" in their lives. Worden believes that "One never loses memories of a significant relationship" [2, p. 16]. That relationship lives on within them through love, through remembering, and through the continuing bonds with the deceased, bonds which can be fostered even after death (see Chapter 3, "The Healing Process Model©").

Bereaved parents have a great need to have their experience of loss recognized and validated. Parents can remember privately or with other families through public memorials created in remembrance of their deceased children. Among the many such memorials which have been established in various parts of the world, the following are just a few examples: the Matthews Child Caressed sculpture in Australia; the Angel statue in Salt Lake City, Utah; the wooden prayer plaques and dolls symbolizing babies in Japan; and two memorials in Canada, one in Saskatoon and the other in Montreal. By visiting these memorials, grieving families can seek solace and take comfort in remembering their children.

Australian Babies Remembered

The "Matthews Child Caressed" sculpture which is dedicated to Australian babies, was established by the Bonnie Babes Foundation in Necropolis Springvale Cemetery in Victoria, Australia. The Bonnie Babes Foundation is a non-profit organization that was established in 1994 to counsel families grieving after the loss of a baby due to miscarriage, stillbirth, and prematurity. The following news release describes this memorial:

> On February 7, 1996, Matthews International Corporation's new Caressed Child sculpture was unveiled by the Honorable Marie Tehan, M.P., Australia's Minister for Health. The cast bronze feature depicting an infant sleeping in the hand of Christ sits atop a bluestone rock in a tranquil garden. An inspiring verse is cast on a bronze plaque which is positioned on the front side of the base. The garden also includes an area adjacent to the new feature where families can memorialize their children on individual bronze plaques [7].

In referring to the sculpture as a beautiful addition to Necropolis Springvale Cemetery's Remembrance Garden, the general manager of Matthews' Arrow plant, Bob Romah, commented, "It is hard to describe the outpouring of emotion that occurred when the feature was unveiled" [7].

The inspiring verse inscribed on the bronze plaque of the "Child Caressed" memorial sculpture reads:

> THOSE SPECIAL MOMENTS WE SHARED ON EARTH
> MEMORIES FOREVER ALIVE FROM YOUR BIRTH
> NO CHILD WHO LIVED UNTIL OLD AGE
> COULD BE MORE LOVED AT ANY STAGE . . .

Salt Lake City's Angel Monument

The Angel statue memorial in Salt Lake City, Utah, has also evoked an outpouring of emotion similar to the response of people who visit the Child Caressed sculpture in Australia. People visiting the Angel statue are deeply touched by this memorial and are often moved to tears. Richard Paul Evans writes about the Angel statue on the last page of his book *The Christmas Box:*

> In Memoriam
> The Angel statue, of which the author makes mention, was destroyed in 1984 by the great floods that came through the Salt Lake Valley.
> A new Angel monument, in remembrance of all those who have lost children, was erected in the same Salt Lake City cemetery and dedicated December 6, 1994.
> The author wishes to invite all those who find themselves in Salt Lake City to lay a white flower at the statue's base [8].[1]

Evans' inspiration to write the book came from knowing his mother had suffered a stillbirth when he was a child. No one was more surprised than Evans himself when the book became a phenomenal best seller, touching as it did the hearts of grieving parents; this overwhelming response to his book is described in a magazine article:

> Evans received hundreds of letters from women who had miscarried; he also got 200 white roses from a woman whose child had been killed in a car accident. "People say 'thank you' to me and I don't totally understand," says Evans; "But I'm moved by their pain" [9, p. 24].

A dedication to his stillborn baby sister appears in the front of his book: "For my sister Sue. Whom I love and I miss" [8].

Memorial in Japan

The Japanese memorial dedicated to deceased babies is another "place to remember" which helps grieving parents to deal with their loss. A personal friend who had visited a Buddhist temple described this memorial to me. Located on the grounds adjacent to a Buddhist temple, the memorial is filled with rows of model baby statues which the mother buys and which symbolize her aborted or miscarried baby. Some of these models are dressed with bonnets or other baby clothing. Most of the babies were given names which are inscribed on vases in front of the dolls. Parents can go there to light candles and to bring toys and flowers. In addition to wooden prayer plaques, parents can write messages expressing their love and asking for forgiveness.

---

[1] Reprinted with the permission of Simon & Schuster from *The Christmas Box* by Richard Paul Evans. Copyright © 1993 by Richard Paul Evans.

Woodlawn Cemetery—The City of Saskatoon, Saskatchewan

In a joint community partnership involving the combined efforts of the Saskatoon District Health Agency, the city's three hospitals, a local funeral service provider (the W. A. Edwards family), Woodlawn Cemetery, and Remco Memorials, a comprehensive service project was developed to provide a special burial and memorialization program for bereaved parents and families who have suffered the loss of a child. Part of this project involved the placement of a large shared monument in Woodlawn Cemetery on November 21, 1997 as a permanent and everlasting tribute of a parent's love. Dedicated to babies who have died at or before birth, this monument which has space available for the inscription of the babies' names, is designed with a simple single rose and is inscribed with the words, "Our Children Live In Our Hearts Forever."

Challenges Posed by Task IV

While finding "a place to remember" through private and public memorials helps to accomplish this fourth task, Worden explains the difficulty this task poses for some individuals:

> For many people, Task IV is the most difficult to accomplish. They get stuck at this point in their grieving and later realize that their life in some way stopped at the point the loss occurred [2, p. 18].

Many bereaved individuals who have suffered a reproductive loss are afraid to let go of the pain of grief, as if somehow that painful feeling is the same as holding on to the deceased baby. They fear that they might forget the baby if they are not experiencing pain. They often feel guilty if they begin to smile and laugh again or if they do not feel at least some degree of pain. Elaine could only remember her premature twins in the intensive care nursery, even after they had been buried. For several weeks, she had difficulty locating them in another place, or indeed, even accepting the reality of the loss. In her mind, she still expected them to be in the nursery. After several counseling sessions with me, she decided to visit the intensive care nursery as a way to deal with the loss. Although it was a painful encounter, she was able to face the reality that her twins were not in the nursery. Using visual imagery, she could now picture her babies in a safe place that was comforting to her. Helping her to emotionally relocate her babies thus enabled her to continue the bonds of love she felt for them and eventually to be more at peace.

Doreen felt surrounded by death for many years after her abortion. Through the telling of her story, she realized that emotionally she had never left the abortion clinic. Through appropriate counseling using visualization, she was able to leave the abortion scene and to emotionally relocate her deceased baby; the feeling of death and depression that had engulfed her for years had also disappeared.

In helping parents accomplish this task, the counselor can encourage them not only to let go of the pain but also in its place to foster the continuing bonds with the baby instead, and to reassure them that letting go of the pain does not mean forgetting the deceased baby.

Helen Schulman, author and co-editor of the book entitled *Wanting a Child,* describes the emotional impact that her three miscarriages had upon her life. Her story reflects this fourth task of mourning:

> Even though I love my daughter more than life itself, I doubt I will ever forget the babies I carried that were never born, and the power of the grief still catches me by surprise. You have children—not in the world inhabited by other people, but in the private world of your heart—you have children you will never get to mother. They are secret children, like those children you read about, confined to an attic or a closet. No one but you recognizes their existence; you yourself don't even know their form, their genders, the shape of their noses, the color of their eyes, and yet the strength of their souls flutters inside your heart like a caged bird's wings. As a mother, it is your job to get them out into the world, but you have failed them hopelessly, and so they haunt you, inhabiting a hyperreality that in the middle of the night feels truer and more real than any reality you have ever known. They are your children, and you are their mother. And yet you do not stop your life for them. Instead, you go on [10, p. 39].[2]

It has been said that grief is the price we pay for love. While that does not make it hurt any less, it is nearly impossible to avoid the pain of grief, even though we may try to avoid that pain as much as we can. Worden explains how avoiding the pain of grief hinders the completion of the fourth task:

> The fourth task is hindered by holding on to the past attachment rather than going on and forming new ones. Some people find loss so painful that they make a pact with themselves never to love again [2, p. 17].

"Not loving" is the phrase that Worden uses to define the incompletion of the fourth task. After experiencing the tragic loss of a pregnancy, bereaved couples, contemplating a subsequent pregnancy with the possibility of suffering another loss, often say such things as, "Do we really want to feel this terrible pain of loss and grief again?", "I don't think I can bear the pain of losing another baby." Deciding on a subsequent pregnancy following a previous pregnancy loss poses a serious dilemma for couples. While they may want to have a child or other children, they may not want to risk the hurt that comes from loving and losing a baby. The decision to resolve "never to love again" in order to avoid the pain of grief can be a very powerful temptation indeed. While everyone must face the pain of these losses in their own unique way, most bereaved couples can and do rise above that temptation "never to love again"; they can find hope and courage to risk loving once more; and they can discover within themselves the strength to grapple

[2] Excerpt from *Wanting a Child* edited by Jill Bialosky and Helen Schulman. Copyright © 1998 by Jill Bialosky and Helen Schulman. Reprinted by permission of Farrar, Straus, and Giroux.

with the mystery of healing through grieving, as well as the mystery of seeking and finding the gifts that grief and loss can bring and be brought to bear upon the healing of body, mind, and spirit. The mystery of finding gifts through grief and loss and the paradox of healing through grieving has been captured in a beautiful heartfelt poem on miscarriage entitled "Just Those Few Weeks" by Susan Erling Martinez:

> For those few weeks—
> I had you to myself.
>
> And that seems too short a time
> to be changed so profoundly.
>
> In those few weeks—
> I came to know you . . .
> and to love you.
> You came to trust me with your life.
> Oh, what a life I had planned for you!
> Just those few weeks—
> When I lost you,
> I lost a lifetime of hopes,
> plans, dreams, and aspirations . . .
> A slice of my future simply vanished overnight.
>
> Just those few weeks—
> It wasn't enough time to convince others
> how special and important you were.
> How odd, a truly unique person has recently died
> and no one is mourning the passing.
>
> Just a few mere weeks—
> And no "normal" person would cry all night
> over a tiny, unfinished baby,
> or get depressed and withdraw day after endless day.
> No one would, so why am I?
>
> You were just those few weeks my little one
> you darted in and out of my life too quickly.
> But it seems that's all the time you needed
> to make my life so much richer
> and give me a small glimpse of eternity [11, p. 7].

REFERENCES

1. T. R. Golden, *Swallowed by a Snake. The Gift of the Masculine Side of Healing,* Golden Healing Publishing L.L.C., Kensington, Maryland, 1996.
2. J. W. Worden, *Grief Counseling & Grief Therapy,* Springer, New York, 1991.

3. C. M. Parkes, *Bereavement: Studies of Grief in Adult Life,* International Universities Press, New York, 1972.
4. A. Janov, *The New Primal Scream,* Enterprise, Wilmington, Delaware, 1991.
5. G. D. Gorer, *Death, Grief, and Mourning,* Doubleday, New York, 1965.
6. J. Bowlby, *Attachment and Loss: Loss, Sadness, and Depression* (vol. III), Basic Books, New York, 1980.
7. *Matthews News Release,* Matthews International Corporation, Victoria, Australia, March 4, 1996.
8. R. P. Evans, *The Christmas Box,* Simon & Schuster, New York, 1993.
9. E. Seidman, The Good Son, *Good Housekeeping,* p. 24, December 1995.
10. H. Schulman, A Child of Her Dreams, *Time* (Canadian Edition), pp. 36-39, May 18, 1998. Book excerpt from *Wanting a Child: 22 Writers on Their Difficult but Mostly Successful Quest for Parenthood in a High-Tech Age,* J. Bialosky and H. Schulman (eds.), Farrar, Straus & Giroux, New York, 1998.
11. S. E. Martinez, *Rainbow After a Storm,* A Place to Remember, a division of deRuyter Nelson Publications Inc., St. Paul, Minnesota, 1984, with permission from the author (www.tjsusan.com).

CHAPTER 3

The Healing Process Model©

Give Sorrow words. The grief
that does not speak
Whispers the o'er fraught heart
and bids it break.

Shakespeare, *Macbeth, iv, iii*

OUTLINE OF THE HEALING PROCESS MODEL©

- Acknowledgment
- Telling the Story: Facts and Feelings
- Reproductive Loss History
- History of Other Losses and Stress
- Explain, Describe, Normalize Grief Reactions/Manifestations
- Establish, Reconnect, Continue Relationship
- The Questions? Encounter with Mystery, Spirituality, and Growing through Grief
- Grief Work vs. Guilt Work
- Forgiveness and Anger
- Closure—Letting Go of the Pain: Creating "A Place to Remember"
- Care for Self: Body, Mind, Spirit
- Reaching Out to Help Others: Compassionate Outreach

OVERVIEW

The Healing Process Model© is a way of viewing grieving that can guide bereaved individuals and their helpers through the grieving/healing process in order to bring about constructive healthy grieving of reproductive losses. Some of the operations/actions of the process are those of the bereaved (for example, telling the story, establish the relationship, forgiveness, etc.); some are the actions of the helper (reproductive loss history, explain/normalize grief manifestations).

33

Acknowledgment can be both—acknowledgment on the part of the helper and on the part of the bereaved ("accepting the reality of the loss"). This model can benefit the bereaved most effectively when used with a grief counselor/therapist or others who have an understanding of the nature of grief. Although the model was not intended to be used as a self help tool by the bereaved, it can, nevertheless, give them an understanding of the nature of grief and provide guidelines for them to follow, especially if there is no one else available to walk with them on their grief journey. It is important to remember the non-sequential, to and fro, back and forth nature of this model which is one way it differs from others. Even though acknowledgment is the first and reaching out to others is the last, any of these actions or components may arise in any order, according to the uniqueness of each person's grief journey as well as how much grief work bereaved individuals have already done at the time they sought help from a grief counselor. For example, since naming the miscarried baby helps to establish the relationship with the child, some parents may have named the miscarried or stillborn baby even before coming to a grief counselor, while others who never thought of doing that on their own were greatly comforted by this action when it was suggested to them. Each of the operations/actions/components covers one, two, or three categories of the body, mind, spirit connection although no operation/action is strictly one or the other.

DEVELOPMENT OF THE MODEL

This model grew out of the fruit of my clinical practice and observations from my work with the bereaved who were in fact my best teachers. Among other things, they taught me how essential acknowledgment of their loss was for healing. Acknowledgment of loss, as a significant reality of the grief experience, thus became one of the operations/actions/components in the healing process model. Through the telling of their stories, an essential therapeutic component, bereaved parents disclosed other factors and similar realities of the grief experience which they appeared to have in common with other bereaved parents; factors such as the grief manifestations of body, mind, and spirit and their need to normalize them (see Chapter 1); the comfort that comes from telling their stories and remembering their babies; the issues of anger and forgiveness; the unfinished business of previous losses; the importance of caring for one's self as well as their desire to reach out to others, to name just a few.

From these common factors or rather, factors in common, a pattern emerged which provided guidelines and a broad overview of the grieving/healing process from beginning to end. These guidelines proved to be helpful initially for the bereaved in my clinical practice and later on for health professionals who requested from us at the Centre for Reproductive Loss a training program on how to help those individuals who were grieving reproductive losses. Through further development, these guidelines became the Healing Process Model© which was subsequently used as a teaching tool in our training programs and seminars of the Centre for Reproductive Loss in Montreal. The purpose of these seminars was and is intended to give a broad overview of those components that appear to be the most essential in helping bereaved individuals to grieve reproductive losses such as miscarriage, stillbirth, abortion, infertility, and other related losses. Because the seminar participants, who were comprised of health professionals and volunteers, had very little or no exposure to grief education, especially vis-à-vis reproductive loss, it was necessary to give a broad yet concise view of the healing process from beginning to end in order to accommodate the day-long seminar format. This clinically-based model provided that overview and emphasized a holistic way of looking at the healing process of grieving through the body, mind, spirit connection.

GRIEVING AND THE HEALING PROCESS MODEL©

A process, defined as a group of operations or actions, is not passive. Operation, as action, effort, performance, and working, is active. The healing process, then, requires effort, action, and work on the part of the bereaved. Hence, the term "grief work." Since no one can grieve for another, "good grief" comes about through "grief work." At the same time, however, there are helpers who can walk this healing journey with the bereaved so that no one needs to grieve alone.

These operations or actions undertaken during the process of grieving are not the only ones required for constructive, healthy grieving; they are, however, in my estimation, the most essential. Other healing actions, found in the literature on grieving, are not excluded.

In actual practice, these operations do not necessarily follow a specific sequential order. Even though "reaching out to others" is placed at the end of the guidelines, in grief support groups, for example, grievers may reach out to others to help and be helped from the very beginning. The internal logic of the model (our way of viewing grieving) does not require a particular chronological order to the operations/actions since each grieving individual is unique.

This process does not follow the stage, step, phase, or other models of grief theory. It takes its cues from the grieving person. The process is essentially fluid in nature and follows the way people usually experience grief. This experience of grief proceeds not in an orderly linear fashion but more in a zig-zag manner, much like a lightening bolt. Parents often describe it as an emotional roller coaster. In other words, there is not an even progression from point A to point B, or from number one to number two. Grieving persons may need to go back to one or more of the parts to grieve again in a different time and place. Re-grieving a loss is normal. For example, the telling of the story may need to be told again and again. This is very different from a medical history (of the particular loss) that is taken once and for all, with only the bare bones facts recorded.

The helper who is guided by this Healing Process Model© presents grieving persons with suggestions that they can choose to do or not do, at their own pace and in their own time. One grieving mother who had lost twins, said she appreciated these suggestions which she called her "homework." "Homework," such as journal writing and reading material on grief and reproductive loss (bibliotherapy), is helpful to some because it provides structure by giving grieving persons something concrete to do. This, in turn, helps them to gain a sense of control and empowerment, especially in the face of feeling helpless, powerless, and experiencing a loss of control. Because many grievers report that their memory is adversely affected, "homework" is always written down on paper. Thus, "homework" can facilitate "grief work" for some bereaved individuals.

The process respects the individuality of grieving persons because it is fluid and must be adapted to the uniqueness of each individual. To put it another way, one size does not fit all. For example, while having a ritual or memorial service or ceremony is helpful for putting closure on the pain of the loss, each person chooses to individualize what is most meaningful for them. Then again, others may choose not to have any ritual or memorial service at all. Respect for the individuality of grieving persons requires that the therapist/helper must be sensitive to where the bereaved are on their grieving/healing journey by taking cues from each individual through compassionate and non-judgmental listening. Not everyone will travel this journey at the same pace nor proceed in the exact same order. Some individuals have entered counseling by wanting to help others, which is usually the last component. Once again, the grief therapist or other helping persons—family, friends, health professional, or pastoral counselor must ascertain if that particular bereaved individual is ready to reach out to others; this they can do by assisting the bereaved to determine their state of readiness, renewal, and healing.

The healing process can also be called the grieving process or the grieving/healing process. "In the grieving is the healing," is the axiom which appears on the brochures of the Centre for Reproductive Loss and which expresses the close relationship between grieving and healing. Another quotation that expressed this close relationship even earlier is the Beatitude from the New Testament, "Blessed are those who mourn for they shall be comforted" [1]. This Beatitude gives permission to the bereaved to grieve and to mourn their loss so that healing and comfort can come.

To summarize, each of the separate components within this model is not unique. They have appeared in the grief literature and in numerous other publications. Most of these components also apply to other types of grief and loss, not just reproductive loss. Yet, by bringing together these operations/actions/components, this model becomes unique due to its composition. These components or essential elements required for healing make for a holistic way of looking at grieving since they represent a body, mind, spirit connection. This model thus presents a broad overview of constructive, healthy grieving, in particular, grieving related to reproductive loss.

DEFINITION

The Healing Process Model© for reproductive loss is a clinical based model which is derived from the realities of the grief experience, that is, what the bereaved themselves manifest (see "Development of the Model," p. 34). These realities of the grief experience then become the components for the guidelines in the Healing Process Model©. The objectives of these guidelines are to heal, to comfort, to soothe, to grow sound again, to encourage, restore, and renew the body, mind, and spirit of those who grieve and mourn.

COMPONENTS OF THE
HEALING PROCESS MODEL©

Acknowledgment

Normally in our society, acknowledgment is the first response to anyone who is bereaved. We extend condolences to the bereaved with such expressions as, "I'm sorry about your loss," or "Please accept my deepest sympathy." When we acknowledge another's loss, we identify with and accept their grief. We allow ourselves to become involved in their pain and carry some of the burden of their sorrow. Just as with deaths other than through reproductive loss, parents who have suffered a miscarriage or stillbirth also need to hear words of consolation and comfort. Sympathy and empathy must be communicated either in words of condolences or non-verbally through a simple touch, hug, or embrace. It is not enough simply to "feel bad" for them.

Acknowledgment of reproductive loss can also be the first healthy response on the part of the bereaved to the loss. This acknowledgment gives permission to the bereaved themselves to grieve their loss (see Chapter 2, Worden's first task of mourning, "To Accept the Reality of the Loss"). Thus, to acknowledge loss is to allow, own, permit, recognize, and accept the reality of one's loss. Its opposite is to deny, dismiss, reject, and shun.

When we do not acknowledge and accept the reality of loss, reproductive or otherwise, it is as if we were saying that we do not want to get involved, and so we have given ourselves permission to become detached and distant from the bereaved. It lets us "off the hook," as it were, of becoming involved in their pain. When health professionals, family, or friends do not acknowledge these reproductive losses, they minimize, dismiss, deny, and thus disenfranchise the grief and loss of bereaved parents [2]. Not knowing what to say or do at the time, they will often resort to clichés such as "You're young. You can have another," or "That's nature's way," or "It was probably deformed anyway." These clichés are not helpful and may further compound the distress of the grieving parents.

Lack of acknowledgment on the part of a significant other can be very hurtful and may even forestall the grieving process. One woman reported that her husband had not acknowledged a miscarriage she had suffered or even the fact that she had been pregnant. Could it be that acknowledgment of this loss implies a recognition of the fact that some events are not under our control and thus make us feel helpless, vulnerable, powerless, and out of control? Is it a case of denying the reality of the event and its accompanying manifestations of grief? Another example is that of the mother who cannot acknowledge, who even minimizes her own daughter's miscarriage because she had not grieved her own reproductive losses. In another situation, a woman who had had an abortion followed by a miscarriage was inconsolable as she tried desperately but unsuccessfully to become pregnant. She received no comfort or sympathy from her husband, even though he had tacitly approved of her abortion. He blamed her saying, "Well, it was your decision, you're the woman. After all, you're the one who had it done." He also blamed her for the miscarriage saying that it probably happened because she really did not want to be pregnant.

Acknowledging and accepting the reality of reproductive loss is perhaps the most effective healing intervention that anyone can do to help the grieving parent.

When a woman calls our Centre for Reproductive Loss to say she's had a miscarriage, the first thing we do is to offer sympathy and condolences on the death of her baby. We often hear these women say, "You're the first person to call it a baby." While this simple intervention of acknowledgment sometimes elicits tears from the woman, it tells her that her loss is understood and that she has permission to grieve. Sometimes that is all she may need to hear. With these simple words of acknowledgment, the healing process has begun. Some other women have told us that just knowing we exist is a comfort to them; our very existence is a form of acknowledgment. Another woman said that to her the fact that we were there serves as a witness to her loss and grief.

One study, "Parental Grief Response to Perinatal Death," examined the effect of several variables on the grief response [3]. The findings suggest that it is not the variables (sex, type of loss, number of losses, and subsequent pregnancy) which influence the grief response as much as the parents' perception that their loss was not understood. In other words, when parents perceived that their loss was not properly acknowledged, their grief was more intense. Conversely, it would also suggest that acknowledgment can lessen the grief response.

Closely related to this is another study entitled "Satisfaction with Hospital Care and Interventions after Pregnancy Loss" [4]. In this study, the researchers examined the recommended interventions at the time of pregnancy loss in a longitudinal study of 138 women and 56 of their husbands or partners who experienced miscarriage, ectopic pregnancy, stillbirth, or newborn death. They found that the bereaved's greater satisfaction with overall care was related more to the attentiveness and sensitivity of health care personnel than the numbers of interventions alone.

Hospital personnel such as nurses, doctors, ultrasound technicians, pastoral team members, and even secretaries, ward clerks, and admitting personnel play a key role in initiating the healing process. Their sympathetic acknowledgment of the loss gives the grieving parents permission to mourn their child. Parents felt comforted by their doctors' and nurses' expression of care and concern especially if the latter were themselves also moved to tears or showed other signs of acknowledgment of the loss. On the other hand, one mother said that it brought her no comfort to have her doctor dismiss the death of her full term stillborn baby by saying, "It's unfortunate but these things happen." Another woman in a similar situation who also perceived a lack of compassion, described the hospital and her doctor as being "tainted." Consequently, she looked for another doctor at a different hospital. When parents are treated in such an apparently cold and dismissive manner, seemingly devoid of compassion and comfort, they have usually changed doctors and sometimes hospitals.

Telling the Story: Facts and Feelings

Telling the story and re-telling the story of grief and loss to a compassionate, non-judgmental listener is essential to healing. Telling the story helps to process the grief and to facilitate other tasks of mourning. The story is much more than the facts of when, where, how, etc., as in the manner of the medical history taking. That is only the beginning. Most parents will readily manifest a "crystal clear" memory recall of facts and feelings of the loss as if it happened yesterday. However, some other parents who have experienced a particularly traumatic loss might not remember all the details. One way to help them remember is to have them picture everything around the event, even seemingly insignificant details such as time of day, weather conditions, clothing worn, people they encountered, what they ate, any particular sights, sounds, smells that would jog their memory. For example, one woman could recall the loss but not the feelings surrounding the loss. When we began to explore those factual details, she was then able to recapture the feelings associated with the loss and then work with those feelings. Telling the story can be done also by using a tape recorder. Writing out the story in a diary or journal or more simply on looseleaf paper are other ways to tell the story. Some parents have written poetry and even books about their loss.

Reproductive Loss History

Taking a history of reproductive loss must be done with sensitivity and compassion. In addition to the presenting problem (for example, miscarriage, stillbirth, etc.), I ask the question, "How many pregnancies?" and "What was the outcome?" I usually do not ask directly if there were any abortions. Some women may not wish to tell even their physicians of a previous abortion for any number of reasons. One woman told me she lied about her four abortions to her doctor when he recorded her medical history. One couple took offense when the nurse used the term abortion to refer to the therapeutic abortion they were about to have. They insisted on calling it a "pregnancy termination." It is important to record all the pregnancy losses, however they occurred, since they represent "unfinished business"; they also must be acknowledged and grieved. Pacing is also an important consideration when obtaining a history of reproductive and pregnancy losses. One must be sensitive to too much being recalled too fast.

For those women who present for post abortion counseling, I assure them that I am not there to judge their actions but rather to help them heal. Therefore, if I do not tell them that their decision was the wrong one, neither do I tell them that their decision was the right one; both statements would be judgmental.

History of Other Losses and Stress

In addition to a reproductive loss history, it is important to know what other losses a person has experienced, especially if they are recent or concurrent losses. These losses might also be death related—other relatives, friends, pets—or non-death related—accident, flood, trauma, earthquake, divorce, downsizing, unemployment, a move or any other significant life change or transition. It is helpful to know how these losses/transitions are normally dealt with by this particular person. In other words, what is their usual pattern, if any, of coping with such events. Lisa, a young woman of 22 who had experienced the death of her premature twins, was understandably devastated by this loss and became obsessed with getting pregnant again; she wanted to replace the loss rather than grieve it. Since she had never even attended a funeral, she had not had an occasion to learn how to cope with a death related loss.

Losses and life transitions, even the happy ones, are stressful experiences. The Social Re-adjustment Rating Scale developed by Holmes and Rahe [5] rates many stressful life events and gives each one a numerical position on the Scale from 0–100. For example, the death of a spouse is rated at 100, the highest; divorce at 73; marital separation at 65; death of a close relative at 63. These numbers serve as a guide to the degree of stress in one's life. Interestingly, most of these events listed are losses. It is not difficult to understand that a person experiencing a loss is also experiencing stress.

Infertility as a reproductive loss is also a stressful life event. In a study done by Doctors A. Epstein and Helane S. Rosenberg, professors of psychology at Rutgers State University in New Brunswick, New Jersey, 59 infertile women were asked to rate infertility as a stressor, using the Holmes and Rahe Social Re-adjustment Rating Scale. The findings of this study placed infertility sixth on the scale at 59.7. Dr. Epstein commented:

> There are about 43 events on this scale, and this was among the top six. To find that this (infertility) is not even included on the list of major life stresses would suggest that if you're going through infertility, although you feel this is a major life stress, the rest of the world doesn't even acknowledge it. It turns out that of the infertile population, the major proportion are secondary

infertile patients, and this is the population that family physicians tend to see the most [6].

Dr. Epstein believes that many family physicians are not aware of the stress that infertility causes their patients, in particular the secondary infertility patients who have had one child but appear to be unable to have another child. Secondary infertility refers either to the inability to again conceive or to conceive but not carry to term, after having only one successful pregnancy. In many cases the reasons for this condition are unknown and cannot be anticipated. This condition of secondary infertility has profound implications in regard to abortions, especially when done because the time was not right. Unfortunately, for many women there was never another time that they were able to conceive.

Bereaved individuals often experience a sense of little or no control following a loss and they would be well advised to reduce stress as much as possible during the time of their grieving. The presence of stress hormones can alter the body's physiology. Dr. Robert Carney, professor of medical physiology at Washington University in St. Louis, said that stress hormones can trigger higher levels of fibrinogen, a protein that binds blood cells together to form clots; when levels of fibrinogen are elevated, the risk of a heart attack is increased. Stress hormones can also increase the pulse rate, and "make the heart less flexible in responding to changing demand" [7]. Carney's comments were related to a British study which associated higher plasma fibrinogen concentrations with workers who had a feeling of little or no control at work. Pregnant women should also heed the same advice in order to prevent the adverse effects of the presence of stress hormones upon the body's physiology.

Explain, Describe, and Normalize Grief Reactions and Manifestations

While "grief work" is largely "heart work," in many ways it is also "head work." When the helper gives to grieving parents an overview of how grief affects body, mind, and spirit, they have a sense that what they are experiencing is normal, that they are not alone, and that others have experienced similar reactions (see Chapter 1 "Grief: The Body, Mind, Spirit Connection," p. 1). There is comfort in knowing that they are normal, that they are not "going crazy," even though they feel as if they are. Several of our grieving parents told us how reassuring it was to be told that they were not "going crazy," but rather they were grieving. It is equally important for them to keep in mind that having grief reactions similar to those of others does not take away from them their individuality and their own unique way of responding to their loss. Even when grief reactions approximate the statistical "bell shaped curve" of normal distribution, it does not reveal the whole picture of how uniquely parents experience reproductive loss. For example, there is a wide variation in one's reaction to miscarriage according to Limbo and Wheeler as stated in their book *When a Baby Dies: A Handbook for Healing and Helping:*

Parents may mourn deeply, not at all, or somewhere in between. One mother may be devastated, calling it "the most terrible thing a family has to go through." Those who mourn little initially may mourn the baby months or years later. Other women may consider it just another learning experience. Some are relieved because they did not want to be pregnant. It is as normal for parents not to grieve as it is to be devastated by the miscarriage [8, p. 42].

As a help to explain and describe grief manifestations and reactions, I make available to grieving parents articles, pamphlets, books, and audio and video cassette tapes on grief and reproductive loss. At the beginning, the information given is usually quite simple and brief. Because many grieving persons report inability to concentrate and memory loss, it is more beneficial to give information that is easy to understand, in small doses, and in written form. If information and instructions need to be given verbally, they may have to be repeated and given slowly. Sometimes the bereaved just do not comprehend as quickly as they might do under different circumstances. They are in a different emotional space and slowed down time frame. Some may feel out of "sync" with the rest of the world around them.

Establish, Reconnect, Continue the Bonds of the Relationship

Establishing, reconnecting, and continuing the bonds of the relationship with the miscarried, stillborn, or aborted baby is a most effective and comforting component in the healing process.

Giving the child a name helps to establish the relationship and make real the loss. The effect of naming affirms the child's unique individuality as a person and gives that child a place on the family tree. Naming can prevent subsequent children from carrying the burden of a replacement baby who then must not only fulfill his or her own potential but carry the unfulfilled shattered dream of a previous loss. Naming a child is a way of dealing with the "unfinished business" of not addressing previous reproductive losses and parents report a sense of peace and comfort after they have given their miscarried baby a name (see Appendix C, "Letter to Sandi"). Interestingly, many of these parents have instinctively and spontaneously named their babies on their own, as though prompted by some innate natural wisdom to do so. Even in early miscarriage, it is important to name the baby, so as to separate the child's identity from the mother's. The first trimester of pregnancy, when the majority of miscarriages usually occur, is referred to as the narcissistic stage of pregnancy, states Dr. J. M. Stack [9]. Grieving the loss of a baby at this stage of pregnancy can be very difficult. Dr. Stack lists several factors which may contribute to prolonged, inadequate, or delayed grief reactions and which help explain this difficulty:

1. Frequently, people do not even know that the woman is pregnant.
2. A woman who has miscarried is often embarrassed or reticent to mention that she was, but is no longer, pregnant.
3. Frequently, she had not resolved the ambivalence that is typical of the early narcissistic stage of pregnancy.
4. She had not identified the fetus as a new person who was a part of herself. Grieving the loss of one's self is often different and more difficult than grieving the loss of an outside love object.
5. She is unable to identify with the "lost person" even to the extent of having felt fetal movement and recognized "someone else" was there [9, p. 162].[1]

Delayed grief reactions have been noted, too, in women who have abortions in the first trimester of pregnancy. The same contributing factors for such a reaction, as cited by Dr. Stack, also apply. Health professionals should not overlook this as a possibility when caring for these women.

In addition to naming the baby, letter writing is a simple tool that parents can use to establish, reconnect, and continue the bonds of relationship with the baby. Journal writing, keeping a diary, poetry and prose, are other forms of writing that bring comfort to grieving parents. In fact, many of our parents surprised themselves at the depth of emotion that writing to the baby or about the baby elicited. For most, it was the first time they had ever written poetry.

Writing as a form of emotional catharsis and healing is not a recent development of 20th century psychology; for centuries, poets and novelists have recounted the devastating effects of the loss of a child. In the book *The Poetry of Childhood* [10], several well-known poets, from Milton's (17th century), "On the Death of a Fair Infant" to Rossetti's (19th century) "Empty Cradle," express the deep sorrow and devastation of losing a child.

These poems seem to reflect a natural instinct which prompted the written expression of these losses and which continue to bear silent witness to the agelessness and universality of such grief (see Appendix D).

While there are some skeptics who believe that naming the baby (especially a miscarried one) or writing a letter or poem to and about the baby are "morbid," one cannot deny the evidence of healing and comfort that grieving parents have reported from these interventions. Nor can one overlook the proliferation, in recent years, of reproductive loss newsletters founded by and for grieving parents as a forum for sharing their remembrances and memorials of their deceased children. Some of these newsletters include "Pen Parents of Canada," "Centre for Loss in Multiple Birth" ("C.L.I.M.B."), "Infertility Awareness Association of Canada"

---

[1] Reprinted with permission from the *American Journal of Orthopsychiatry*. Copyright © 1984 by the American Orthopsychiatric Association, Inc.

("IAAC"), "Loving Arms," "The Baby's Breath," and "The Dove," the newsletter of the Centre for Reproductive Loss (see Appendix E).

In addition to the grassroots approach of writing in newsletters as a means of continuing the bonds with the deceased, current grief literature further supports this important healing intervention. One such example is the book *Continuing Bonds: New Understandings of Grief* [11]. Another is Alexandra Kennedy's *Your Loved One Lives on Within You*. She comments:

> An inner relationship with the person who has died continues on after death. This relationship, constantly unfolding within, offers powerful and mostly untapped opportunities for healing, resolution, and even guidance [12, p. 6].

Grieving parents who write prose or poetry to or about their deceased children can derive much comfort from this powerful tool which is helpful for achieving internal communication and thus continuing the bonds. Kennedy further explains :

> When you practice internal communication with the person you have lost, you'll experience the release of what has been bottled up inside and be more at peace with the loss as the love you feel begins to flow freely to its object [12, p. 9].

The Questions?—Encounter with Mystery, Spirituality, and Growing through Grief

The question "Why?" is often raised with any loss, but it is especially poignant when parents follow the "why" with the statement, "But babies aren't supposed to die." "Why" is not the only question that arises after a reproductive loss. There are many others as well.

One woman who presented with a miscarriage wondered if her present loss was related to a previous abortion. Others might ask or wonder if the loss was a punishment from God; a woman who had difficulty getting pregnant believed her infertility was a punishment from God because she was living with a man to whom she was not married. Some parents have blamed God for their loss even when they held no religious beliefs at all.

Other questions bring up issues of blame toward self, spouse, partner, health professionals, and even some diagnostic procedures. Several couples have blamed themselves for agreeing to the diagnostic procedure "amniocentesis," since a miscarriage occurred shortly afterwards. Catherine believed her baby died due to her fears and the stress of anticipating the amniocentesis; her baby died in utero at four months, shortly before the procedure could be done.

Being able to assign blame, real or imagined, to a concrete event or action or even to oneself seems preferable to attributing blame to nothing in particular or to the randomness of the universe. It is almost as though parents find a sense of order or control over the loss when blame for it can be named; a strange and paradoxical comfort is thus provided. In the film *There was a Child* [13], Maureen attributed the stillborn death of her son to a plane trip that she had taken. She stated that he had been "incredibly active" due to the pressure in the cabin on the plane and she believed that his vigorous movements caused him to become tangled up in the cord and consequently to die.

Encounter with mystery and spirituality is inevitable in the search for a purpose and meaning of the loss. Believing in some form of spirituality, even if only to make sense of the loss, may give parents some measure of peace and comfort but only if the meaning comes from them. For the therapist or helper to suggest a meaning or purpose for reproductive loss too early in the grieving/healing process is not advisable. The cue for addressing this issue must come from the parents themselves, at their own pace, and in their own time.

Although Marie-Josée was absolutely shattered by the death of her premature twins, she believed this tragic event helped her to be less afraid of death since "I know I have two children waiting for me in heaven."

Caroline's baby lived only 12 hours but she felt that her life had been transformed by the birth and death of her daughter. "She really saved my life because I was going downhill before I got pregnant. But she got me back on track. I began to take care of and respect myself during my pregnancy because I loved her and I knew she loved me in return."

Sometimes parents believe in a purpose right from the start even when they do not know what it is. The following notice in the Birth/Death column of a local newspaper is a poignant example of that belief. I have omitted last names out of respect for the privacy of the family:

> Michael and Charlene proudly announce the birth of their first child, Jordan Brooke Teionientate, on January 19, 1997 at 15:13 at 6 lbs., 4 ozs. and 19¾". Proud grandparents are Margaret M. and Ken and Irene, fifth grandchild on both sides and first granddaughter for Margaret. Great-grandmother Velma L. Numerous aunts and uncles and cousins joined in the celebration of her birth. Regretfully, and with great sorrow, they also announce that their little angel (Bright Snow) was taken from them at 16:44 the same day. Her beauty and strength were insurmountable. Her face was that of an angel. Her message, still unclear, will one day give us the strength to be at peace again [14].

This touching announcement intermingled as it is with joy and great sorrow, affirms the reality that reproductive loss is a family affair by acknowledging the members of the extended family; it confirms the placement of the baby on the family tree by the identification of the role relationships to the deceased child; it honors the uniqueness of the baby's identity by giving her a name; it offers the hope of finding a purpose, through the message, "still unclear," that this child brought and that one day its meaning will be revealed through continuing the bonds of the relationship with her.

Asking the question "Why?" eventually leads to questions about meaning and then to focus on spiritual concerns—the meaning of life and death, the purpose and mystery of suffering and grief, and in particular the meaning parents give to their own loss. When the spiritual issues go beyond our limitations as therapists, we refer parents to an appropriate spiritual director or pastoral counselor, priest, minister, or rabbi.

Grief Work vs. Guilt Work

Guilt, remorse, and regret often accompany self blame following reproductive loss. Feelings of guilt are more prevalent than most people realize. In his book *Swallowed by a Snake,* author Thomas R. Golden comments: "People who experience a significant grief will usually experience some form of guilt. The guilt is characterized by searching for the responsibilities we did or did not take prior to the death. It usually takes the form of shoulds and shouldn'ts" [15, p. 66].

Parents who have suffered a reproductive loss berate themselves with questions and recriminations: "If only I had not driven on that long trip"; "Why didn't I take better care of myself?"; "Why did we agree to the amniocentesis knowing the risks of miscarriage, especially after seven years of infertility and trying so hard to get pregnant?"; "Why did I stay on birth control pills for ten years instead of trying to get pregnant sooner? I wonder if I had fertility problems and never even knew it when I started on the birth control pill." Usually there are no answers to such questions. Parents often say that they "beat themselves over the head" because of their guilt. One mother who miscarried felt very guilty because she could not protect her baby from death. "My body failed me. I'm supposed to protect my baby. I feel I'm to blame." Regarding miscarriage, Dr. Stack also confirms this universal guilt experience:

> Guilt is a nearly universal feeling experienced by women suffering from a miscarriage. Explanations as to cause are often inadequate or non-existent, leading the woman to feel that she may have done something to cause the miscarriage. As do many survivors, the woman may feel that she didn't care enough, didn't pray enough, didn't go to the doctor soon enough or went too soon, took the wrong foods or drugs, and sometimes even wished consciously not to be pregnant and got her wish [9, p. 162].

Just as "grief work" requires effort and energy, so too does "guilt work." But sometimes "guilt work" can be non-productive, does not always lead to healing, and is often counter-productive to genuine "grief work." Because of that, it is necessary to differentiate non-productive guilt from productive guilt. Golden explains:

> Guilt is somewhat different from the other feelings of grief. We need to differentiate the guilt we are speaking of from other forms of guilt, particularly the guilt that has a productive message for us. For instance, maybe our guilt over drinking and driving and causing an accident has an important message for us about our need to change that behavior. In the typical guilt of

grief, many people don't think that guilt is a feeling at all. They see it more as a process of thinking comprised of negative self-thoughts [15, p. 68].

Guilt feelings, however, do need to be acknowledged and explored so that the non-productive "guilt work" can become productive "grief work" once again. However, Golden believes that most of the irrational guilt that stems from grief can be summarized in the sentence, "Guilt is putting today's knowledge on yesterday's problems" [15, p. 68]. Sometimes bereaved parents get stuck in their healing journey, bound, as it were, by the ties of guilt which keep them from moving forward. The advice of Golden is worth heeding when he states: "Don't hunt yourself down in a lethal chase with guilt. If you do, you are positioning yourself for paralysis" [15, p. 67].

If irrational guilt persists, even after reality testing, then the way out of that paralysis of guilt, the way out of "guilt work" and back to "grief work" is through forgiveness. When parents believe that they were *actually* responsible for the loss, they must come to forgive themselves for those actions they thought caused the loss. If they only *imagine* that they were responsible for the loss, even when it could not possibly be their fault, parents must forgive themselves for that as well. Worden believes that the "seeking and granting of forgiveness" is a critical aspect of the resolution of guilt in grief therapy [16, p. 84].

Forgiveness and Anger

There are other occasions and situations where the "seeking and granting of forgiveness" is needed. Just as guilt can accompany grief and loss, so, too, does it seem that grief and anger are partners as well. Parents may experience anger toward themselves and others; or they might hold a grudge against family, friends, or health professionals who dismissed or minimized their loss, who may have said or done the "wrong thing," who did not give sufficient support or who otherwise appeared to be cold and distant. One woman was angry at her obstetrician who, she felt, abandoned her once she was about to miscarry. Another young woman hated and resented her parents, her husband, and her mother-in-law for having coerced her into having an abortion prior to her wedding. One parent can blame the other for the loss or feel angry about not receiving from the partner all the help desired during the grieving process. Ironically, parents have experienced anger at the baby that they lost; they feel that their child has abandoned them and they even resent the baby for coming into their life at all at that particular time.

"Life After the Death of a Child," a study which examined the source and continuity of support received by bereaved parents, also documents the feelings of anger and hostility brought about by a lack of support from family and friends. Although she has learned to forgive, one mother who lost a child still feels hostile sometimes. Her comments illustrate this feeling: "The neighbors never mention her name or anything; act like nothing happened. They want to talk about their children and all their grandchildren. At first, I wanted to punch them in the face or scratch their eyes out. They can't know what they haven't experienced" [17, p. 73].

A very beneficial intervention that can be utilized for bringing about forgiveness is the Gestalt "Empty Chair" technique [18]. In her article, "Abortion: An Issue to Grieve?," a counselor described the use of this technique with post aborted women; it "allows the client to 'talk' to the fetus, explaining the factors that contributed to the decision to abort, expressing feelings of sorrow and, finally, asking forgiveness. Next, the client speaks for the fetus and offers understanding, compassion, and forgiveness" [19, p. 376].

When forgiveness is released too early, before the anger has been adequately addressed, this healing component might remain incomplete. Therefore, it should be noted that prior to seeking and granting forgiveness, feelings of anger, rage, and hostility must be acknowledged first. In addition to the "Empty Chair" technique, letter writing has proven helpful for exploring and expressing those feelings as a way for releasing forgiveness. There may even be a need for repeated rituals of forgiveness over time.

Closure—Letting Go of the Pain:
Creating "A Place to Remember"

Although there are similarities between this component and another one already discussed, namely, "Establish, Reconnect, Continue the Bonds of the Relationship," they are treated separately in the healing process model in order to emphasize the different aspects of remembering. For our purposes, we define closure as a process of letting go of the intense pain of the loss. It must be clearly understood that closure does not mean forgetting the deceased child. Sometimes parents are reluctant to let go of the pain since the pain represents a tangible reminder of the loss, the child "who could have been." A health professional who had attended one of our seminars reacted very strongly and negatively to the word closure. She thought it meant turning her back on the loss and forgetting about her miscarried baby. Anyone using the term closure must, therefore, carefully and sensitively explain its meaning.

Achieving healthy closure begins by remembering and by preserving memories, keepsakes, and mementos of the loss. Such items could include a doctor's appointment card, an ultrasound picture, the mother's and baby's identification bands, footprints, handprints, crib card, lock of hair, a photograph of the parents holding the baby, and certificate of birth and death.

In their book *When a Baby Dies: A Handbook for Healing and Helping,* authors Limbo and Wheeler offer the following advice:

> Anything used in caring for the baby while in hospital, be it a brush, baby lotion or powder, should be given to the parents. The blanket in which the baby was wrapped should remain unwashed and be put in a sealed plastic bag. "I opened the plastic bag that had Lisa's blanket and its smell made me feel

like she was still a part of us," explained a mother. "This was her blanket. It touched her body. She was real" [8, p. 109].

While taking a photograph of the deceased baby may sound strange, it is not a new or recent practice. Bereavement photographs of parents holding their stillborn child in a formal pose were done in the early 1900s. Today, with consent of the parents, many hospitals take pictures of the deceased baby and keep them on file until the parents decide they want them. When the parents' permission is asked beforehand, some of them may at first refuse to have the picture taken; later they may regret not having this precious memento of their baby. Parents have reported that they were too much in shock to be able to make even the simple decision to have a photograph taken. It would be more helpful for grief-stricken parents not to have to make such a choice while they are in shock and great distress. Hopefully, over time, this practice will become part of routine care, just as the taking of the footprints and handprints of a baby is done now. Parents can be informed later that the baby's picture was available for them whenever they felt ready to see it. One health professional, a support group facilitator, listed the following suggestions for taking pictures of the newborn and stillborn babies who had died:

1. Take more than one picture.
2. Fill the picture frame with the baby.
3. Take some with the baby wrapped in a blanket, some with the baby unwrapped if possible, some with the parents holding the baby.
4. Make sure the lighting makes the baby look attractive.
5. Add a stuffed animal or baby toy to the picture.
6. Use your imagination and think about how the baby can look its best. Many parents like to share these pictures with their friends and relatives [20, p. 9].

There is also available another resource which describes how to take sensitive pictures of deceased babies. Caregivers will find this manual, *A Most Important Picture,* very helpful [21].

The Perinatal Bereavement Services Ontario have available *Perinatal Bereavement: A Caregiver Guide* which is a very well written and visually appealing manual for dealing with miscarriage, stillbirth, or neonatal death [22].

In addition to keepsakes and mementos, having a memorial service or simple ritual, especially of the parents own choosing, contributes to meaningful closure, as the following illustrates:

One family whose baby died before the 20th week of pregnancy held a memorial service in the mother's hospital room. Immediate family members were present, and a local minister performed the service. Their baby, swaddled in a warm blanket, was brought to the mother's room. "Just to know she was there with us during the service helped us to say good-bye," the mother said. "The service provided us with a feeling of closure from the past two day's experience, though we knew her loss would keep on hurting for many days to come."

Parents can write and conduct the service themselves or ask a minister or other comforting person to do so. A prayer or blessing also may be said in memory of the baby, especially when baptism is not possible or desirable.

A funeral, either public or private, is another option. It may be at the graveside, a church, the hospital, or at home [8, pp. 74-75].

Care for Self: Body, Mind, Spirit

Just as grief affects body, mind, and spirit, so also caring for self includes body, mind, and spirit. As mentioned previously, losses are stressful life events (see Holmes and Rahe Social Re-adjustment Rating Scale [5]) and since stress places additional burdens upon the immune system, the bereaved are more likely to become ill after a loss. Therefore, it is advisable for the bereaved to have a medical examination within the first three months of their bereavement. In addition to the bodily effects of grief, the effect of grief upon the mind is manifested by reports of some who claimed to be more accident prone while they were grieving. This may be related to such common grief manifestations as an inability to concentrate, memory loss, and the lack of focus which many bereaved individuals have experienced. The effect of grief upon a person's mental capacities (mind), has profound implications in the workplace. One of our grieving mothers who had experienced a stillbirth, commented upon her lack of concentration at work saying, "All I could do was shuffle papers, I was so pre-occupied with the thoughts of the death of my little girl." Employers need to be aware of how grief can affect their employees and their work performance. Hopefully, those individuals in such critical occupations as air traffic controllers and airline pilots will receive adequate grief support when needed through their Employee Assistance Programs.

The bereaved may also experience lack of appetite and so may not be eating properly. Vitamin supplements might be needed at this time. Often the bereaved do not sleep well and can accumulate a sleep debt, resulting in sleep deprivation, yet another stress factor. Many experience lack of energy and extreme fatigue to the point where they lack interest or motivation to do any of the activities they normally once did easily. This in turn could also lead to social isolation, thus cutting themselves off from the support of family and friends. Sometimes the bereaved may not even have sufficient energy to make a telephone call to ask for help. Caregivers need to be aware of this and to be pro-active in their follow-up to grieving parents, rather than wait for the grief stricken parent to make the first move. It is also important that caregivers be aware of those bereaved individuals who have an underlying (or chronic) depression, anxiety, or other mental conditions which may require more intense help and/or medication.

Some bereaved individuals may neglect exercise while others may throw themselves into too much physical activity, including work, in an attempt to ease the pain of their loss. A few may resort to unhealthy behaviors, such as increased smoking, drinking, or even abusive, aggressive acting out.

The third aspect of caring for self focuses on the spiritual, and bereaved individuals should not neglect this critical component of their healing. Studies have shown that incorporating and nurturing the spiritual element in holistic health care cannot be ignored. This is no less true in counseling anyone who has suffered a reproductive loss. One article, entitled "Get Spiritual for Better Health," stresses the link between physical well-being and spirituality:

> Spirituality is good medicine. A growing body of scientific research shows that those who believe in something more than their physicians not only enjoy life more but also live longer and are physically healthier.
> This new version of preventative medicine holds the promise of reducing medical bills, because prayer, meditation and attendance at religious services are cheaper than surgery and other medical treatment [23].

"Be caring of your spiritual health" and "don't end your search for spirituality" advises Rabbi Earl A. Grollman, popular speaker and writer. Although his words were intended for caregivers, individuals who have suffered reproductive loss will find his advice helpful as well. He suggests some things to do that will keep one "spiritually in tune."

> Take time for spiritual care. Worship, walks, prayer, meditation, reading, or listening to music may be ways that you attend to your own spirituality. Despite the busyness, do not separate yourself from your sources of spiritual nourishment and strength. Now they are even more critical [24, p. 153].[2]

In the not-too-distant past, spirituality had often been overlooked or regarded as unimportant in much of the health care literature. More recently, however, research into the connection between spirituality and physical health has sparked some new medical interest in spirituality. One reason for this renewed interest is given by Dr. John D. Morgan, philosophy professor at the University of Western Ontario, who believes that "the love affair with science is no longer working. In the 1960s, the attitude was that science was going to cure all our problems. I don't think anybody believes that anymore. Now people are looking for solutions other than the scientific" [23].

While spirituality may not be the only "solution" people are looking for, especially when the encounter with the mystery of the meaning of life, death, and loss may not yield an acceptable answer, nevertheless, it remains an integral part of the holistic caring for self in the grieving/healing journey. Rabbi Grollman offers these words of comfort:

---

[2] Copyright © 1997 from *Living with Grief: When Illness is Prolonged* by K. J. Doka [24]. Reproduced by permission of Routledge, Inc., part of the Taylor & Francis Group.

> Spirituality is something you may wish to use, not lose, with a wisdom that has nourished the souls of humankind for untold generations. And sorrow can be a spiritual pilgrimage.
>
> Spirituality may not take away heartache. But spirituality may help you to better live with adversity and to accept the unacceptable [24, pp. 157-158].

To sum up, caring for self should also include learning about grief, what one can expect to experience about the grieving process as well as the normal reactions and manifestations of grief. Parents can read articles and books about what others have written of their experience of reproductive loss. They can also join a support group and/or seek individual counseling through educational and support organizations such as the Centre for Reproductive Loss. In addition, they can connect with other support organizations which provide helpful newsletters on grief and reproductive loss.

The bereaved need to be encouraged to be gentle and patient with themselves, not be too hard on themselves during this difficult time of bereavement and avoid, if possible, making any major decisions. The caregiver/helper can assess the grieving individual in terms of nutrition, sleep, rest, exercise, relaxation, recreation, or just taking time out perhaps for spiritual retreats, offering support and encouragement to the bereaved, and helping them to be aware of how important it is to care for self in the holistic manner of body, mind, and spirit at this critical time.

Reaching Out to Help Others— Compassionate Outreach

According to our Healing Process Model©, the final operation/action in the grieving process is usually reaching out by the bereaved to help others who had experienced a similar reproductive loss.

Many of our parents have volunteered to act as peer support helpers either through telephone support or personal contact with those persons who were recently bereaved. However, this should not be done too soon, at least not until the volunteer parents have sufficiently done their own grief work. Volunteers may need help to determine and to assess their own state of healing and readiness to reach out to others. Having done that, bereaved parents have volunteered their time, talent, and energy to help the organization that supported them in their grief. Parents can also subscribe to newsletters provided by such organizations as Pen Parents of Canada, the Centre for Reproductive Loss, and others already mentioned. These newsletters provide helpful information about grief and serve as a compassionate forum for outreach not only locally but across the country as well. Through their own experience, the bereaved themselves participate in grief education when they take to the community a better understanding and knowledge of the grieving/healing process.

Bereaved parents have reported being comforted by speaking with peers who had experienced a similar reproductive loss. It helped to reduce their sense of isolation and to encourage them in their grieving/healing journey in the knowledge that others have not only managed to survive but have been transformed by their experience of loss and grief.

*   *   *

POSTSCRIPT

This Healing Process Model© in its present form is one way of conceptualizing constructive healthy grieving, taking into account the body, mind, spirit connection. But will it remain in its present form or will it evolve over time is a question that can only be posed, not answered. Hopefully, the Healing Process Model© for reproductive loss will undergo its own refining process, as new insights are gained and new understandings of grieving and healing become known.

REFERENCES

1. Matthew 5:4.
2. K. J. Doka, *Disenfranchised Grief*, Lexington, Toronto, 1989.
3. A. Smith and S. Borgers, Parental Grief Response to Perinatal Death, *Omega: Journal of Death and Dying, 19*:3, pp. 203-214, 1988-89.
4. J. Lasker and L. Toedter, Satisfaction with Hospital Care and Interventions after Pregnancy Loss, *Death Studies, 18*:1, pp. 41-64, January-February 1994.
5. T. H. Holmes and R. H. Rahe, The Social Re-adjustment Rating Scale, *Journal of Psychosomatic Research, 11*:2, pp. 213-218, 1967.
6. K. Johnson, Infertility High on List of Major Causes of Stress, *Infertility Awareness, 10*:4, p. 6, December 1994.
7. Canadian Press, Out-of-Control Killer, *The Gazette*, Montreal, p. C-1, July 25, 1997.
8. R. K. Limbo and S. R. Wheeler, *When a Baby Dies: A Handbook for Healing and Helping*, RTS Bereavement Services, Gunderson Lutheran Medical Foundation, La Crosse, Wisconsin, 1998 (revised edition).
9. J. M. Stack, The Psychodynamics of Spontaneous Abortion, *American Journal of Orthopsychiatry, 54*, pp. 162-167, 1984.
10. S. Carr, *The Poetry of Childhood*, B. T. Batsford Ltd, London, 1981.
11. D. Klass, P. R. Silverman, and S. L. Nickman, *Continuing Bonds: New Understandings of Grief*, Taylor & Francis, Washington, D.C., 1996.
12. A. Kennedy, *Your Loved One Lives on Within You*, Berkley Books, New York, 1997.
13. *There Was a Child*, Video, Canadian Learning Company, Toronto, 1991.
14. *The Gazette*, Montreal, January 1997, with permission from the family.
15. T. R. Golden, *Swallowed by a Snake: The Gift of the Masculine Side of Healing*, Golden Healing, Kensington, Maryland, 1996.
16. J. W. Worden, *Grief Counseling & Grief Therapy*, Springer, New York, 1991.

17. S. Brabant, C. Forsyth, and G. McFarlain, Life After the Death of a Child: Initial and Long Term Support from Others, *Omega, 31*:1, pp. 67-85, 1995.
18. J. Fagan and I. L. Sheperd (eds.), *Gestalt Therapy Now: Theory, Techniques, Applications,* Science and Behavior Books, Palo Alto, California, 1970.
19. S. S. Joy, Abortion: An Issue to Grieve?, *Journal of Counseling and Development, 63,* pp. 375-376, February 1985.
20. K. Hardy, How to Help When a Newborn Dies—A Health Care Provider's Guide for Perinatal Loss, *Health Provider's Manual for Helping After Perinatal Death,* H.A.N.D., Los Gatos, California, 1987.
21. J. Johnson and S. M. Johnson, *A Most Important Picture: A Very Tender Manual for Taking Pictures of Stillborn Babies and Infants Who Die,* Centering Corporation, Omaha, Nebraska, 1985.
22. U. Nunes, J. Pearce, and A. Smith, *Perinatal Bereavement: A Caregiver Guide,* Perinatal Bereavement Services Ontario, Markham, Ontario, 1996.
23. B. Harvey, Get Spiritual for Better Health, *The Gazette,* Montreal, p. A-10, July 29, 1996.
24. E. A. Grollman, A Decalogue: Ten Commandments for the Concerned Caregiver, in *Living with Grief: When Illness is Prolonged,* K. J. Doka (ed.) with J. Davidson, Hospice Foundation of America, Washington, D.C., Taylor & Francis, Bristol, Pennsylvania, Chapter 11, pp. 149-158, 1997.

CHAPTER 4
Facilitating the Healing Process

Where there is sorrow there is holy ground.

Oscar Wilde, "De Profundis"

* * * *

Sorrow is not an intruder any more than joy is an intruder. It is part of the threads out of which life is woven, and we can accept it on that basis. It is part of life, as much as any other thing is a part of life . . . one of those ties that bind all mankind together. Sorrow is something we choose when we elect to love, the other side of the coin of joy.

Sorrow is a priceless possession, causing us to remember with a sadness that interprets the meaning of love. Surrender is the key to comfort and love. You have to admit that you have lost that which you loved, instead of giving in to the urge to pretend that it isn't so. . . . Where we cannot find the way, it means everything to believe that God does know the way.

Minister Vernon S. Broyles [cited in 1][1]

As stated previously, reproductive losses due to miscarriage, stillbirth, abortion, perinatal death, SIDS (Sudden Infant Death Syndrome), etc., generate grief reactions which are manifested as characteristic thoughts, feelings, and behaviors, affecting the bereaved in body, mind, and spirit. Many bereaved individuals will be able to cope with these reactions on their own while some others will seek help in coping with those distressing thoughts, feelings, and behaviors arising from or associated with the loss. A few bereaved parents reacted negatively when referral to a psychiatrist was suggested by their physicians or other health professionals; although they recognized their need for help in grieving, they reported that they did not feel the need for psychiatric intervention for something which we now know to be a normal, necessary, and natural experience of the human condition. As Worden comments: "There is always the risk of making grief seem pathological

---

[1] Copyright © 2002 *The Atlanta Journal—Constitution.* Reprinted with permission from *The Atlanta Journal—Constitution.*

because of the formal intervention of a mental health worker, but with skilled counseling this need not be the case" [2, p. 38].

There may be some bereaved individuals or, indeed, health professionals who question the need for this formal intervention for grief counseling and whether or not bereavement counseling is even effective. Colin Murray Parkes, asking the same question in his journal article, "Bereavement Counseling: Does It Work?," came to the following conclusion after examining several research studies about bereavement support:

> The evidence presented here suggests that professional services and professionally-supported voluntary and self-help services are capable of reducing the risk of psychiatric and psychosomatic disorder resulting from bereavement. Services are most beneficial among bereaved people who perceive their families as unsupportive or who, for other reasons, are thought to be at special risk [3, p. 6].[2]

PATHWAYS TO HEALING

There are many pathways to healing for reproductive loss that can guide the grief counselor to help bereaved clients work through the pain of their loss. For example, Worden suggests ten principles for effective grief counseling. The first four principles parallel his four tasks of mourning. For a detailed description of these principles, see Worden's *Grief Counseling & Grief Therapy* [2, pp. 42-52]. An outline of those ten principles follows:

1. Help the survivor actualize the loss.
2. Help the survivor to identify and express feelings.
3. Assist living without the deceased.
4. Facilitate emotional relocation of the deceased.
5. Provide time to grieve.
6. Interpret "normal" behavior.
7. Allow for individual differences.
8. Provide continuing support.
9. Examine defenses and coping styles.
10. Identify pathology and refer [2, pp. 42-52].

THE HEALING PROCESS MODEL©

The components within the Healing Process Model© (see Chapter 3) also suggest guidelines for healing interventions which the grief counselor can use to help the bereaved along the path of constructive, healthy grieving. These healing interventions are:

---

[2] Reprinted with permission from the BMJ Publishing Group.

- Acknowledge the Loss with Empathy
- Listen to the Story without Judgment
- Identify all Reproductive Losses
- Identify Other Losses and Stress Factors
- Interpret Grief Reactions as Normal
- Facilitate Continuing the Relationship with the Deceased Baby
- Honor the Ultimate Questions about Life, Death, and Spirituality
- Explore the Meaning of "Guilt Work" within "Grief Work"
- Allow for Expression of Anger and Release of Forgiveness
- Facilitate Closure through the Creation of Memories
- Encourage Caring for Oneself in Body, Mind, and Spirit
- Assess Readiness in Reaching Out to Help Others

Acknowledge the Loss with Empathy

A primary task of the grief counselor is to acknowledge the reproductive loss of the bereaved client and to communicate that acknowledgment in a supportive, empathic, and non-judgmental manner. Not all expressions of acknowledgment of the loss communicate empathy. In fact, some expressions fall terribly short of genuine acknowledgment and, indeed, may even be judgmental. Several bereaved clients reported being told: "It's been three months now since your miscarriage. Why aren't you over it yet?"; "How can you feel so bad when you never got to know the baby?"; "It's unfortunate but these things happen."; "Your abortion could not possibly be bothering you still. That happened over ten years ago. Let's talk about your alcoholic father instead."

Acknowledgment, especially of a disenfranchised reproductive loss such as miscarriage, abortion, and stillbirth needs to come not only from the bereaved themselves but also from others—family, friends, health professionals. Not only is this a key component to set the healing process in motion, it also gives the freedom and permission to the bereaved to grieve their loss, which in fact they have every natural right and reason to do. Comments which communicate that the loss does not need to be grieved minimize their freedom or permission to grieve, resulting in disenfranchised grief. When this occurs, the bereaved might go through a time of denial and subsequently be unable to accept the reality of their loss. Compassionate acknowledgment of the loss can overcome denial and facilitate accepting the reality of the loss. The grief counselor can communicate acknowledgment non-verbally through appropriate touch or through words in simple expressions of sympathy as "I'm sorry about the death of your baby" or "Even though I can't imagine how painful this must be for you, I'm here to listen to you whenever you feel like talking. You don't have to go through this alone." Acknowledging the loss leads into and facilitates the telling of the story.

Listen to the Story without Judgment

The grief counselor must be an empathetic non-judgmental listener who enables the bereaved to tell their story of the loss as often as necessary and who provides a safe effective environment for the telling of their story. The environment in which the bereaved tell their story is not limited to the office of the grief counselor. There are times when the bereaved prefer to tell their story by telephone, sometimes even anonymously. For those individuals, the telephone was their safe environment. On other occasions, I have made home visits to bereaved parents who were physically or emotionally not able to leave their homes to seek counseling. For them, home was their safe environment.

Worden has used a variety of informal settings, including the garden on the hospital grounds, for grief counseling and he supports the home setting as an effective environment as well:

> Grief counseling does not necessarily have to take place in a professional office, although it might. One setting that can be utilized effectively is the home setting; counselors who make home visits may find that it is the most suitable context for their interventions [2, p. 39].

The grief counselor could suggest to the bereaved that they start telling their story with the facts and include as much detail as possible. Starting with the facts of the story provides a safe, structured way to allow distressing and problematic feelings to emerge, especially feelings of guilt, anger, rage, hostility, and blame.

One bereaved father described his need for support in telling his story: "I desperately needed people who could listen without judgment or advice" [4, p. 64]. A friend of his who although he "didn't say much," nevertheless conveyed to the bereaved father support, acknowledgment, and empathy in these few simple words: "Please consider us as members of your community. We're here for talking, visiting, telephone calls, anything you need" [4, p. 64]. While the father was grateful for his friend's expression of sympathy, it stirred up other emotions in him as well:

> Nobody had ever said anything like that to me before—or, alternatively, I had never let myself acknowledge the need for such support from others before. In any case, I was deeply grateful. Other friends let us know that if we needed anything, they would be there. Many couples who had lost children of their own contacted us. While all the support felt good, it was also painful. For one thing, I feared emotional dependence and found it much easier to give love than to receive it [4, p. 64].

The grief counselor can reassure the bereaved that grief-care support does not in and of itself foster "emotional dependence." However, if the client were to experience some dependence for a time, this would be normal and would only be temporary.

Identify All Reproductive Losses

The grief counselor should always obtain a reproductive loss history of other pregnancies of the bereaved and their outcome. This provides an opportunity to address the "unfinished business" of previous losses—miscarriage, abortion, giving up a child for adoption—losses which might not have been adequately grieved or, indeed, acknowledged as losses, acting as if the loss never happened. Ignoring such losses or dismissing them as unimportant can hinder the effectiveness of grief work that is being done for the presenting problem. Worden believes that this is the way some people deal with abortion. He writes:

> Many single young women who get pregnant choose to terminate the pregnancy. One problem here is that the decision is often made in isolation—the man often is not told about the pregnancy and the woman's family is not involved, often because of fear. So the woman has the abortion and then buries the incident deep in her mind, as if it did not happen. But the loss still needs to be grieved and if it is not, it may surface later in some other situation [2, p. 69].

To summarize, the grief counselor must use sensitivity and compassion when asking about the number of pregnancies and their outcome. Because some women may be reluctant to disclose the fact of a previous abortion, I do not ask directly if they ever had one. However, in nearly every case I have seen, women were relieved to be able to talk about their abortions, especially when the emphasis is placed upon the healing of the grief experience and listening to their story in a sympathetic and non-judgmental manner. Often these women have said, "You're the only one I ever told about the abortion."

Identify Other Losses and Stress Factors

The grief counselor should also obtain a history of other losses and stress factors as these can compound the present reproductive loss, thus intensifying the grief experience. It is helpful for the bereaved to know that all losses are stressful and to take into account those other sources of stress in addition to their reproductive loss. Such stress factors could include chronic or acute medical and mental health conditions, conflicting or toxic interpersonal relationships at home or work, divorce, death of other family members or friends, economic difficulties, unemployment, lack of social support, addictions, alcoholism, and other substance abuse.

Since grief and loss always occur in the midst of other life events, changes, and transitions (which themselves are accompanied by their own stresses, challenges, and difficulties), the grief counselor can point out to their bereaved clients that not all of their perceived or experienced distress is due to reproductive loss; other factors can contribute to their distress as well. These factors should be teased out and appropriate referrals and interventions made, if necessary. By doing this, the grief counselor places the grief work in proper perspective, thereby giving hope and encouragement to the bereaved. In addition, the grief counselor should identify the bereaved clients' abilities to cope with loss and stress in general, and assist with these when needed. Regarding his tenth counseling principle of identifying trouble and knowing when to refer, Worden says:

> A person doing grief counseling may be able to identify the existence of pathology which has been triggered by the loss and the subsequent grieving and, having spotted such difficulty, may find it necessary to make a professional referral. This particular role is often call the "gatekeeper" role. For some people, grief counseling or the facilitation of grief is not sufficient and the loss or the way that they are handling the loss may give rise to more difficult problems [2, p. 52].

Interpret Grief Reactions as Normal

This intervention parallels Worden's sixth principle, interpret "normal" behavior. As Worden explains, "If the counselor has a clear understanding of what normal grief behavior is, then he or she can give the bereaved some reassurance about the normality of these new experiences" [2, p. 50]. One of the most distressing and frequently experienced grief reactions is the feeling of "going crazy" reported by parents who have suffered a reproductive loss. This particular grief reaction, however, is not exclusive to reproductive loss. "After a significant loss many people have the sense that they are going crazy," states Worden [2, p. 50]. When told that this feeling is normal, bereaved individuals are greatly relieved. With my clients I use the body, mind, spirit connection as a structure to explain, describe, and normalize those thoughts, feelings, and behaviors that make up grief reactions and manifestations (see Chapter 1). I also describe the nature of the grieving process. I explain how it is like an emotional roller coaster and that its progression does not move in a linear fashion from point A to point B; but, rather that its movement has more of a back and forth, up and down characteristic pattern.

Facilitate Continuing the Relationship with the Deceased Baby

Before continuing the relationship with the deceased baby, that relationship must be established if it has not already been done. The grief counselor can encourage the bereaved to do this by suggesting that they first name the baby. Naming the baby and placing the baby on the family tree establishes and reconnects that relationship by acknowledging that something of significance took place here; a baby, a person that was loved is now gone but not forgotten. Writing letters and poetry about the baby; keeping a journal; planting a tree, rosebush, or evergreen; making or building something; celebrating rituals of remembrance—especially anniversaries (due date, birth date, death date); collecting mementos of the baby and thereby creating one's personal "place to remember"; visiting a memorial cemetery or garden dedicated to deceased babies, all foster continuing that relationship. Bereaved parents that I have seen took readily to these suggestions; in fact, some parents, following their own instincts, had already initiated many of these actions in their attempts to continue that relationship. Some had given their baby a name; others had written letters to the baby; some told their stories of loss and love in poetry and books; all of them wanted to create memories to honor the life and memory of their beloved child.

Robert Jonas, a bereaved father whose premature baby daughter Rebecca died in his arms, recalled the consoling words of his priest-friend, Henri Nouwen. These words communicated to Jonas that his friend "understood the transcendent dimension of my grief." Jonas writes:

> Listening silently to my story, he understood immediately and affirmed what my heart was telling me, that Rebecca was becoming a doorway to God for me. After our talk I could only remember a few of the phrases that touched me. "Let her have a name among you," he offered. "Your love for her has not been in vain. . . . Let your relationship with her continue. . . . Know there is a mystery here. Let yourself enter into the mystery this reality brings. . . . Somehow, if you can meet this tragedy in God, your wisdom will deepen" [4, pp. 66-67].

Honor the Ultimate Questions about
Life, Death, and Spirituality

The questions "Why?", "Why did this happen?", or "Why was our baby given to us for such a short time?" are questions bereaved parents struggle with at the time of loss. These questions inevitably lead to other spiritual questions and reflections on the mystery, meaning, and purpose of life, death, and suffering. The grief counselor can help the bereaved to voice these questions as they arise in their encounter with the mystery of loss, offering hope, support, and encouragement, and guiding them in their search for the spiritual strength they need for this painful journey of grieving and healing. Many bereaved parents have revealed to me that they were able to find some purpose or meaning or greater good from their loss and, although it seems like a paradox, they discovered, through their pain, the transcendent and transformative gifts that grief can bring. The grief counselor needs to be open to this dimension of the grief experience and encourage the bereaved to look for these gifts of grief in due time.

Henri J. M. Nouwen, in his book *Sabbatical Journey: The Diary of His Final Year,* described the transcendent power of a father's grief. Nouwen recalled the telephone conversation with him about Rebecca's birth and death. "His grief was immense, but his willingness to let his pain lead him to gratitude was there also from the very beginning" [5, p. 43]. Jonas' pathway to healing culminated in a book that he wrote as a tribute to his daughter Rebecca. Nouwen, who had been asked to write the forward to Jonas' book *Rebecca: A Father's Journey from Grief to Gratitude* [4], described it as a "remarkable and hope-giving book, in which sorrow leads to joy and grief to gratitude" [5, p. 44]. Although Rebecca lived only three hours and forty-four minutes, her short life had a profound effect on Jonas. Nouwen describes this profound effect in the forward to Jonas' book:

> Gradually it dawned on him that Rebecca had come to reveal the mystery that the value of life is not dependent on the hours, days, or years it is lived, nor on the number of people it is connected to, nor on the impact it has on human history. He realized that the value of life is life itself and that the few hours of Rebecca's life were as worthy to be lived as the many hours of the lives of Beethoven, Chagall, Gandhi, and indeed Jesus [4, p. xiii].

Explore the Meaning of "Guilt Work" within "Grief Work"

After a loss, bereaved individuals often experience guilt feelings. Worden states that "guilt feelings are normal after any type of death" [2, p. 94]. Reproductive loss, especially miscarriage and abortion, is no exception. The grief counselor must not dismiss these guilt feelings even when they seem unrealistic. These guilt feelings still need to be addressed, evaluated, and reality tested. This intervention is especially crucial when a baby or child dies. Worden comments:

> Parents whose children die are highly vulnerable to feelings of guilt that are focused on the fact that they could not help the child stop hurting or prevent the child from dying. Some feel guilty that they are not experiencing what they believe to be the appropriate amount of sadness. Whatever the reasons, most of this guilt is irrational and centers around circumstances of the death. The counselor can help here because irrational guilt yields itself up to *reality testing* [2, p. 45].

It is especially challenging for the grief counselor to help bereaved individuals in the case of real guilt or real culpability. As Worden explains:

> It is important when dealing with real guilt to include the seeking and granting of forgiveness between the deceased and the patient. In facilitating this, certain role-playing and imaging techniques may be useful [2, p. 84].

Parents may blame themselves for the loss of their child especially in miscarriage, despite the absence of any responsibility on their part for the child's death. They may continue to berate themselves, blame one another, and inflict upon themselves imagined guilt for something that their actions couldn't have realistically caused. Even when there is this kind of imagined guilt, the "seeking and granting of forgiveness" should not be overlooked as it may be needed here as well.

Allow for Expression of Anger and Release of Forgiveness

The grief counselor must adequately acknowledge the presence of anger in the bereaved person following a reproductive loss. While the feeling of anger is only one among the many manifestations or reactions of normal grief, I want to give it special emphasis because the resolution of anger plays an important part in the grieving/healing process.

Bereaved parents are often perplexed and confused when anger eventually surfaces but they are relieved to hear that the feeling of anger is commonly experienced after a loss and is a manifestation of normal grief. They are also surprised when they realize that their anger is often directed at the baby who died and whose death generated within them intense feelings of abandonment, as well as the pain of loss and hurt. The grief counselor can help bereaved parents to get in touch with this anger and to suggest safe ways to facilitate its resolution. After her miscarriage and subsequent D & C in the emergency department, one of my clients was very angry and filled with rage and hostility toward the hospital staff for treating her loss in what she perceived as a dismissive and cavalier manner. I suggested that she write out those feelings in a letter to the hospital administrator and describe in detail the actions and comments of the personnel involved that were upsetting to her. She was greatly relieved by this action because she could express her anger concretely in writing—six pages of typed single-spaced text! Sometimes these letters are only written but never sent; yet they are effective nevertheless. In any case, the purpose of getting in touch with and expressing this anger has been achieved. Worden comments on the importance of helping the bereaved deal with anger after a loss:

> This anger is real and it must go somewhere, so if it is not directed toward the deceased, the real target, it may be deflected onto other people such as the physician, the hospital staff, the funeral director, the clergyperson, or a family member.
>
> If the anger is not directed toward the deceased or displaced onto someone else, it may be retroflected—turned inward and experienced as depression, guilt, or lowered self-esteem. In extreme cases, retroflected anger may result in suicidal behavior, either in thought or in action. The competent grief counselor will always inquire about suicidal ideation [2, p. 43].

Just as with guilt resolution, the "seeking and granting of forgiveness" has a healing part to play but only after the acknowledgment and expression of anger has been addressed. Through role playing or in writing, some bereaved parents were moved to forgive their baby for abandoning them through death; others sought forgiveness from the baby and for themselves for not being able to protect their baby from dying.

With some other reproductive losses, bereaved individuals find that forgiveness is difficult to seek and to grant, especially for themselves. I have seen this quite often, especially in the post-aborted woman who not only regretted her decision to abort her baby but continued to live her life in self-condemnation and self-punishment for her action. By saying, "I'll never forgive myself," these women seemed to confuse the feeling of remorse and regret with the act of forgiveness. Although they may always regret their decision for having aborted their baby and may feel some degree of sadness, the grief counselor can nevertheless help these women by pointing out the difference between feeling regret and remorse and being willing to seek and to grant forgiveness from the deceased and for themselves.

Facilitate Closure through the Creation of Memories

The word closure literally means "a bringing to an end; conclusion" [6, p. 280], and its use is often associated with grief and loss. To some people, its connotation may convey the notion that the grief is over and now it's time to forget and move on. Bereaved parents resist this meaning of closure because they feel it betrays the memory of the baby. They also resent the implication that they should forget about the loss and stop talking about the baby, something that has been suggested to them by a few well-meaning, albeit misguided, health practitioners, family members, and friends of the bereaved.

Explaining to bereaved parents what closure is and what it is not can prevent misunderstanding of this emotionally charged concept and can offer some degree of comfort when they see closure in terms of remembering rather than forgetting the baby. In my work with bereaved parents, I have come to understand closure as a kind of transition from a place of disorganization to a place of re-organization, a coming together of acceptance of the loss accompanied by a feeling of peace. Parents have come to this feeling of peace when they can envision the baby in the care of other relatives who have died; placed under the protection of spiritual or religious figures such as angels, God, Jesus, Mary, saints; biblical persons such as Rachel; or whatever imagery is compatible with their set of beliefs.

In reproductive loss, the grief counselor facilitates closure by encouraging bereaved parents to collect and create memories of the deceased baby and, in due time, to let go of the intense pain of the loss. Some people may believe that forgetting the death of the baby rather than remembering that baby is the preferred way to bring about healing of the grief experience. One grieving parent said that "creating memories does not prolong the pain but comforts the soul." Bereaved parents do not forget; they want to honor that baby at whatever age or stage of gestation the baby was with them. Another grieving mother expressed it so well when she said, "Our babies are carved in our hearts forever." Bereaved parents need reassurance that letting go of the intense pain does not mean forgetting or letting go of the memory of the baby. The grief counselor can suggest finding a place to remember, gathering mementos of the baby and keeping them in a memory box or other special place (for specific suggestions see Chapter 3). This intervention also helps to continue the bonds of the relationship with the baby.

Bereaved parents in asking "How long will this pain last?", fear that they will never get over their intense anguish of the loss nor that they will ever be happy again. Because each person's timeframe for dealing with grief is so unique, the grief counselor does not impose an artificial timetable for processing grief but instead honors and respects whatever time is needed to heal.

Sherokee Ilse, who herself suffered several reproductive losses and is the author of many books on the subject, speaks with the authenticity of her experience. In her book, *Empty Arms: Coping with Miscarriage, Stillbirth, and Infant Death,* she captures what I believe to be the essence of closure:

> Hope . . . Time . . . Love . . . Healing. Tomorrow will come. The pain will ease. But you will never forget your precious child. It takes hope and time and love for the healing to take place. Remember along the way to accept, but never forget [7, p. 67].

The grief counselor can offer hope by assisting bereaved parents in gaining perspective that their pain will decrease over time, that their loved one will live on in them through the bonds of love, and that eventually they will arrive at that place of acceptance and peace.

A bereaved father offers hope and comfort in a poem he wrote about his grief following the deaths of his three sons:

> In this sad world of ours, sorrow comes to all . . .
> It comes with bitterest agony . . .
> Perfect relief is not possible, except with time.
> You cannot now realize that you will ever feel better . . .
> And yet this is a mistake.
> You are sure to be happy again.
> To know this, which is certainly true,
> Will make you become less miserable now.
> I have experienced enough to know what I say [7, p. 66].

That bereaved father was a former president of the United States, Abraham Lincoln.

Encourage Caring for Oneself in Body, Mind, and Spirit

Just as grief affects body, mind, and spirit, so also should its healing interventions focus upon body, mind, and spirit. Using this focal point of the body, mind, spirit connection provides a structure around which both the grief counselor and the bereaved themselves can assess progress along the grieving/healing journey. I find this conceptualization to be a very useful tool with grieving individuals, who, because they often feel disorganized, confused, forgetful, and unable to deal with too much or too complex information at one time, need a simple structure which this format provides. The key to its effectiveness lies in its simplicity; by centering attention on three broad areas of body, mind, and spirit, it reduces somewhat the complexity of the grieving process, a process which itself is very complex. The grief counselor can encourage the bereaved to look at all of these areas and suggest to them constructive ways of coping.

This format of focusing on body, mind, and spirit reflects the better understanding we have acquired in recent years of the interconnectedness of how grief does affect the person in a holistic manner. There is much more attention given to the physical aspects of grief-care today; for example, earlier writings about grief centered primarily upon the emotional aspects and rarely alluded to the physical. Because we now know that stress adversely affects the immune system and that grief and loss are stressful, we are more attentive to the physical aspects of grief-care; even to the extent of suggesting to the bereaved that they see their physician for a medical exam soon after the loss. Some other aspects for physical well-being that the bereaved should be mindful of include:

- sleep and need for extra rest
- nutrition and vitamin supplements
- recreation
- exercise, especially walking
- stress management
- relaxation techniques
- deep breathing exercises
- massage therapy
- eliminate or reduce smoking, caffeine, alcohol

The grief counselor can also remind the bereaved not to overlook the healing benefits of nature. As one bereaved mother wrote:

> I found much of what I needed in nature. I frequently walked down to the beach, where I listened to the waves, watched the dolphins play, and lay on the sand getting tan. I spent hours wandering around the landscaped grounds of my apartment complex. I needed to see earth again, to listen to the birds and to gaze at the trees and the flowers that grew there in profusion [8, p. 15].[3]

Once a neglected area of grief-care, the spiritual component is gradually becoming more prominent due in large part to such authors and speakers as Dr. John D. Morgan, Dr. James Miller, Rabbi Earl Grollman, Rabbi Harold Kushner, and many others whose writings on loss, grief, and spirituality have contributed greatly to our understanding of this facet of grief-care. As an example of the topical importance given to the spirituality of grief-care, the theme for the King's College Conference in London, Ontario, Canada in the year 2000 was "Attending to the Spiritual Needs of the Dying and the Bereaved." For some bereaved individuals, the spiritual realm may be foreign to them; for others, there may be a loss of faith or an increase of faith; one woman said that her spiritual journey took years to come

---

[3] All quotes from [8], *Giving Sorrow Words*. Copyright © 1990 by Candy Lightner and Nancy Hathaway. By permission of Warner Books, Inc.

together after the loss of her baby. While the grief counselor is not required to assume the role of spiritual director, there are several suggestions that can be made to the bereaved to help create a climate for reflecting upon spiritual concerns:

- Take time for silence, solitude, meditation, prayer, inspirational reading, and music;
- Create private rituals to honor the memory of the baby;
- Attend memorial services dedicated to remembering babies who have died;
- Use meaningful symbols to remember the deceased;
- Commemorate anniversary dates;
- Plant a tree or rosebush or other flowering shrubs;
- Care for living things such as pets, plants, flowers;
- Make a spiritual retreat;
- Talk with a spiritual advisor.

In counseling bereaved parents, I explain to them that grief-work involves not only the head but also the heart, both of which come together as the emotional and intellectual aspects of the mind component of grief-care. There may be some individuals who believe that "just thinking through" their loss is all they need to do in order to deal with their grief; but this is not how grief works. In her book of meditations for healing, *A Time to Grieve*, Carol Staudacher, author, lecturer and grief consultant, poignantly reflects upon the equally important roles played by heart and head in grief's healing journey:

> Some survivors try to think their way through grief. That doesn't work. Grief is a releasing process, a discovery process, a healing process. We cannot release or discover or heal by the use of our minds alone. The brain must follow the heart at a respectful distance. It is our hearts that ache when a loved one dies. It is our emotions that are most drastically affected. Certainly the mind suffers, the mind recalls, the mind may plot and plan and wish, but it is the heart that will blaze the trail through the thicket of grief [9, p. 7].

In respecting and honoring the wisdom of the heart and the mind in the grieving process, the grief counselor can be supportive of those emotional and intellectual needs of the bereaved even when they themselves think their actions seem unusual or strange. For example, after the loss of her premature twins, one grieving mother could not leave her house without taking along the teddy bears she had bought for her babies. Bereaved parents need support and encouragement for taking whatever time they need for grieving, even though this notion is a counter cultural one in a society which says to get over it as soon as possible. During the grieving process, the bereaved may need to be reminded to:

- Pamper yourself from time to time;
- Appreciate simple pleasures;
- Be gentle and patient with yourself;
- Ask for help;

- Accept help from others when it is offered;
- Let others know what you need;
- Take time to grieve and to remember;
- Listen to your heart and don't dismiss its wisdom;
- Keep a journal. While the benefits of this exercise are primarily emotional and psychological, they can also be physiological; some studies have suggested that immune system functioning is enhanced by writing in a journal [8, p. 210].

In addition, there are some other ways of coping with grief which the grief counselor can effect:

- Encourage active grieving. A bereaved mother describes her experience of active grieving:

> Throughout that period, I actively grieved, by which I mean that when I felt pain, I gave in to it; I allowed it precedence over everything. It had been there all along, of course, but for the most part, I pushed it back. I'm pretty good at holding back tears. This time, I wanted to let them come through [8, p. 15].

- Give the bereaved the tools (grief-care) to help themselves such as educational newsletters about grief and loss, information on support groups, access to peer support, and telephone support.
- Stress the importance of writing their thoughts and feelings in a journal.
- Suggest visiting a Memorial Garden and attending commemorative services. In Montreal, the Mount Royal Cemetery has created a special children's perpetual memorial garden for the burial of babies who have died before and after birth. Also, they have inaugurated, as of October 1999, a commemorative service, "Forever a Baby" Memory Service, to remember those babies who have died through miscarriage, ectopic pregnancy, stillbirth, or newborn death. This annual service is held in October to coincide with the National Pregnancy and Infant Loss Awareness month.
- Encourage them to learn about grief through books (bibliotherapy), articles, video, and audio tapes.
- Explain and describe the grieving/healing process and normal grief reactions. One author wrote about how she experienced the grieving process:

> Nothing is more painful than grief, which is why it cannot be ignored. So I've learned to express my grief. Grief, I have discovered, ebbs and flows, and I've learned to ride those waves. When I feel it, I'll go into my room as soon as I can and immerse myself in it.
> When I need to, I call a friend. Or I walk down to the beach and watch the tide come in. Sometimes, I just lie on the bed and cry. And then I can go on. It's all part of the process [8, p. 16].

Assess Readiness in Reaching Out
to Help Others

When bereaved parents express a desire to help others in their pain of loss, the grief counselor must ascertain if that desire to reach out is in sync with their degree of readiness and the healing of their own grief experience. Looking back over their journal writings as well as the progress notes of the grief counselor are extremely useful ways in determining whether or not the bereaved have sufficient physical, emotional, and spiritual strength for this task. For example, would they be able to talk about their loss and listen to someone else's loss without breaking down to the point where they are being helped rather than helping another bereaved individual? Because the bereaved have so little energy after a loss, they must attend to resolving their own grief first. Even when their pain is fresh, raw, and intense, they still may want to reach out prematurely as a way to avoid facing that pain.

The grief counselor can review with the bereaved how thoroughly they have worked through the components of the healing process. The Healing Process Model© itself (see Chapter 3) can be used also as an assessment guide when its components are posed as questions:

- Have the bereaved adequately acknowledged and accepted the reality of the loss or are they avoiding it by attempting to have a replacement baby instead?
- Have they told their story enough times to process the details of the loss?
- Have they identified and grieved all other reproductive losses?
- Have they taken into account other losses and stress factors in their life during the grieving process?
- How well do they understand the nature of the grieving process and normal grief reactions?
- What actions have they taken which would lead them to continue the relationship with the deceased baby?
- Have they found some meaning in their questions about their loss?
- Have they been able to work through their guilt associated with the loss?
- Were they able to resolve their feelings of anger and seek and grant forgiveness?
- Were they able to achieve some sense of closure, peace, and acceptance through the creation of memories?
- Are they mindful of the importance of caring for themselves in body, mind, and spirit?
- What motivated their desire to reach out to help others?

To summarize, among the several tools the grief counselor can use in determining the bereaved's readiness to reach out to help others, I have found the bereaved's journal writings, my own progress notes, and the Healing Process Model© used as an assessment guide to be extremely helpful.

REFERENCES

1. C. Sibley, Coping with Death: Sorrow is the Flip Side of Love, *The Gazette*, Montreal, p. B3, November 26, 1997, © 2002 *The Atlanta Journal—Constitution*.
2. J. W. Worden, *Grief Counseling & Grief Therapy*, Springer, New York, 1991.
3. C. M. Parkes, Bereavement Counseling: Does it Work?, *British Medical Journal, 281*, pp. 3-6, 1980.
4. R. A. Jonas, *Rebecca: A Father's Journey from Grief to Gratitude*, The Crossroad Publishing Company, New York, 1996.
5. H. J. M. Nouwen, *Sabbatical Journey: The Diary of His Final Year*, The Crossroad Publishing Company, New York, 1998.
6. *The Random House Dictionary of the English Language*, Random House, New York, 1973.
7. S. Ilse, *Empty Arms: Coping with Miscarriage, Stillbirth, and Infant Death*, Wintergreen Press, Maple Plain, Minnesota, 1990.
8. C. Lightner and N. Hathaway, *Giving Sorrow Words*, Warner Books, New York, 1990.
9. C. Staudacher, *A Time to Grieve*, Harper, San Francisco, 1994.

CHAPTER 5

Obstacles to Grieving and Healing

No one ever told me that grief felt so like fear.

C. S. Lewis [1, p. 1]

There are many reasons why people fail to grieve or why they fail to enter fully into the grieving/healing process. Grief reactions of incomplete bereavement have been described as abnormal, arrested, delayed, inhibited, suppressed, postponed, exaggerated, unresolved, prolonged, pathological, complicated, inconclusive, incomplete, masked [2, pp. 65-91]. Just as these labels describe the various types of incomplete bereavement, so, too, are there numerous factors which operate as obstacles to grieving in reproductive loss. Those obstacles leading to incomplete bereavement which I have found to be the most prevalent are the following:

- Looking for the "Quick Fix"
- Lack of Commitment to Counseling Sessions or Healing Process
- Pregnancy
- Therapy
- Medication
- Lack of Previous Experience with Grieving Losses
- Inability to Comprehend Suffering or Endure Hardship
- Underlying Problems (Pathology)
- Inability to Identify One's Own Needs or Feelings
- Inability to Tolerate Feelings of Helplessness
- Guilt
- Fear and Trauma
- False Beliefs or Myths
- Reproductive Loss Not Important
- Relational Factors
- Absence of Social Support
- Not Facing the Pain

71

LOOKING FOR THE "QUICK FIX"

The expectation of the "quick fix," the instant remedy, is a frequently encountered obstacle to grieving. Bereaved parents want to find relief as quickly as possible, since nobody wants to be in pain, especially the devastating pain of losing a baby. When their grief and anguish have not disappeared instantly in the first session, some will not continue in counseling but may choose instead to bury the pain, try to forget, or fall into maladaptive behaviors (drugs, alcohol, aggressiveness, acting out) or adaptive behaviors (channeling their grief into projects, activities, work, exercise) in an attempt to find relief and comfort.

LACK OF COMMITMENT TO COUNSELING SESSIONS OR HEALING PROCESS

Not everyone will seek nor will they need grief counseling. However, for those who do seek counseling, it has been my experience that it takes at least three sessions for the bereaved to comprehend the nature of the grieving/healing process, to enter into it, and to trust the working of that process. While everyone's timetable and grieving patterns are unique, generally speaking, people do seem to make better progress if they can commit to at least three to five sessions.

PREGNANCY

It may seem strange that pregnancy (subsequent pregnancy) itself can be an obstacle to grieving a previous reproductive loss. Couples who had begun to attend our support groups to grieve a previous loss suddenly dropped out when they became pregnant because they wanted to focus only on the pregnancy. They did not want to dwell upon something sad like grief work so they delayed their grieving until the baby was born, after which they would return to the support group to finish their grief work.

THERAPY

A grieving parent who had just lost a baby at the same time as being in therapy for other issues occasionally would seek additional help with grief work. While in general it is not advisable to receive help from two different therapists at the same time, it is possible to do so, depending upon both the nature and intensity of the other conditions. However, in a few instances, it had not worked at all and the grieving person discontinued grief therapy.

MEDICATION

Some bereaved parents have stopped their counseling sessions when they began to take antidepressant medication because they felt better. However, when they discontinued taking the antidepressants, they reported that they were right back to where they were when they had started taking the medication. Another obstacle to adequate grief work which taking such medications presents, is the lack of dreaming that is reported. Dream work is an important dimension to grief work that may be hindered due to taking those medications which could interfere with dreaming or remembering dreams. When normal grief is treated as mental illness, some physicians may tend to overprescribe and prolong medication therapy, and in a way use medication as a substitute for grief work. This is not to say that medication does not have its place for the bereaved. Some people need to postpone grief work until they are stronger and may have more energy to deal with the painful reality of their loss. Several clients have reported that their spiritual life was affected while they were taking medication. For example, one bereaved mother commented that she "had no spiritual life" when she was on Prozac.

LACK OF PREVIOUS EXPERIENCE
WITH GRIEVING LOSSES

Since most reproductive losses happen to women in their twenties and thirties, many of them may not have experienced any significant loss or indeed ever attended a funeral. Such was the case with one 21-year-old mother who had just lost twins, born prematurely. She had never experienced the death of a friend or a relative nor had she ever attended a funeral. Her pain was so intense that she could not focus on the grieving process; instead, she was obsessed with wanting to become pregnant again right away to replace the babies she had lost. Unfortunately, she discontinued therapy after only two sessions.

Worden's reference to the recently widowed person seeking a replacement relationship, has application also to the replacement baby:

> If people rush in for a quick replacement, this may make them feel better for a time, but it may also preclude experiencing the intensity and the depth of the loss. This intensity needs to be experienced before the grieving can be completed. Also for the relationship to work, the new person must be recognized and appreciated for himself or herself [2, p. 49].

INABILITY TO COMPREHEND SUFFERING
OR ENDURE HARDSHIP

This obstacle to grieving is closely related to the previous one regarding lack of experience in grieving losses. When people have not had any experience facing life's difficulties and challenges, or even in reflecting on their own mortality or the meaning of life, death, and suffering, they may be ill-equipped to handle the grieving process on their own without someone to guide them through it.

UNDERLYING PROBLEMS AND/OR PATHOLOGY

The grieving process can be hindered or complicated by other underlying problems, unfinished business of resolving previous grief issues, or a pre-existing pathological condition. As Worden states: "Those people who have had a history of depressive illness also run a higher risk of developing a complicated reaction" [2, p. 67].

INABILITY TO IDENTIFY ONE'S OWN NEEDS OR FEELINGS

One of my clients who presented for grief counseling following her miscarriage manifested this inability to identify her own needs or feelings due in part to unresolved grief issues in the past. She was very hard on herself and could not even determine when she was fatigued and needed to rest. Before she could fully enter into the grieving process, she required several sessions just to identify her needs and to practice meeting those needs. Similar exercises were used to help her describe and define her feelings apart from the present grief issue. Once that obstacle was removed, she was then able to begin the grieving process.

INABILITY TO TOLERATE FEELINGS OF HELPLESSNESS

The experience of grieving inevitably leads people to feel vulnerable, helpless, and dependent. This inability to tolerate those feelings of helplessness and dependency is another obstacle to grieving. In her book, *A Time to Grieve: Loss as a Universal Experience,* Bertha Simos writes:

> Because the resolution of grief demands the experiencing of universal feelings of helplessness in the face of existential loss, those individuals whose major defenses are built around avoidance of feelings of helplessness may be among those likely to have dysfunctional reactions of grief. Thus the individuals who normally function most competently on the surface may be the very ones thrown more heavily by a major loss as it strikes at the core of their defensive system [3, p. 170].

GUILT

Although guilt is almost always present in any reproductive loss as well as other losses, it can become an obstacle to grieving if the individual remains stuck in guilt. In order to bring grief toward a healthy and satisfactory conclusion, it is necessary to move out of guilt work and back into effective grief work. As Worden has pointed out, the seeking and granting of forgiveness is the key to this resolution. (See Chapter 3, section on "Guilt Work vs. Grief Work.")

FEAR AND TRAUMA

There are many fears that bereaved parents may experience after the death of their baby, which can present obstacles to grieving; for example, they may be fearful of:

- feeling the pain
- actively grieving
- the unknown (e.g., only imagining but not seeing the deceased baby)
- the future (e.g., life without their baby)
- their spouses/partners leaving
- how they will respond
- death
- showing emotion
- breaking down
- not being able to be the strong one
- seeing and holding their deceased baby

Fear can also cause bereaved parents to want to "run away," if not physically then emotionally, from having contact with their deceased baby. Patricia Simone, licensed funeral and bereavement specialist, stated that a flight response is typical for newly bereaved parents [4, p. 7]. Fear can inhibit bereaved parents from exercising their right to parent their deceased child, by touching, holding, and loving them. This intervention helps to create memories, to say good-bye, and to facilitate closure, all of which are part of the healing process. Hospital personnel can minimize those fears by providing private quality time for bereaved parents to hold their deceased baby and by reassuring them that these healing interventions are necessary to the grieving process. Bereaved parents need help to allay those fears that would prevent them from entering into the grieving process; they need to be gently encouraged to exercise their parental care and love for their children even in the face of death. Simone explains:

Perinatal Bereavement Services of Ontario states that newly bereaved parents have some specific rights that need to be fulfilled, and that the baby has some important rights too. Some of the deceased baby's rights are:
- the right to be touched and held,
- the right to be recognized as a person, who was born and has died,
- the right to have his/her life ending acknowledged [4, p. 7].

Moreover, the exercise of these rights is not tied to any particular gestational age as evidenced by the fact that fetuses are now accepted for proper funerals in England. Having a funeral service helps to acknowledge the loss, especially a disenfranchised loss, and facilitates the grieving process. *The Dodge Magazine,* a funeral service publication, featured an article which described the impact that the social evolution of the fetus has had upon funeral practices:

> The societal norms which guide when parents may mourn over the death of a wished-for child have changed; this can now occur twenty to thirty weeks before expected delivery. The social evolution of the foetus seems to have occurred since about 1991. Where once a funeral was considered unnecessary, it is now considered quite appropriate. What was disposed of with no ceremony or perceived value less than a mere decade ago is now considered worthy of a legitimate social event [5, p. 22].[1]

It is also important for parents not to allow fear to prevent them from seeing their deceased baby, even in the case of viewing a stillborn baby who was born very deformed and discolored. Julie Peterson, editor of *Canadian Funeral News,* in a personal letter to me, related the story of a father who insisted on seeing his child despite everyone's insistence that he not. She writes: "As he held the child, he looked down at the poor baby and said, 'He has his mother's eyes.' People see what they want to see—all that father remembers is that his baby had his wife's eyes."

In situations involving traumatic bereavement, the trauma itself can be an obstacle to grieving a loss unless attention is given first to the trauma by providing a feeling of safety or trauma mastery. Thus, trauma mastery plays an important part in facilitating healthy mourning [6].

FALSE BELIEFS AND MYTHS

Social, cultural, and familial expectations, beliefs, values, conditioning, and codes of conduct influence and shape how effectively we grieve. Some people believe that they must be the strong one at the time of loss and so will not give themselves permission to grieve or to express their feelings. They may also falsely believe that tears are a sign of weakness, or that they do not need help from others, therefore feeling that they can and should grieve alone.

Another myth about grief relates to the time grieving takes. Society's expectations seem to reflect a "one size fits all" attitude, that everyone must "get over it" in a rigidly prescribed amount of time which is always shorter than the time it actually takes. Not having enough time to grieve can be an obstacle for the bereaved whose outward mourning may be enough to satisfy social expectations while their inner grieving is insufficient to process the loss. Worden encourages

---

[1] Copyright © 1997, The Dodge Company. Reprinted with permission.

providing enough time for the bereaved to grieve when he says that "it takes time . . . to accommodate to the loss and all its ramifications" [2, p. 49].

In answer to the question, "How long does it take?", Dr. Sandra Elder, noted authority on bereavement, commented, "It takes as long as it takes" [7].

While it is true that grieving takes time, many people simply believe that "time alone heals." Certainly, pain may be lessened over time, but if the grief is buried, it could manifest itself as "something else" or it could surface years later when triggered by a situation or event which may or may not be related to the initial loss. Worden cited the example of a woman he treated who lost four close family members in three years: "She was so overwhelmed that she did not openly grieve, but experienced her grief as disabling anxiety" [2, p. 67].

Fourteen years after her miscarriage, one of my clients, a mother of three living children, was finally able to grieve her loss when I asked her, "What name did you give the baby?" This question triggered an immediate and dramatic response; she suddenly burst into tears and without hesitation uttered the child's name, so touched was she by this healing intervention. Afterward, she reported that this opportunity to release her grief had a profound life changing effect upon her, including positive changes in her worldview, as well as giving direction to her occupational decisions. Prior to this she felt that she had "dealt with" the loss, and that time alone would heal her grief. However, looking back at the past 14 years, she came to realize she had been using a great deal of energy to bury the grief, by wearing a mask of self-sufficiency and bravado, encountering life situations only on the surface, and relating to people superficially, as she described it.

REPRODUCTIVE LOSS NOT IMPORTANT

Regarding any reproductive loss as unimportant can be an obstacle to grieving. Some women who have suffered a reproductive loss, especially miscarriage and abortion, may believe those losses are unimportant and consequently will not grieve them. Yet they may be troubled by this unresolved grief for years after without even realizing that loss as the root cause. Their distress brought about by this "unfinished business" could manifest itself as depression, anger, anxiety, hostility, guilt, lowered self-esteem, and even somatic complaints as well. Because they see such losses as unimportant, they might not mention them unless a loss history is routinely taken by the grief counselor or other health professionals who might encounter the bereaved for reasons other than loss. Worden stresses the importance of a loss history as part of the intake procedure:

Most intake procedures require a fairly detailed history from the client or patient, but deaths and losses can be overlooked, and these can have a direct relationship to the current problems. It is very important to take a loss history when doing a formal intake procedure [2, p. 75].

FACTORS OF RELATIONSHIPS

Women who experience ambivalence in a pregnancy which then ends in miscarriage or by abortion are at risk for not adequately grieving their loss, as ambivalence in a relationship can be an obstacle to effective grieving. Worden explains how such relational factors affect the grieving process:

> The most frequent type of relationship that hinders people from adequately grieving is the highly ambivalent one with unexpressed hostility. Here an inability to face up to and deal with a high titre of ambivalence in one's relationship with the deceased inhibits grief and usually portends excessive amounts of anger and guilt which cause the survivor difficulty [2, p. 65].

In cases where the pregnant woman wants to continue her pregnancy, but instead is coerced into having an abortion which she does not want, she will often experience this "unexpressed hostility" (and in some cases "expressed hostility") toward the person or persons coercing her, including the health professionals involved in the abortion. Not only has she needlessly suffered the loss of her baby, but also in over 90 percent of death losses through abortion, the relationship with the partner has ended. This non-death related loss of the relationship further complicates the resolution of her grief.

Both miscarriage and abortion in the first trimester of pregnancy pose additional relational obstacles to grieving. As noted previously, the first trimester is referred to as the narcissistic stage of pregnancy because at this stage the woman perceives the developing baby as a part of herself rather than as a separate entity. Worden describes how this highly narcissistic relationship causes difficulty in grieving: "In this relationship, the deceased represents an extension of oneself. To admit to the loss would then necessitate confronting a loss of part of oneself, so the loss is denied" [2, p. 65].

ABSENCE OF SOCIAL SUPPORT

The absence of a social network can be an obstacle to grieving and bereaved individuals who do not have such support, especially women who have had abortions, are at risk for developing complicated grief reactions. As Worden explains: "Grief is really a social process and is best dealt with in a social setting in which people can support and reinforce each other in their reactions to the loss" [2, p. 69].

With my clients who are lacking social support, I encourage them to telephone me between sessions if necessary, join a support group, or speak to other bereaved individuals who have experienced similar losses, in one-to-one contact peer support.

NOT FACING THE PAIN

Most of the preceding obstacles to grieving could account for why bereaved individuals do not or cannot face the pain of loss. Moreover, there are circumstantial factors that cause people to delay their grief or to put their grief on hold. Women who suffer a miscarriage but who have other children to care for, have said that they had no time to grieve (even though they may have wanted to) and had to put their grief on the "back burner." It is not unusual for these women to seek help a year after the loss, when triggered by the anniversary date of the loss or perhaps the due date of what would have been the birth. Such triggering events can give rise to grief reactions just as if the grieving was taking place for the first time. Other types of losses such as divorce, death of a friend, or a parent can stimulate delayed grief. Worden elaborates:

> Delayed grief reactions are sometimes called inhibited, suppressed, or postponed grief reactions. In this case the person may have had an emotional reaction at the time of the loss, but it is not sufficient to the loss. At a future date the person may experience the symptoms of grief over some subsequent and immediate loss, but the intensity of his or her grieving seems excessive. What is happening here is that some of the grieving, particularly as it is related to Grief Task II, which was not adequately done at the time of the original loss, is carried forward and is being experienced at the time of the current loss. The person generally has the distinct impression that the response they are experiencing is exaggerated vis-à-vis the current situation. Such delayed reactions can occur not only to a subsequent loss, which is directly related to the individual undergoing the experience, but also when watching someone else go through a loss or when watching a film, television, or some other media event in which loss is the main theme [2, p. 72].

Not facing the pain for losses in the past which resulted in a complicated grief reaction can influence bereavement outcome in the present. Social worker Bertha Simos explains: "Past losses and separations have an impact on current losses and separations and attachments and all these factors bear on fear of future loss and separations and capacity to make future attachments" [3, p. 27].

Unresolved grief for a former loss such as miscarriage can also be triggered not only by loss but also by happy events or occasions. One perinatal bereavement coordinator comments: "I've counseled women, who, when they finally deliver a healthy baby, cry not tears of joy, but of sorrow for the child they never mourned" [8, p. 180].

Since grief work takes a great deal of energy, there may not be enough energy to mourn when there are too many losses at once. In such cases, the person shuts down the mourning process due to overwhelming feelings and "bereavement overload" [2, p. 67]. Bereavement overload itself could also be considered another obstacle to grieving and not facing the pain.

To sum up, these obstacles to grieving are examples of what I have encountered with my clients and constitute only a partial listing of the many factors which operate as obstacles to grieving. In fact, while some of these factors may overlap, others could possibly be combined or even grouped differently. Indeed, there may be yet other factors that we can learn about from our bereaved clients when we listen carefully and pay attention to what they have to teach us.

REFERENCES

1. C. S. Lewis, *A Grief Observed,* Bantam Books, New York, 1961.
2. J. W. Worden, *Grief Counseling & Grief Therapy,* Springer, New York, 1991.
3. B. G. Simos, *A Time to Grieve: Loss as a Universal Experience,* Family Service Association of America, New York, 1979.
4. P. Simone, Is it Fear? Is it Grief?, *The Baby's Breath Newsletter,* The Canadian Foundation for the Study of Infant Deaths, Issue 37, September 1999.
5. P. Gore, From the Other Side of the Atlantic Part 1: The Social Evolution of the Foetus, *The Dodge Magazine,* 3/97, pp. 9, 22, 23, 1997.
6. T. A. Rando, *Clinical Considerations in Understanding and Responding to Traumatic Bereavement: It's More Than Merely Trauma Added to Grief,* conference paper presented at King's College, London, Ontario, Canada, May 14, 2002.
7. S. Elder, *Pathways Through Grief: A Tool for Healing and Growth,* Conference at King's College, London, Ontario, Canada, May 1996.
8. R. Polaneczky, Mourning What Might Have Been, *Parenting,* pp. 175-183, November 1999.

CHAPTER 6

Issues Related to Reproductive Loss

> Grief is, in a sense, a gift that the dead give to the living, their final legacy. From the grieving process, we can gain empathy, wisdom, an appreciation of life. We gain something of what they were, we incorporate their values, and we continue to be influenced by them—in our actions, in our values, in the ways we treat others, in the ways we see the world, and in our memory. Death changes the living. Grief is the journey you take from the person you used to be to the person you will become.
>
> C. Lightner and N. Hathaway [1, p. 206]

In addition to grieving the heart-breaking loss of a baby, bereaved parents are faced with other difficult issues including additional losses resulting from and related to the nature of a reproductive loss as well as the unique characteristics of the parental bond to the child.

LOSS OF PART OF SELF

Whether the loss they experienced was due to miscarriage, stillbirth, abortion, or other infant death, bereaved parents have often said that they felt as if they had lost a part of themselves. This response can be attributed to the strong bond that exists between parent and child as well as the nature of a death experience itself.

> The parent/child relationship is the most intense that life can generate. The child was literally a part of the parent at one time. When you lose a child, you lose part of yourself [2, p. 11].

Regarding the nature of a death experience, Worden believes that death confronts the bereaved with having to adjust to their own sense of self:

> . . . for women who define their identify through relationships and caring for others, bereavement means not only the loss of a significant other but also the sense of a loss of self [3, p. 15].

LOSS OF SELF-ESTEEM

Closely related to the sense of a loss of self is the loss of self-esteem. This is often accompanied by social isolation and emotional withdrawal which in turn affects relationships with others. [...] or women in particular to experience [...] tiness after a miscarriage, stillbi[...] [...] e to realize just how much her [...] nd how this was manifested in h[...]

> I shut down emo[...] When
> he asked me wha[...] worry
> that I didn't love[...] truth
> [4, p. 180].

When communication [...] at risk for developing a troubled [...] reconcile their uniquely differen[...] of their different ways of grievi[...] be more accepting and supportiv[...] knowing about such differences a[...]

LOSS OF IDENTITY

> When a child is born, parents take on the identity of parent. When that identity is threatened by the child's death, they are hit at the most basic level. They lose the sense of who they are [2, p. 11].

A woman's identity as a woman who is capable of conceiving and bearing a child can sometimes be adversely affected by a reproductive loss. She may feel like a failure in not being able to do what everyone else apparently seems able to do so easily. Because bonding can take place very early in the pregnancy for some, women who have miscarried can grieve as intensely as they would grieve the death of a full term baby. Such was the case with Becky:

> I miscarried only two weeks after I found out I was pregnant, but my whole life changed in that time. I fell in love with my baby. I imagined how I'd feel when she got on a school bus for the first time and how I'd help her learn to like vegetables. When I lost her, I felt guilty. I wondered why I couldn't do what every woman is supposed to be able to do [4, p. 179].

LOSS OF INNOCENCE

Reproductive loss can rob parents of their innocence about pregnancy. Bereaved parents who had suffered such a loss, almost always use the term "loss of innocence" to describe their feelings of not only the loss of the baby, but also the loss of a dream ("shattered dreams"), the loss of the "assumptive world" (things are not as they *should* be), the loss of the expectation of a perfect pregnancy, and the loss of a worry-free, innocent, and joyful subsequent pregnancy.

With all the recent medical advances in technology, people's expectations are very high regarding a successful outcome in pregnancy, almost taking for granted that nothing will go wrong but if it does then it can be fixed; yet when things do go wrong, they are devastated. Today the technology exists for women to find out early for themselves if they are pregnant:

> That sense of lost innocence has spiked sharply with the introduction of home pregnancy tests. Because they allow you to discover whether you're pregnant at a very early stage, they also make you aware of an early miscarriage [4, p. 179].

MOTHERING INSTINCT AFFECTED

After a reproductive loss which has not been fully grieved, the mothering instinct can either be heightened or diminished; women can either become over-protective toward their children or they may fail to bond with them, becoming emotionally distant, neglectful, or in extreme cases, abusive. One bereaved mother who had a full term stillbirth, said she felt "paranoid" after the death of her baby. When I asked her what she meant by this term, she explained that she was afraid of losing everybody else, especially the young children in the family, and was extremely watchful and protective of their well-being. In another case, a woman who had miscarried experienced similar feelings, even after the *birth* of her full term baby. She wrote: ". . . almost a full year passed before I stopped worrying that she could die at any moment" [4, p. 176].

Lisette, a 43-year-old mother, presented for counseling because of the difficulty she was experiencing in her relationship with her two-year old child. She said that because she felt so much anger toward the child, she was afraid that she would harm her in some way. When I took a reproductive loss history, she reluctantly disclosed that she had had four abortions, the last one of which was an abortion of a much wanted child. None of these abortions had been fully grieved; the first three had never been acknowledged as losses and she herself said, "I even lied about them to my doctor." After going through the healing process with her and dealing with her unresolved grief, she said that she felt as though a tremendous weight had been lifted and that she experienced a sense of peace. Because she had a better understanding of where her anger was coming from, she was then able to resolve that anger instead of directing it toward her child. She believed that doing this grief work for her previous losses helped her to become a more patient and loving mother.

In another case, this one an unmourned stillbirth followed by the birth of a live baby, the mother was depressed and had great difficulty in mothering. She said she hated her baby and was afraid that she would either harm her or commit suicide if they were not separated. Only later, as she was able to express her feelings and to grieve that previous loss, did she realize she had resented her living child while her son, the "idealized" stillbirth, was dead.

These examples illustrate the necessity of grieving previous losses, whether it be due to abortion or stillbirth, and the implications for mothering behavior that not doing so would entail.

FEELINGS OF ANGER

The feeling of anger is frequently experienced after a loss and although it is a manifestation of normal grief, it is one that bewilders bereaved parents the most. They often express surprise when they discover this anger but are even more surprised and confused when they realize they are angry at the baby who died and abandoned them.

Because Lisette's grief and anger were not adequately acknowledged after the abortion of her wanted child, they complicated her bereavement to the point where her anger was directed (displaced) toward her two-year-old child instead of toward the baby who died due to her abortion. Worden explains:

> The anger that the bereaved person experiences needs to be identified and appropriately targeted toward the deceased in order to bring it to a healthy conclusion. However, it often is handled in other less effective ways, one of which is displacement, or directing it toward some other person and often blaming them for the death. The line of reasoning is that if someone can be blamed, then he is responsible and, hence, the loss could have been prevented. People blame the physician, the funeral director, family members, an insensitive friend, and often God [3, p. 23].

Furthermore, parents often blame themselves, believing that they may have done something wrong to bring about the miscarriage or stillbirth. One woman blamed herself for reluctantly agreeing to the abortion of a Down (also spelled Down's) syndrome child because she felt she was capable of raising such a child. Her self-blame and anger intensified when she watched a television program featuring an actor who had Down syndrome. She also blamed herself for, and now regretted, the three previous abortions of what she believed might have been perfectly healthy children.

ATTACHMENT AND BONDING

Bonding with the baby in utero normally takes place quite early and is an essential component for attachment in the mother-child relationship. However, some parents who have not finished grieving for their deceased child may find it difficult to develop such a bond with a subsequent child [5-7]. Many will intentionally avoid bonding behaviors either until they have passed the point at which the previous loss occurred or until the baby is born. Some parents may avoid bonding behaviors out of fear that if they do become attached their grief would be overwhelming should this baby die also. Others were reluctant to attach themselves to the subsequent baby, because they felt they were being disloyal to the memory of the child who died, and in a sense "abandoning" the dead child. Parents might also feel guilty about the quality of their relationship with the baby if they feel that they have had to hold back their love in order to protect themselves from unbearable grief in the event of another death.

One couple who attended our support group felt very tentative during the pregnancy; they feared becoming attached to a baby they might lose again. Although they avoided bonding behaviors (talking to the baby, stroking the mother's abdomen, etc.) throughout most of the pregnancy, they did continue to attend the sessions to finish grieving for their miscarried baby. Fortunately, they realized a successful pregnancy and were overjoyed at the birth of their baby.

AMBIVALENCE DURING PREGNANCY

Every woman, to some degree, has ambivalent feelings about her own pregnancy. Ambivalent feelings are so common that they were at one time regarded as a presumptive sign of pregnancy. Ambivalent feelings can be present even for women who waited a long time for a much wanted child; they may express some hesitation when faced with the awesome imminent reality of becoming a mother and, so, they may have occasional feelings of not being up to the task. Often they would express their ambivalence or hesitancy in words such as, "I'm not ready to be a mother," or "I don't know how to be a mother when I hardly know how to be myself," or "How can I handle another child at this time?" In the case of miscarriage or stillbirth, these ambivalent feelings can often compound her grief, causing her to blame herself for the loss and to feel guilty as she recalls those times during her pregnancy when she was not a perfectly happy expectant mother.

Sadly, one young woman interpreted her feelings of ambivalence and of not feeling perfectly happy to mean that she should seek an abortion; she did so and later regretted her decision. She said that she had wished someone had told her what to expect during a *normal pregnancy,* including those feelings which prompted her mistakenly to have the abortion. Had she known that these were normal feelings, she said she would never have had the abortion because she loved children and wanted to be a mother. She also expressed fear that she may have aborted her one and only baby.

Even women who consciously do not want their babies experience ambivalent feelings as well. Should the child then be lost through miscarriage or stillbirth, these women will also grieve, despite conscious rejection of the child and the pregnancy. Such women may also feel guilt so profoundly that it leads to great anguish and despair [8].

SUBSEQUENT PREGNANCY

A pregnancy following a reproductive loss has been referred to as the longest nine months. Deciding when or even whether or not to try again to have a child is a primary consideration for couples after the death of a baby. While there are no hard and fast rules to guide them in this decision, couples must take into account many concerns which affect their physical and emotional well-being.

WHAT TIME IS THE RIGHT TIME?

Couples are concerned about how long they should wait before they can try again to become pregnant. Their physician's response is usually based upon the physical readiness of the woman, at about three months. Yet, even if a woman's body is physically able to carry another baby three months after a pregnancy loss, she may not be emotionally ready to do so. The couple may have been in shock since the loss and probably only started to grieve at three months. They might not feel emotionally ready at such a time even though they may be physically ready. One woman believed that she should wait until the remainder of the full nine months had passed out of respect for the baby who died.

IF IT HAPPENED ONCE . . .

Parents may feel emotionally vulnerable, fearful, and tentative throughout a subsequent pregnancy. Their sense of reality about a "perfect pregnancy" has been greatly altered and changed by their previous loss:

> The parents have lost their innocence and realize that life and medical technology cannot guarantee a healthy outcome. This can result in feelings of vulnerability and powerlessness not only during the pregnancy but during the labor and birth. A common parental expression is "If it happened once, what prevents it from happening again?" The fear of losing the pregnancy may be omnipresent for some parents [9, p. 11].[1]

---

[1] Copyright © 1987, *Health Providers Manual for Helping After Neonatal Death.* This work originally appeared in a publication of HAND. For more information, please visit HAND at http://www.handonline.org.

CHOOSING A HEALTH CARE PRACTITIONER

After a pregnancy loss, parents have to consider if they will return to the same physician or other health care practitioner, such as a midwife, or if they should consult with a high-risk obstetrician instead. Some parents refuse to return to the hospital where the loss occurred because of the painful memories associated with the place of their trauma; they often use the word "tainted" in reference to the hospital or clinic in question. One woman who was given a referral for grief-care follow-up in the psychiatry department of the hospital where her baby died, could not bring herself to go back there even though the psychiatry department was located in a different area of the hospital. This kind of response from bereaved individuals supports the need for community based organizations concerned with grief-care for pregnancy and infant loss—such as the Centre for Reproductive Loss—which are not attached to a hospital or clinic setting where the death most often occurs.

SEXUAL CONCERNS

Sexual intimacy may also be affected during a subsequent pregnancy. Couples might worry that sexual intercourse could harm the developing baby or precipitate a miscarriage or premature labor. Aside from physical prohibitions such as an incompetent cervix, in general these fears are unfounded. However, the couple should express their concerns to their physician or other health care provider.

SUPPORT GROUPS

During a subsequent pregnancy, parents might find it helpful to attend a support group of other expectant parents who had also experienced a previous loss. Expectant parents have found it awkward to be in a support group with newly bereaved parents who were not expecting.

THE REPLACEMENT BABY

The replacement baby is one who "takes the place of" the deceased child and, because of this, might not be "valued as a beautiful and unique human being in her own right, but as a place holder for the child who has died" [10, p. 24]. Considering a subsequent baby as a replacement baby denies the uniqueness of that individual since one child can never replace another; every child is entitled to a special place on the family tree. Not every subsequent pregnancy is automatically considered a replacement baby just as a replacement baby is not the same as a subsequent pregnancy. After a previous loss, if a couple rushes into another pregnancy (or adoption) without taking enough time to grieve, this places the subsequent baby at risk for becoming a replacement baby, one who would carry the double burden of the deceased child in addition to having to realize his or her own potential:

> The child herself may have trouble establishing her own identity in the face of unrealistic expectations on the part of the parents, who are constantly comparing her to a "perfect" child who didn't live long enough to dirty the carpet or challenge their authority [10, p. 24].[2]

A replacement baby is often sought as a means to avoid grieving for the child who died. Not only does this short circuit the grieving process for the deceased child, it can also affect bonding with the subsequent baby:

> When parents bring a new baby home too early in the grief process, it is often an attempt to rewrite history, to "undo" the death which has occurred. This is potentially harmful both to the parents and the child. Focusing on the new baby may delay the parents in their journey toward acceptance and resolution of their grief, and this delay in turn may interfere with normal parent-child bonding [10, p. 24].

This combination of insufficient grieving and lack of bonding can affect the parent-child relationship even later on just as it did in Lisette's case where her anger from unresolved grief due to an unmourned abortion was directed toward her replacement child.

WHEN IS POST PARTUM DEPRESSION
SOMETHING ELSE?

The birth of a child can bring tears of joy, tears of sorrow, and sometimes both, bittersweet tears. There are many reasons other than post partum depression that can bring about sadness and tears at such a time. A woman can feel sad that she is no longer pregnant even with the successful outcome of her pregnancy, a baby. She experiences the "loss" of her pregnant condition, the "loss" of that special feeling of closeness with the baby inside her, and the "loss" of the attention and recognition a pregnant condition brings. In the article "Failure to Mourn a Stillbirth: An Overlooked Catastrophe," the authors Lewis and Page offer this observation: "Even with a live birth the mother feels a sense of loss but the consolation of a surviving 'outside baby' helps the mother to overcome her puzzling and bewildering sadness at losing her 'inside baby.' With a stillbirth the mother has to cope with an outer as well as an inner void. There is even more of a

---

[2] Copyright © 1992, 2000, *Unsung Lullabies: A Parents' Guide to Healing After Childbearing Loss*. This work originally appeared in a publication of HAND. For more information, please visit HAND at http://www.handonline.org.

puzzling sense of nothingness for a mother who is anaesthetized at delivery as with a caesarian section" [7, p. 237].

A woman might also grieve if her own mother is not present to share her joy either because her mother is deceased or in poor health, perhaps estranged from her daughter, or simply living too far away to be with her at this time.

An unplanned C-section or unusually difficult birth can trigger sadness and depression for the mother causing her to feel like a failure at not being able to have a "natural" childbirth as she had planned and expected. Her sense of inadequacy is further intensified as she hears stories of other women who breezed through childbirth. Her self-esteem can plummet and she can doubt her own abilities as a mother which also can affect her mothering skills.

Health care providers must be alert to teasing out causes for sadness and depression when discriminating among factors related to a true post partum depression, hormonal influences, or grief reactions brought about by a current or previous loss.

Even a joyful event such as childbirth can act as a trigger to bring back the memory of a previous loss (death-related or non-death related) accompanied by the emotions associated with it. The woman might also remember any previous reproductive loss she experienced (miscarriage, stillbirth, abortion) which can elicit a grief reaction as intensely as if it had happened yesterday. This can also bring tears as she re-grieves that loss or perhaps grieves a previous loss for the first time. One woman describes her reaction:

> I couldn't believe she was alive. I kept saying . . . she lives! I thought I'd cry at the birth but didn't. I was in shock. Tears came later when the baby was brought to my room. I simply could not believe I had a living baby in my arms and I cried for the babies who were denied both life and the love I had to give [9, p. 11].

PRE-NATAL DIAGNOSTIC TESTS

There are a growing number of procedures, both invasive and non-invasive, that are used for detecting and diagnosing fetal problems prenatally that expectant couples must consider in the course of pre-natal care. Most of these tests carry little or no risk while some others do. Two of these tests, amniocentesis and ultrasound, are most pertinent to reproductive loss issues.

Amniocentesis

Amniocentesis is an invasive procedure in which a hypodermic needle is used to take amniotic fluid from the mother's womb for analysis for screening of a variety of potential conditions, including Down syndrome. This elective procedure has a risk factor for miscarriage at the rate of one per hundred cases.

This fact alone can cause great distress for expectant parents, as they fearfully anticipate the procedure itself, anxiously await the results, and then, depending on the outcome, face the decision to end the pregnancy by abortion or not, or consider medical or surgical intervention for the fetus if that is what is suggested. Despite the elective nature of this test, some couples reported that they were pressured into having it done and were told that unless they agreed to it, they would have to "find yourself another physician." As one bereaved mother commented, "It was like starting a process in motion we could not stop." After learning about the amniocentesis early in her pregnancy, one mother's fear in anticipating this test was so great that she denied the reality of the baby's *presence* and only acknowledged her pregnant condition. She did not want to bond with a baby she might lose to miscarriage. Unfortunately, she did lose the baby after the amnio and had difficulty grieving the child because the *reality of the baby's presence had been denied* as she had not been able to acknowledge the baby as an entity separate from herself. Another mother believed that her overwhelming fears caused the miscarriage the day before she was to have the procedure done. Both of these mothers had terrifying nightmares and were under a great deal of stress in anticipation of this test.

When this procedure goes awry and the result is miscarriage, parents feel tremendous anxiety and guilt and take upon themselves responsibility for the loss, and regret the fact that they consented to the procedure at all. The extent of the pain and grief is illustrated in the following story.

This 35-year-old married woman who became pregnant after years of infertility was urged by her doctor to have an amniocentesis because of her age. She thought it was a regular part of routine prenatal care, much like a blood test, rather than an elective procedure with attendant risks to the fetus. In hindsight, she believed the procedure and risks were not explained clearly to her. An accident occurred during the amniocentesis in which the amniotic sac was torn and amniotic fluid began leaking faster than it could replenish itself. The doctor told her he was going to perform a D & C, but when she later saw "abortion" written on her chart, she became very upset. Results of the amniocentesis proved to be negative, that is, the baby was normal. This couple lost the only child they have been able to conceive through an accident caused by an elective procedure resulting in an abortion. They also stated that had they known that the end result of amniocentesis would be abortion, they would not have agreed to this elective procedure in the first place; because they were Catholic, they would not have consented to abortion in any case.

Another bereaved mother also lost a baby after an amniocentesis. Not only has she given permission to tell her story, she also urges great caution regarding this procedure especially to couples experiencing infertility:

> This letter is an attempt to allow you to see and feel the realistic possibilities of a family choosing an amnio following six years of infertility

drugs at a cost of $1500.00 for 5 days, as well as 3 surgeries, and 8 inseminations. All of the above do not include the emotional experience for which I felt there was not enough staff to attend to this major component at all.

We started trying to conceive in 1985. After six years, which felt like twelve, we conceived at the age of 34. We were referred for genetic counselling at the [Hospital A]. After this counselling, we were more confused and the decision to experience the amnio was not too clear for us, so we decided, yes, maybe it's best to have one. At 16 weeks gestation, we had our amnio at [Hospital B] with what seemed like no side effects. At 17 weeks our scheduled U/S (ultrasound) showed less amniotic fluid than previously. The combination of the unmeasureable stress and emotional pain of waiting 3 weeks for results and the decrease in fluid certainly contributed to my blood pressure (B.P.) becoming quite elevated and this led to my having a 6 week hospital and I.C.U. admission for what was told to my family "a life threatening toxemia." So they delivered my daughter at 27 weeks and she died 3 weeks later. Please, what I ask is to always be cautious with advice for amnio in all couples yet more so with infertile couples who were blessed to conceive.

This couple experienced great difficulty in their relationship while grieving this heartbreaking loss. The woman still needed to talk about the loss for a long time after, while for her husband it was over quite quickly, at least on the surface. Eventually, she presented for counseling and she was comforted by the fact that, "This is the only safe place where I can talk about Kayla, my daughter, and my miscarried son Austin. No one else wants to listen to me because they think I should be over it by now." Fortunately, they were able to conceive again, this time adamantly refusing the amniocentesis, even though she was now older and statistically more "at risk" for congenital conditions. They were overjoyed at the birth of a full term, beautiful, healthy boy.

Not all couples refuse a second amnio after a loss, as this couple did. Several of our couples who did have another amnio for a subsequent pregnancy apparently experienced, at least to our knowledge, no ill effects from the procedure.

Ultrasound

Ultrasound (or sonogram) is a non-invasive diagnostic procedure using high-frequency sound waves to create an image of a particular body part. When used prenatally it has several uses; it can determine the baby's position within the womb, identify the sex, the baby's movements, and detect fetal abnormalities, such as spina bifida, or a neural tube defect, just to mention a few..

When the ultrasound reveals that the baby has a congenital anomaly or has died in utero, parents are in shock and disbelief and in great distress; yet, they are offered little comfort at this crucial time, sometimes not even a word of sympathy. Mothers who receive this "bad news" are often alone when they hear it, after which they need to get themselves home on their own while in shock, confusion, and distress. One woman said she nearly caused an accident when she drove herself home because of her difficulty in concentrating and inability to focus after she was told her baby was dead. Another woman was sent to her doctor's office to have him tell her the "bad news." Before she could see him, she had to wait in a room full of pregnant women, which caused her further distress. Other women are so grief stricken that they exhibit a "flight" response and want the baby out right away. Parents have told stories of the additional trauma they experienced due to a lack of compassion and insensitivity from health care providers when the "bad news" was given that their baby was dead.

HOW TO DELIVER "BAD NEWS"

No one likes to hear "bad news" or to give "bad news." But there are compassionate ways of relating to people as human beings at this difficult time. Dr. Bernie Siegel tells the story of one woman's experience when receiving "bad news." He writes:

> The truth without compassion is hostility. I had a patient come to my office the other day who had had a mammogram in Spain, and she told me that when the time came for her to get the results, both the technician and the physician walked out and embraced her before telling her the news that she would need surgery. When she came to this country for treatment, she was shocked by the difference in physicians. The first surgeon she was referred to talked to her with his back toward her as he completed a chart, and got angry at her for asking how her breast would look after surgery. She found a similar coldness in the radiology suite she visited. She felt so uncared for that she left and ultimately found her way to my office [11, pp. 130-131].[3]

Bereaved parents are most comforted by compassionate gestures and genuine, heartfelt expressions of sympathy for their loss. One couple told how they were helped in their grief by their doctor's healing words and kindness as he, with tears in his eyes, expressed his sympathy while holding both their hands and sitting on the hospital bed. They never forgot his kindness and compassion, healing expressions of his "shared humanity." Dr. Siegel writes:

> Once the shared humanity of doctor and patient is acknowledged, doctors can be relieved of the burden of thinking that the responsibility for life and death lies with them alone [11, p. 137].

A SUDDEN DEATH EXPERIENCE

The term "sudden death" most often calls to mind those deaths that are due to suicide, accidents, heart attack, and homicides. We don't usually associate reproductive loss with such an experience. Yet, it is noteworthy that in the

---

[3] Reprinted by permission of HarperCollins Publishers Inc.

index to Worden's book, *Grief Counseling & Grief Therapy,* under sudden death are included the terms miscarriage, stillbirth, and SIDS (Sudden Infant Death Syndrome). Several of the features of sudden death described by Worden are ones I have seen manifested also in bereaved parents following a reproductive loss. These characteristic features are a sense of unreality, strong sense of guilt, need to blame someone, helplessness, sense of rage, and agitation [3, pp. 98-99]. As mentioned above, upon learning that their baby had died in utero, many women adamantly stated that they wanted the baby out right away. Some parents leave the hospital as soon as possible after a stillbirth. This is not because the parents did not love or care for the child; rather, their behavior is tied more to the nature of a sudden death. Worden sheds light on this behavior: "The stress of sudden death can trigger a "flight or fight" response in a person and lead to a very agitated depression. A sudden increase in levels of adrenaline usually is associated with this agitation" [3, p. 99]. Of particular note is the effect of the sense of helplessness that the bereaved experience after a sudden death. As Worden explains:

> This type of death is an assault on our sense of power and on our sense of orderliness. Often this helplessness is linked with an incredible sense of rage, and it is not unusual for the survivor to want to vent his or her anger on someone. Occasionally, hospital personnel become the targets of violence or the survivor expresses a wish to kill certain people for having been involved in the death of a loved one [3, p. 99].

This sense of rage has been manifested in several of my clients who had experienced abortions, especially the ones that were coerced; sometimes, they expressed a wish that the doctor who had performed the abortion would die or that some harm would come to him. Even though some of these women were relieved not to be pregnant any longer, they still experienced a grief reaction and profound feelings of emptiness. In one especially sad case, a woman turned her sense of rage upon herself after being coerced into an abortion; tragically she committed suicide. Miscarriage, stillbirth, and abortion interrupt the pregnancy, a natural process, and leave behind an incredible feeling of emptiness. They also leave behind other manifestations of a sudden death. Weizman and Kamm describe the tremendous impact this type of unexpected death has upon the grieving person:

> There is nothing to compare with the impact and profound shock of sudden unexpected death. The assault is a jolt to the system. After a sudden death, the period of shock and disbelief is long lasting. Those who have suffered the sudden death of a loved one will experience a long period of numbness and denial [12, p. 101].

Therese A. Rando, in her book *Grief, Dying, and Death,* says this about sudden death:

> When . . . the loss comes from out of the blue, grievers are shocked. They painfully learn that major catastrophic events can occur without warning. As a

result, they develop a chronic apprehension that something unpleasant may happen at any time. It is this lack of security, along with the experience of being overwhelmed and unable to grasp the situation, that accounts for the severe postdeath bereavement complications that occur in cases of sudden death [13, p. 52].

Reflecting upon the above characterizations of sudden death, my attention was drawn to certain key words which can also describe the experience of reproductive losses such as miscarriage, stillbirth, abortion, or other infant death:

"profound shock"
"assault, jolt to the system"
"long lasting shock and disbelief"
"numbness and denial"
"major catastrophic event"
"chronic apprehension"
"lack of security"
"experience of being overwhelmed"
"unable to grasp the situation"
"severe postdeath bereavement complications"

If reproductive loss was truly understood as a sudden death experience, would these losses then be so readily dismissed as unimportant or as ones not needing to be grieved? If health professionals acknowledged these losses as a sudden death experience, would they allow their patients to leave for home unaccompanied after they delivered the "bad news" that their baby had died in utero? It is only in the last 30 years or so, that reproductive losses, also referred to as perinatal losses, have received the long overdue and much needed attention and recognition they deserve. One health professional commented upon the far-reaching implications of the severity of the problem of reproductive losses:

In my own experience, I was struck by what seemed to be a high incidence of hospitalized psychiatric patents whose histories uncovered some guilt related to miscarriages, stillbirths, and birth defects [5, p. 2053].

Devastating is a word that is often used to describe the emotional and psychological trauma of the impact of reproductive losses which seem to share, at least to some degree, many of the same manifestations that characterize a sudden death experience. Just as in the case of sudden death which happens without warning, there is no time for goodbyes, no time for hellos, and usually no time to express the love the parents may already feel towards their baby. Not everyone will manifest those features of sudden death with the same intensity; but, for those who do, it is imperative to remember that their behavior may be appropriate for the circumstance of a sudden death experience. Even an early miscarriage can be traumatic and its effects should not be readily dismissed [6].

TRAUMA AND REPRODUCTIVE LOSS

We are beginning to realize that reproductive loss is a tragedy with implications similar to those manifested in other losses and trauma. A victims-services consultant commented upon such aftermath following a devastating loss:

> One of the things we often see after a mass tragedy is higher divorce rate, an increase in alcohol and drug use, and more car accidents, all because of the trauma people suffered [14].

Trauma, shock, injury, wounds, physical or emotional harm, hurt, and loss are not only related by definition but also by similar effects. Grief reactions and the manifestations of post traumatic stress also share many of the same characteristics. Sometimes its effects may not become evident until years later. For 12 years after her abortion, one woman seemed to have no ill effects from it until the triggering event of giving birth produced a post traumatic stress reaction to the abortion, including panic attacks, intrusive thoughts, flashbacks, nightmares, in addition to other manifestations of a grief reaction.

"Trauma is not all in your head," declared post-trauma expert Frema Engel in her acceptance speech as the 1999 recipient of the Montreal Council of Women "Woman of the Year" event. She emphasized that everyone has the tools to help people who have been traumatized. "Let them talk about their experience. Ask what you can do to help and then do it. When they get enough support and understanding, they begin to recover." While trauma may not be "all in your head" (in one sense), it has been demonstrated through Magnetic Resonance-Imaging (MRI) brain scans that trauma can alter pathways in the brain and that "a traumatized person's bloodstream is chemically different from a non-traumatized person's" [15].

Whether the trauma was due to a mass shooting tragedy, a miscarriage and the tragic loss of a baby, or abortion, the aftermath can be the same—"higher divorce rate, an increase in alcohol and drug use, and more car accidents" [14].

When the trauma of loss and grief is not adequately processed, its effects can even be felt across generations. Jane Middleton-Moz, author of *Children of Trauma,* comments on the inter-generational effects of unresolved trauma:

> Without intervention, the painful effects of the unresolved trauma and the resulting denial of the identities and emotions of subsequent family members, lives on generationally. Each generation attempts to undo the pain of the previous generation [16, p. 118].

In reproductive loss, this is seen in the absence of bonding between mother and child, especially when previous reproductive losses have not been resolved and the resulting trauma has not been adequately processed.

However, when crisis intervention is put in place as soon as possible after the trauma, the person is helped to process that event and with appropriate counseling over time, the aftermath of the loss or trauma can be minimized or prevented and the person can recover.

REFERENCES

1. C. Lightner and N. Hathaway, *Giving Sorrow Words*, Warner Books, New York, 1990.
2. M. H. Gerner, *For Bereaved Grandparents*, Centering Corporation, Nebraska, 1990.
3. J. W. Worden, *Grief Counseling & Grief Therapy*, Springer, New York, 1991.
4. R. Polaneczky, Mourning What Might Have Been, *Parenting*, pp. 175-183, November 1999.
5. C. C. Floyd, Pregnancy After Reproductive Failure, *American Journal of Nursing*, *81*:11, pp. 2050-2053, November 1981.
6. T. M. Stephany, Early Miscarriages: Are We Too Quick to Dismiss the Pain?, *RN Magazine*, p. 89, November 1982.
7. E. Lewis and A. Page, Failure to Mourn a Stillbirth: An Overlooked Catastrophe, *British Journal of Medical Psychology, 51*, pp. 237-241, 1978.
8. L. Peppers and R. Knapp, Maternal Reactions to Involuntary Fetal-Infant Death, *Psychiatry, 43*, pp. 155-159, May 1980.
9. E. Miller-Karas, Subsequent Pregnancy After Miscarriage, Stillbirth or Infant Death, in *Health Provider's Manual for Helping After Perinatal Death*, H.A.N.D. of Santa Clara County, Los Gatos, California, p. 11, 1987.
10. Reclaiming the Future: Accepting Loss, Resolving Grief, in *Unsung Lullabies: A Parents' Guide to Healing After Childbearing Loss*, H.A.N.D. of Santa Clara County, Los Gatos, California, p. 24, 1992.
11. B. S. Siegel, *Peace, Love, & Healing*, Harper, New York, 1989.
12. S. G. Weizman and P. Kamm, *About Mourning, Support and Guidance for the Bereaved*, Human Sciences Press, New York, 1985.
13. T. A. Rando, *Grief, Dying and Death*, Research Press Company, Champaign, Illinois, 1984.
14. M. Janofsky, Columbine Shootings Still Claiming Victims, *New York Times*, reported in *The Gazette*, Montreal, October 24, 1999.
15. J. Davenport, Post-Trauma Expert Wins, *The Gazette*, Montreal, November 25, 1999.
16. J. Middleton-Moz, *Children of Trauma—Rediscovering Your Discarded Self*, Health Communications, Inc., Deerfield Beach, Florida, 1989.

CHAPTER 7

Types of Reproductive Loss

On Visiting the Grave of My Stillborn Little Girl

Sunday, July 4th, 1836

I made a vow within my soul, O child,
When thou wert laid beside my weary heart,
With marks of death on every tender part,
That, if in time a living infant smiled,
Winning my ear with gentle sounds of love,
In sunshine of such joy, I still would save
A green rest for thy memory, O Dove!
And oft times visit thy small, nameless grave.
Thee have I not forgot, my first born, thou
Whose eyes never opened to my wistful gaze,
Whose suffering stamped with pain thy little brow:
I think of thee in these far happier days, and thou, my child,
from thy bright heaven see
How well I keep my faithful vow to thee.

Elizabeth Gaskell (1810–1865) [cited in 1]

As well as not recognizing the great sorrow associated with reproductive loss, our modern society perpetuates the false notion that previous generations took little notice of perinatal loss since death, from various causes, occurred with such frequency. Yet poets tell us that a child's death has always been devastating to parents. In *The Poetry of Childhood* [1, pp. 12-29], there are several poems written between the 8th and the 20th centuries by such poets as Elizabeth Gaskell (1810–1865), John Milton (1608–1674), Po Chii-1 (772–846), and W. H. Davies (1871–1940), describing the sadness of losing a child. Thus, we can see that this has been recognized as a universal sorrow in the human condition for many centuries.

Reproductive loss can include miscarriage, stillbirth, infertility, sterility, ectopic pregnancy, relinquishing a child for adoption, and elective abortion, including multifetal pregnancy reduction (MFPR). It can also include women who have never had children. Responsibility for the care of a frail relative, careers that preclude the possibility of having and raising children, not meeting a suitable partner or losing a partner through broken engagements, or death of a spouse can all lead to a sense of child loss. Each of the above events or situations can be a source of intense suffering. Only within the last decade or two has there been recognition on the part of the helping professions and the community that these are significant losses and support is needed for the woman–couple–family in helping them grieve [2-4]. *Webster's New World Dictionary of American English* defines loss as the "damage, trouble, disadvantage, deprivation caused by losing something" [5, p. 799]. Among the examples of loss given is one related to reproductive loss "to suffer the miscarriage or stillbirth of a baby." It is interesting to note that the dictionary gives some idea of the seriousness of the loss of a baby before or at birth, while society at large still tends to ignore or make light of these events. In recent years, however, an increasing number of health care providers are beginning to recognize the seriousness of these losses.

Some discussion of terminology is required to shed light on the extent of the problem and the importance of definition to our clients.

According to the *Standards and Guidelines for Providing Care to the Family Experiencing Neonatal Death* [6, p. 20], fetal death (formerly stillbirth) occurs when the fetus shows no sign of life at birth. The new standard terminology identifies fetal death as death prior to complete expulsion or extraction from the mother of a product of human conception, regardless of the duration of the pregnancy. Neonatal death is death of a live born baby before the age of 28 days. A fetal death occurring before 20 weeks of gestation in which the conceptus remains in utero is called a missed abortion. It has been our experience and that of Maternal and Child Health Nurses that these definitions are useful to health professionals in their discussions, presentations, and record keeping.

However, it should be noted that some terms are repugnant to many women experiencing these losses. They tend to think and use the word baby regarding their pregnancy. To them, they have lost a baby. Some do not even like the word fetus. The term abortion is understood as induced abortion, hence the terms spontaneous abortion and missed abortion are upsetting to many. The *Guidelines* specifically exclude termination of pregnancy from their definition of fetal death; however, it must be remembered that women and men grieving abortion also see induced abortion as the death of a baby.

The Centre for Reproductive Loss will continue to use the terms stillbirth and miscarriage instead of fetal death, spontaneous abortion, and missed abortion.

The American Academy of Pediatrics and the American College of Obstetricians and Gynecologists report that approximately 18,000 neonatal deaths occur each year. "Fetal death accounts for 50% of cases of peri-natal mortality. In 50% of these cases the cause of fetal death is unknown" [6, p. 20].

MISCARRIAGE

Friedman and Gradstein have defined miscarriage as the spontaneous natural termination of a pregnancy prior to the 20th week of gestation. It is reported that at least one in five pregnancies ends in miscarriage. The numbers are probably higher, as miscarriages can occur which are not brought to the attention of a physician. Some may only be perceived as a delayed menstrual period [7, p. 30].

Grief from miscarriage can be very intense for the parents and other family members. Many health professionals still do not see miscarriage as an outcome of pregnancy, an attitude that can be devastating for parents and families. Health care providers who have become aware of the impact of miscarriage on women were initially astonished at the high degree of emotional pain the mothers experienced. This pain can be as great as for any other significant loss but many people do not view miscarriage as a significant loss. The woman who miscarries often does not receive the empathy and support she needs as she goes through a crushing loss. Even worse, her normal grief can be seen as inappropriate or even pathological. In other words, society in general and the mother's potential networks, often with the best of intentions, minimize her loss and do not permit her to grieve. Consequently, she may then repress her grief. We have discovered with our clients that grief repressed will surface sooner or later. Also, problems in relationships can occur as partners may grieve differently. There can also be difficulty in bonding with present and future children. In complicated grief, self-destructive behaviors can be manifested. Perceived lack of social support has been reported to lead to complicated grieving. Lack of recognition of miscarriage as an event to grieve renders mothers and fathers who suffer miscarriages more vulnerable to complicated grief. The skill, knowledge, and understanding shown by health professionals are vital to helping bereaved parents in their shock and pain. Offering condolences helps the parents to begin to accept the reality of their loss. This is the most important task of mourning. Although most of our clients found health personnel kind, a few were not only unhelpful but also rude. Courtesy certainly must be the minimum one should expect in interactions with hospital workers under any circumstances.

A.'s Story

A.'s story illustrates a number of the points discussed above. She is a charming, intelligent, and vivacious woman in her late thirties who had had a miscarriage ten years prior to reaching out for help with her loss. When she began bleeding six weeks into her pregnancy, she went to the hospital where she miscarried. Much of what occurred is still a blur to her. However, she clearly remembers being sharply reprimanded by a nurse. As she was being transferred from the stretcher to the bed, there was a gush of blood which stained the sheets. The nurse seemed inordinately annoyed by the accident. Unfortunately, this is the only interaction with hospital personnel at that time that she remembers.

She had not discussed the miscarriage with anyone. As she said, "I just didn't think about her. I stuffed my grief down. We were always taught not to make a fuss or inconvenience others." She only became aware of her grief when, by chance, she read one of our Centre for Reproductive Loss pamphlets and suddenly burst into tears, to her own astonishment. She contacted our Centre and joined a support group sponsored by the Centre. She told her story and shed many, many tears and received great support from other group members. Her full participation in the group provided the environment she needed to do her grief work, once she recognized that what she had experienced was a painful loss. In addition, she was able to empathize with other group members and offer support to them. A. was able to do her grief work quickly. She was sure the baby was a girl and gave her a name which was a very important step in her healing. The memorial service, which was planned and carried out by the group and facilitators, included giving a rose for each child being grieved and remembered. She found the closure she needed through the group and the service. A.'s experiences show dramatically the need to grieve reproductive loss; the importance of understanding and care by health care providers involved in miscarriage; how the lack of supportive networks can lead to repressed grief; that grief will emerge at some time, in this case ten years later; and that compassion, empathy, and assistance in understanding grief and grief work can greatly facilitate the healing process. Grief is exceedingly painful, but successfully working through the pain can bring new growth and wisdom.

Miscarriage, and certainly any reproductive loss, can affect one's view on the world. To most of us, for a good part of our lives, pregnancy means that a healthy baby will be the end. North American health professionals take great pride in North American medicine. People believe that good prenatal care ensures a positive pregnancy outcome. Because of this, many of our young parents have not experienced the death of a close family member. Parents and grandparents are living longer, often full and active lives. The death of a baby through pregnancy loss can be devastating. Bereaved parents have often said, "Babies are not meant to die." I have also heard many wise older people say, "It is a terrible thing to outlive your children." For the young expectant parents then, the event is doubly shocking. Their predictable world collapses. There is usually a sense of helplessness, a frightening loss of control whenever the death of a close family member occurs. It is magnified when the persons affected have little experience of dealing with loss. This experience is exemplified by the next couple's story.

J. and L.'s Story

J. and L. are an intelligent, healthy, articulate, and devoted young couple. Each set of parents is living, fairly well, and active. The extended families on both sides are close and involved. J. and L. were eagerly looking forward to starting their family and were delighted when J. became pregnant. The expectant grandparents were ecstatic, as were the prospective aunts, uncles, and cousins.

This was J.'s first pregnancy. She felt well except for some of the first trimester discomforts of queasiness and fatigue, which she tolerated very well. However, after the sixth week she had some spotting and cramping, and subsequently miscarried. She was seen at the hospital, and was scheduled for a D & C that evening. J. and L. found the doctor and the nursing staff very kind, empathetic, and supportive. The hospital chaplain saw her first before she went to surgery and again in the morning before she was discharged. Both sets of parents kept in close touch. L. stayed with her during the night and took her home the next morning. Both shed tears and expressed their sadness and disappointment.

J. reported that she felt very well supported both in the hospital and from family and friends. She said she was able to do her own mourning and say "Good-bye" to the baby. I asked if she wanted to name the baby. She was not comfortable with this as she believed that a child must be seen and known and then an appropriate name, which suits the child, can be selected. This was fine, as this was her reality. She was very much in touch with her feelings and was quite clear on what she found healing and comforting. This is a good example of the uniqueness of grieving. J. said, "I've done my grieving, I know. But I feel like I lost my innocence. I won't ever feel quite so sure that everything will turn out fine." This was how her loss affected her view of the world. The world was just not as reliable as she once thought. Although she had three pregnancies after the miscarriage and delivered healthy babies, she said she could not enjoy the pregnancies to the same extent as she had enjoyed her first pregnancy and she could not be totally at ease until the pregnancy was over. While she did not obsess over this, there was a shadow of fear that something might have gone wrong in each of the last pregnancies. Because both parents were secure in their relationship with one another, they were able to attach quickly to each child. They assumed and mastered the tasks of parenting, and enjoyed the process. Had they not done their grief work, it could have interfered with attachment and impeded parenting skills.

J. and L. exemplified a young couple whose first serious loss was the miscarriage of their first child. Through the support they received and their own inner resources they were able to work through their grief together and grow from the experience. It is important to remember that "good grief" is growth enhancing spiritually and emotionally, while loss that is not effectively processed can stultify development.

The statement, "I lost my innocence," was poignantly echoed by two young fathers who, along with their wives, had suffered reproductive loss. These couples had experienced miscarriage. None of the three couples knew each other; yet, each couple, independently, had this realization of lost innocence.

V.'s Story

V. had a history of difficulty getting pregnant. She and her husband had one child, Rose, a girl of eight years who repeatedly asked for a brother or sister. They, too, wanted more children.

V. was treated for infertility for several years so the family was delighted when she became pregnant. Even under the care of her obstetrician who specialized in treating high-risk expectant mothers, she miscarried at ten weeks. She, her husband, and child were very sad and disappointed. V. was under a great deal of pressure; she and her husband needed to deal with their grief and help their daughter to understand *at her level* the loss of her sibling. Since V. was in her late thirties, she believed that she needed to try again for another baby soon. She went back to the fertility clinic after the waiting period of several months, as her doctor advised. While she was undergoing treatment for infertility she joined a support group to help work out her grief regarding her miscarriage. She was able to participate well in the group. Her family was supportive, although her parents worried about her health when she became pregnant again. She had a very uncomfortable pregnancy, which added to her stress, although she handled it well. She had a professional career, but arranged to take time off to eliminate pressure from that source.

V. delivered a healthy baby girl, to everyone's delight. V. recognized the need to do her grief work so that she would be free to bond with her daughter. Even though this was a difficult time for her, she came through it well. She had a supportive husband, parents, and friends, and she had the material resources and the insight to care for herself. She was privileged to be able to take time off from a stressful job. She utilized her resources well, sought appropriate help and used it effectively. She benefitted from the support group for parents with reproductive loss, and several one-to-one contacts with grief counselors.

Unfortunately, not all individuals who suffer miscarriage have the same support as the couples mentioned above. Some of the mothers we saw told us that they received little help from sources that they had relied on. One woman reported that her doctor was "so cold, and acted as though our miscarriage was trivial. He told me to wait a month and then try again. He didn't want to be bothered by questions about the loss, and said curtly, 'Nobody knows.' I wasn't ready to think about another baby. I wanted to find some way to care for the baby I just lost." It is often impossible to tell what causes a miscarriage or even a stillbirth, but brushing off the parents' concerns about their loss is hurtful.

Sometimes, parents of the couple cannot be helpful because they are grieving too. They have lost a grandchild, and find their children's pain too much to bear. One young couple was very hurt when her mother drew away and could not discuss the miscarriage. The prospective grandmother had lost three babies through miscarriage. Because of her own pain, she could not be available to the couple. Grief counselors in such cases can help these couples to deal with their own grief and come to understand and forgive the lack of support from family and friends.

Neighbors and colleagues at work can be very insensitive. Worden reminds us a person has been lost [8, p. 104], but many people do not realize this. The need for education to help society to understand this as a death is obvious.

Some parents are very insightful and aware of their own needs. The importance of listening carefully and being open to the clients' ideas cannot be overly emphasized. As grief counselors we learn so much from our clients. Responding to what they tell us they need helps them and broadens our own understanding and gives us new ideas for helping other bereaved persons.

M.'s Story

M. gave us much to think about and motivated us to find new resources in the community. She was a young mother of two children who had just experienced a miscarriage, twelve weeks into her pregnancy. M. was concerned that her baby might be discarded in the hospital garbage, so she wrapped the remains in a small blanket, took her tragic little bundle home, and stored it in her refrigerator freezer in the kitchen. Then, she called the Centre to tell us that she wished to bury the baby. Her parents had a family plot that she was permitted to use. There was a fee for opening the cemetery plot which neither the parents nor grandparents were able to afford since her parents were on pension, and her husband was out of work. M. wanted to know how we could help her to arrange for the burial of the baby. This was a deeply spiritual young woman, with a closeness to and a love of nature. She is a good communicator and had helped her family to share their grief with her. They named the baby, which they believed was a girl. Now M. needed help to do this final important task to fulfill her strongly felt obligation to her baby. Although we did not have the answers right away, we sought out the advice of a funeral director who was able to assist M. This director was a very compassionate and generous man, sensitive to the grief of his clients. He owned and maintained a special area in a cemetery which assisted families such as M.'s who wished to bury an extremely tiny baby and have neither the place nor the finances to do it. He arranged for the burial without charge. They had a memorial service with the family and a burial service at the graveside. Later, she explained "It takes nine months for that baby to grow in the womb. It takes nine months for the buried person to completely return to earth. That is why it was so important to bury her." How well this young woman knew the spirit, mind, and body connection! In our role as facilitators, we helped her to find the means to meet her own needs and those of her family, to work out their grief. She called me some months later to report that they were doing well. They had successfully integrated the baby into the family constellation even though the baby was no longer with them physically.

Hippocrates once said, "First do no harm." Here was a woman who knew what needed to be done to process her grief. The health personnel in the hospital did not understand her need to bury her baby. Respect for her, her family, and the baby could have enabled the caregivers involved to respond in new ways. Some of the hospital staff might have found this so unusual as to be bizarre and certainly outside the rules and protocol of hospital policy. Yet, there was a beautiful logic and reasonableness to her request. Some of us recall that colleagues were horrified years ago when we encouraged mothers to view and hold their stillborn babies. These colleagues were very well intentioned in wanting to protect the mother; they thought we were being cruel by helping the mothers grieve their losses in this manner. However, a mother who is anesthetized for the delivery is not aware of the birth; when she learns later of the death and does not see her baby, she may not have closure to the pregnancy which could lead to difficulty in accepting and grieving her loss.

STILLBIRTH

Stillbirth has been defined as the death of the fetus between the twentieth week of pregnancy and birth. Friedman and Gradstein give us the rather chilling statistics that in the United States there is one stillbirth for every 80 live births [7, p. 57]. This loss is much more common than most people realize. There may be more of a perception by the general public that a stillborn birth is a hard and sad event for the parents, one not dismissed as lightly as miscarriage. Still the public does not view stillbirth as a category of the death of a child. Because these losses usually take place in a hospital, in the obstetrical department surrounded by mothers with live babies, mothers who have experienced stillbirth feel even more isolated. The mother tends to blame herself. A sense of guilt and failure seemed to be a universal reaction on the part of women experiencing reproductive loss. Unfortunately, this can be re-enforced by insensitive comments such as, "You really should have taken time off from work earlier," or "Do you think that long drive to Toronto caused it?" This is, to say the least, unhelpful and potentially destructive.

Women can be alarmed about certain changes they sense in their pregnancy. Often these concerns are not seen to be taken seriously. When a woman loses her baby, she may harbor the awful thought that, perhaps with earlier intervention, the baby could have been saved. This thought increases the parent's suffering immensely. In some cases of stillbirth, the physician and parents may know for some time that there is a problem with the pregnancy. The health care team can work feverishly to save the baby with the parents complying and cooperating with the many tests and interventions. Parents hold out hope as long as possible, often longer than the seriousness of the situation warrants. As their hopes begin to dim, health professionals need to give parents the truth, in a sensitive, compassionate manner. It is important that caretakers communicate to grieving parents that they recognize the enormity of their loss. At such times, some pre-grieving can begin.

L. and N.'s Story

L. and N. endured the painful situation described above. They already had two children and had wanted a third child; they were happy in their family, community, and work. When she became pregnant with her third child, she miscarried. She became pregnant again, but there were difficulties in the baby's development. Obstetrical specialists carefully monitored the pregnancy, but it ended in stillbirth. L. and N. were heartbroken. Their obstetrician was very concerned and empathetic to both of them; the nurses also were supportive and helpful in dealing with holding the baby, having pictures taken, etc. Unfortunately, not all the nurses on the various shifts were familiar with the protocol in assisting them in their grief. For the most part, though, the hospital staff treated L. and N. with great kindness and understanding, and they found this very consoling and comforting. They also faced the task of explaining to their two children why they did not bring a baby home. This couple communicates well and were able to share their grief and support each other. Because of their strong faith, they found the rituals of religious service and funeral significant in dealing with their loss.

They joined a support group, shared their grief and what they found helpful, and were very effective in reaching out to other group members. She became pregnant again. Everything went well, even though they were still anxious throughout the pregnancy.

L. and N's story illustrates how one family dealt with an expected stillbirth.

S.'s Story

Parents can experience a stillbirth when they know beforehand that the baby is in difficulty. Then there are the parents who are going through a seemingly normal pregnancy, and yet it ends in stillbirth. S. had this unhappy experience. She was in the 40th week of her second pregnancy, an uneventful one, similar to her first. S. went into the hospital to be checked, and experienced some contractions; the physician considered the possibility of inducing the labor. She felt apprehensive, as the baby who had been quite active was moving less and less. Then the nurses changed shifts and she was unable to get the attention of the nurses to follow up on her concerns. Staff nurses didn't recognize the crisis, until she finally received admission care. In spite of the staff's efforts, by the time she delivered her baby boy, he was not breathing and could not be resuscitated. This was a terrible blow. Both parents had been so looking forward to the birth of their son. There was some nagging question: Could he have been saved by more prompt intervention? Should she have made a scene and insisted on being seen immediately in the case room? As noted before, mothers usually tend to blame themselves and believe if they had only done more or less or. . . . One of the most important tasks of the professional working with parents who have had a reproductive loss is to deal with this guilt. A reality check with the parents usually demonstrates that they are not to blame. Many times a cause cannot be found for stillbirth or miscarriage.

In a situation such as S.'s, it was important that she realize that it was not her fault, that she had done everything that she could. Parents need accurate information. However, the parents are often in shock and cannot absorb much information at the time of the birth. Also, information isn't always immediately available, for example, the results from an autopsy. In the meantime, S. and her husband were grieving differently, as women and men so often do. She knew she needed to share her grief with others who would understand but, he could not bear to talk about the loss, and certainly not to "a bunch of strangers." S. came to the support group accompanied by a friend who came with S. so she did not have to go alone. Her friend's generosity was rewarded, because she also received help from the group with grief issues she had with her father. S. shared some very moving poems she had written to her son. She would write letters to her doctor and the nursing staff explaining her concerns about not being seen promptly. The letters could be sent or not depending on how she felt after. Letter writing was helpful for her to deal with any anger she felt, put to rest her own guilt feelings, and go on with her grief work. She has been doing nicely and is expecting another child.

R.'s Story

R., a woman in her late thirties, had a pregnancy that was going relatively well until the last few weeks. Her obstetrical specialist watched her closely during this time because she experienced some ankle swelling. When she went in for her appointment near her expected delivery date, the baby's heart rate suddenly slowed. In a short time, it returned to its normal count. R. was alarmed and asked the doctor what was happening. He told her everything seemed fine, but just to be sure he had an ultrasound done and rechecked the fetal heart rate. Everything seemed normal so she was sent home. The next day she came into the hospital in labor. When the baby emerged, he was dead. She was in shock, then devastated. The nurses wrapped the baby in a blanket and gave him to R. to hold, a gesture for which she was most grateful. Pictures were taken of her and the baby. These were very important to her and she treasures them, the only pictures she has of her child. She had a very difficult time with no family members living near. Some comments to her were unhelpful to completely brutal: "It's a good thing the baby died, since you and the father were of different faiths," and "Why don't you sue the doctor?" This last comment, of course, exacerbated her concerns that the baby might have lived if some sort of intervention had been done by the medical staff. I did a reality check with her, went over what had been done, and then she was able to realize that the care had been well within the guidelines of good medical practice. This comforted her. It is so difficult to deal with a baby born dead, but it is overwhelming to think that the death could have been prevented.

R. sought help from the Centre in dealing with her grief. Her baby was lost in January and a few months later her father died very suddenly. This was another terrible loss for R. as she was very close to her father. I walked with her through her grief for her son and for her father. She also was dealing with coming to the realization that she might never have a child. As well, this was a time when, with cut-backs from the government, there were few jobs in her field, so economic problems as well as health concerns made her life even more difficult. She used her writing skills to help with her grief and found comfort in trips to the cemetery where her son was buried. R.'s situation illustrates a harsh reality. Loss of loved ones causes grief which is superimposed on individuals who already are dealing with difficulties that themselves alone are almost too much to bear. If grief counselors are to provide holistic care, helping to heal mind, body, and spirit, they must be aware of the resources in the community that are available, and where one can refer clients for assistance.

It is hard to do grief work when you are physically ill, in pain, are malnourished, and/or need a job, spiritual resources, and affordable recreational facilities. With so many young people out of work, businesses downsizing, and laying off of more people, we need to be aware that loss of job, money, and status in the community are also grief issues. There may be health issues or other losses that cross the spectrum of society. Thus, many families who are experiencing reproductive loss are also dealing with other losses. Each loss needs to be recognized and the grief work done but not done in isolation.

Some of our clients were in such dire financial straits that they did not even have bus fare to come for counseling sessions. We solved this by doing telephone counseling. We would have regular telephone appointments with the appropriate time scheduled as for an office session. The clients were also free to call at any other time.

ECTOPIC PREGNANCY

When the egg, fertilized in the fallopian tube, is implanted elsewhere than in the uterus, the pregnancy is known as ectopic. Ninety-five percent of the time, an ectopic implantation is in the fallopian tube. The ovary, abdomen, or the cervix is rarely the site [7, p. 84]. Ectopic pregnancy is very serious, resulting in a compounded loss for the woman—her baby and usually one of her fallopian tubes when the embryo is lodged there. As the baby grows, the capacity of the tube to stretch is limited and the tube can rupture, leading to hemorrhage.

Surgical intervention is required immediately as this is a life threatening situation for the mother. Symptoms of rupture include severe cramping or severe abdominal pain, spotting, fainting, and weakness.

An ectopic pregnancy is hard to diagnose before a crisis occurs, usually about four weeks after fertilization, about two weeks after the first missed menstrual period. The signs of a normal pregnancy are the same as for an ectopic, so it is usually not detected until symptoms appear. This is both a physical and emotional shock to the woman, and very frightening for her and her partner.

The impact of her losses may not set in until after she is home from the hospital. She has been in a situation where she could have died and in some situations the mother very nearly does. She has to deal with her physical recovery, the loss of her baby, and the loss of her tube. The couple must also deal with the very real risk of another ectopic pregnancy as well as her reduced fertility. If difficulties with fertility are already present, this compounds the problem.

J. and B.'s Story

J. and B. experienced all of these difficulties including problems in getting pregnant. They already had a three year old boy but they wanted more children and so they were pleased when she became pregnant. However, J. felt something was amiss early on, as she was experiencing so much discomfort. She went to the hospital, but felt they did not take her concerns seriously at first. As the pain increased in intensity and she went into shock, the staff recognized the crisis. Doctors performed emergency surgery since the tube had already ruptured. Her doctor told her that any further delay could have cost her her life. Because she had hemorrhaged, she was very weak. She was in emotional shock at first; then the loss of her baby hit her, as well as the loss of her tube, and concern for her fertility. She also recognized that this incident triggered her grief over previous serious losses, the deaths of her sister and mother. J. and her family did not discuss these losses. They believed in carrying on and not "bothering" other people with their own troubles. J. and B. presented for counseling about a year after losing the baby. She felt shaky emotionally and did not see any improvement. She had two one-to-one counseling sessions and then joined one of our support groups. She worked very hard on her grief for all of her losses. Her husband accompanied her to the support group sessions and both found the sessions useful.

J. keeps in touch from time to time. She and her husband are reconciled to the fact that they are a complete family of three. It has been a long and painful journey, but facing the pain and walking through it helped them emerge on the other side of grief with strength, understanding, and wisdom.

Tubal pregnancy occurs about once in every one hundred pregnancies in the United Stated according to Friedman and Gradstein [7, p. 84]. Thus, it is more common than most people realize. Women who have experienced ectopic or tubal pregnancies need a great deal of understanding and support from family and friends. Unfortunately, people do not always understand just what they are going through. They have lost a baby, very nearly lost their lives, perhaps their fertility, and a sense of their own bodily integrity. Friedman and Gradstein described a sense of loss of one's wholeness [7, p. 84]. They remind us that there are emotional scars as well as the physical and they are intertwined. J. had quite an extensive scar after her surgery and the sight of it reminded her of her brush with death, and her other losses. There is a tendency on the part of lay people and health professionals to treat this only as a surgical procedure. Much education is needed so that there is understanding and empathy to better support these couples in their emotional and spiritual needs.

REPRODUCTIVE LOSS IN
MULTIPLE BIRTHS

The loss of babies in multiple births can be the death of one, two, or all babies. It is a staggering loss to the parents when all babies die. When one or more babies survive while one or more are lost, the situation becomes complicated. The mother is faced with tasks of bonding with the surviving baby or babies while grieving the loss of the others who didn't make it. At the best of times, it is difficult to attach to one or more persons while grieving the loss of another. The situation is further complicated by the lack of support to the parents to grieve the death of the baby/ies lost, if the twin, one or more of triplets, quadruplets, etc., survive. Often they are reminded by parents, siblings, friends, and even health professionals that they are fortunate in having these other children, implying that the parents are wrong to grieve for the lost one. The parents are often not allowed to express sorrow, let alone begin to process their grief. Even when all the children are lost in a multiple pregnancy, health care workers and others can fail to perceive this as a tragedy.

One woman experienced the death of twins in utero at six months gestation. The physician recommended waiting until labor started, rather than induction. After one and a half weeks, she went into labor and delivered the dead babies. She did not see the babies. When she returned from the delivery room to her own hospital room, the doctor found her in tears. He became very annoyed and said, "What are you crying about? With these words, he abruptly left the room.

The following morning, he again found her in tears. He said, "Are you still crying over those dead fetuses?" Unable to expose her grief to his scoffing, and wondering if her sadness was inappropriate, she denied that she was crying for the babies, but said that she was experiencing postpartum pain. Such shocking behavior on the part of the doctor is, I believe, unusual; his lack of comprehension of the magnitude of such loss is not all that unusual.

Fortunately, she received needed support from her husband, whose pain and disappointment were also very great. Because they had a strong, close relationship, they were able to grieve together. They also received assistance from close friends.

T.'s Story

Another woman, T., had triplets, three little girls. Two survived, one died. She contacted the Centre a year after the birth, asking for support in grieving for her little girl who died. Because she had two surviving babies, many friends and relatives did not understand that she needed to grieve the baby who died. Others, with the best of intentions, did not know how to help her. One incident she found to be very painful was the result of a kindly meant and thoughtful gift. A close relative made a little quilt for each of the surviving girls with their names embroidered on it. There was no quilt for the little girl who died. With the encouragement of the reproductive loss group, T. eventually was able to discuss her feelings about the quilt with the relative who was happy to make a third quilt with the baby's name on it. One of the greatest concerns of mothers experiencing reproductive loss, is that no one will remember the lost child. One mother expressed it well in a video on perinatal death: "There *was* a child" [9].

While T. and her husband had a close relationship, he was in the process of being transferred by his company to another city quite a distance away. He was already located there. He flew back to his family as often as he could, but T. had the responsibility of selling the house, and following up the packing and moving arrangements. All this was in addition to caring for two healthy one-year old girls. We have found that some mothers put their grieving on hold for a while simply because of the press of other life responsibilities which require their immediate and absolute attention. Grief work takes attention, time, and energy. T. was very much aware of this, but also knew that she needed to do her grieving. The birthday of the triplets, which was also the anniversary of the death of one of them, was the catalyst which mobilized her to seek help. She completed her sessions in the support group, and expressed great relief and a measure of peace. After the family had moved to their new home, she kept in touch with us. She continued to process her grief, and sought support in her new setting by contacting the Center for Loss in Multiple Births (CLIMB) (see Appendix). When we last heard from her, she was happy in her new home. She and her husband and extended family were enjoying their children. She continued her association with CLIMB, where she was able to reach out to help other parents in their grief.

When T. first called our Centre, she told the counselor that she had triplets and that one had died. The counselor expressed her sympathy for her loss. T. began to cry and said that most people did not speak about her loss. She needed to have her child acknowledged and her own grief validated. She needed to do her grief work, but life keeps happening even while difficult situations arise. T. had to meet the responsibilities of her children and relocate to a new city. She put her grief work on hold until a year after her loss. Only then was she free to grieve.

Each person is unique, and what is a comfort for one person might be a source of pain for another. Having a quilt made for all three of the girls was very important to T. Someone else could have found it too painful. One can understand the hesitancy on the part of the relative to bring up the subject of the sister who died. As society becomes more aware and accepting of grief, friends and families, it is hoped, will be free to explore with the bereaved to discover what they need, and those who grieve will be more aware of their own needs, and able to ask for and accept help. If the death of a baby at 6 weeks gestation, 16 weeks, or any time during the pregnancy or birth is recognized as a serious loss, the grieving parents will be more likely to receive the community support that occurs at the time of other deaths. Running errands, bringing food, giving rides, helping with chores are practical ways to help that can keep some order for the bereaved who already may feel overwhelmed. Such help also conveys concern and caring, as well as recognition that a momentous event has happened. Thus, acknowledgment plus practical help assists the bereaved to do their grief work.

GIVING A CHILD UP FOR ADOPTION

Some women find themselves in a situation where they feel obliged to relinquish a child for adoption. The initial and ongoing grief of these women is largely ignored, yet the suffering of these women is great. One client confided that there is not a day in her life when she does not think of her child. Anniversaries such as birthdays, holidays, and school reopening in September, all are occasions of pain for her. Evelyn Robinson [10] clearly describes the pain associated with this disenfranchised grief. She explains why these mothers cannot complete the tasks of mourning which Worden outlined (see Chapter 2.) In adoption the grief often is repressed. Robinson reports on studies which showed that mothers who lost their children through adoption reported that their anger and sense of loss actually increased over time. This is in contrast to other kinds of losses where sadness usually diminishes in time. Rituals to assist grieving in other types of reproductive loss are not available to these mothers. Cutting the birth mother completely out of her child's life is an assault on her identity and that of the child.

Ms. Robinson stresses the importance of reunion of adopted children with their birth mothers. She looks forward to the time when there would be no adoption; a time when the financial and professional resources would be such that the birth mother would be able to acquire everything necessary for keeping and caring for her child. This could include financial and housing assistance, health care, education, and skills training (see Resources: The Nurturing Network).

Whether or not it is feasible to eliminate adoption completely, support for the family of origin and help for birth mothers as they plan for their children's future should be considered an inalienable right to mothers and children. In the meantime birth mothers must have the support and opportunity to work through their grief. Some caring adoptive parents have found ways to include the birth mother in the child's life. This needs to be done, and can be done, in such a way as to protect the child's sense of security, through cooperation of birth and adoptive parents, with legal back-up. Recognition and help for birth mothers' grief have been sorely neglected. They receive a mixed message from society. "If you love your child, you will give him up, so he can have a better life." Some birth mothers have been asked point blank by neighbors and friends, "How could you give up your child?" Either way, she is made to feel like a bad mother. These assaults on her self-esteem are monumental, yet she is often left to deal with her grief and battered self-esteem on her own.

ELECTIVE ABORTION
AS REPRODUCTIVE LOSS

One of the most disenfranchised griefs in our society today is post abortion grief. Elective abortion and the subsequent grief experiences of the mother (and often the father) are probably not even recognized as examples of reproductive loss. There is a widespread belief that a relatively simple choice is made and a problem solved. Often the people the pregnant woman would most likely turn to in a crisis are not even aware that there is a pregnancy. Nearly as often she feels she must keep the pregnancy and abortion a secret to avoid censure to herself, or to avoid hurting her family. She may not want to share the information with classmates, if she is a student, or people with whom she is working. The pregnancy may be the result of a casual liaison, and she may not wish to notify the father about the pregnancy. In longer-term relationships, a number of our clients report the male partner abandoned them. Some partners insist on her obtaining an abortion, often using emotional blackmail in threatening to leave if she carries the pregnancy to term. A sad variation on grief and abortion occurs when the male partner wants the baby and is fully prepared to assume responsibility for mother and child, and the woman has an abortion anyway. Many of the women who came to us in distress after an abortion felt coerced by family, counselors, partners, their socioeconomic condition, or the mores of the times. Mary Parthun points out that the stigma of illegitimacy had formerly caused women to seek abortions. Illegitimacy is no longer stigmatized to the same extent but the social and legal stigma are now attached to what she terms "an appropriate pregnancy" [11, pp. 80-82]. Teenagers, mature women, and sophisticated career women are common victims of this stigma. It is a paradox that society encourages sexual expression and bombards us through the media and entertainment with sexual themes but is, on the whole, intolerant of the natural outcome of sexual inter-course. With explicit sex education presented as early as in kindergarten class,

I am baffled by the partners of some of my clients who are astonished and express betrayal when intercourse results in pregnancy. Because of the availability of abortion, fear of pregnancy is no longer seen as a legitimate right to refuse sex [12, p. 72].

The single pregnant woman who is self-supporting may find her career in jeopardy, because she feels unequal to the challenge of being a single parent and full time bread winner.

Studies show that the group of parents who suffer greatly are those who elect abortion because of a medical or genetic problem with the baby [13, pp. 71-82; 14, pp. 901-902]. So often these were babies that were anticipated with a great deal of joy. Outcomes of testing that show Down Syndrome or some other problem come as a shock and the parents feel forced to make a life or death decision regarding their child in a very short time frame.

Abortion is a highly complex event. It is a source of concern that it is often treated so lightly. As Worden says, "Many people take a casual attitude regarding the experience of abortion—at times this seems to border on the cavalier" [8, p. 91]. He also states that abortion is one of those unspeakable losses one would rather forget. Initially there may be a feeling of relief, but if the woman who has an abortion does not do her mourning soon after the loss she may experience the grief at a later time. Dr. Ian Kent reported that a group of women undergoing psychotherapy for reasons other than abortion uncovered deep feelings concerning previous abortions. They expressed intense pain, a sense of bereavement, and identification with the fetus. This occurred even when the client still believed that abortion was the only possible course of action [15].

While our culture has not as a general rule provided any rituals to deal with the aftermath of abortion, some cultures do. In Tami, New Guinea, for example, the woman who aborts wears a short mourning veil, corresponding to the European's half-mourning attire [16, p. 46].

Several years ago, a colleague who had visited Japan told us how grieving parents of aborted children try to deal with their loss in that culture. She showed pictures of hundreds of model babies in the grounds surrounding an immense Buddhist temple. The mother buys a model baby which is then placed in the row upon row of model babies around the temple. The model babies may wear bibs or bonnets, and many have been given toys. Most of the mothers have named the babies. The names are painted on vases standing in front of the dolls. There are wooden prayer plaques with written messages. Translated, some were, "I will never forget you. I love you." "I hope you are happy where you are. I love you." "Please, will you forgive us. We promise to come and visit you every month." These shrines are located in many different parts of Japan. They are a poignant testimonial to the love, grief, and pain these parents feel for their aborted children.

The pain associated with abortion can be complicated in a number of ways. Because it is an event that is not discussed with even the people closest to the woman, she is cut off from a significant part of her usual support system. She may not feel secure in speaking about it to her close friends. She may push her feelings of grief down to the point that she is not conscious of them. This can go on for 20 or 30 years or more, as has occurred with several of our clients. Other losses may be treated the same way (i.e., with denial and repression of grief and pain). But at some time, a particular event may trigger the grief that can then nearly overwhelm her.

L.'s Story

For L., the death of her mother triggered grief for a baby she had aborted some years earlier. In the telling of her story, she expressed how astonished she felt at the depth of her feelings. Using the empty chair exercise, she spoke as though the baby was in the empty chair, and told him how sorry she was, that she wanted him to be happy and asked for forgiveness. Moving to the other chair, she was able to imagine what the child was saying to her. After grieving this loss, she came to terms with her mother's death which had intensified her pain due to some ambivalence in their relationship. It took ten years and the death of a parent to open the door to her grief and allow her to heal.

Just as with L.'s abortion loss, the empty chair exercise is a helpful intervention in other losses. For example, another woman who had experienced two miscarriages used this exercise to express her love for her babies and said that she imagined them together in heaven as little sparks of light.

D.'s Story

D., a young single mother, had an elective abortion when she was 16 years old. She found it very traumatic. The baby's father was in and out of her life. Moreover, D. and her mother have a somewhat troubled relationship. Her mother was very disappointed at the pregnancy because she hoped D. would continue her education and have a successful career. When D. became pregnant again, the mother was very upset. After the baby was born she helped materially but their relationship was still tense. D. became pregnant again. She sought counseling when her grief for her aborted baby came to the surface. She said she could never go through another abortion, and realized that she was trying to fill the empty space of her lost baby. Through her grief work, she has gained insight from the impact of her loss, and she feels more at peace.

In all forms of reproductive loss, there is often a desire to have a baby to fill the place of the lost baby. Family members, friends, and even health professionals may encourage the woman to become pregnant again, but one human being cannot replace another. A child must be welcomed as himself or herself, not as a substitute for someone else. The original loss must be grieved before another child is born for the sake of the child and the parents.

In the case of abortion, this is not understood. Women may continue to become pregnant under circumstances in which they still believe are impossible to have and raise a child. This can lead to multiple abortions for a woman who has not been helped to grieve, and who is desperately trying to fill a void left by her ungrieved loss. Multiple abortions can also be a means of self-punishment. Teenage girls have been quite open in telling us that they got pregnant again to make up for the abortion. They may not be able to face another abortion (young girls are particularly affected by abortion), so a teenage girl who has a replacement baby may well become an impoverished, single young mother without the supports she so desperately needs. All those working with teenagers need to be aware of the effects of unresolved grief.

FATHERS OF ABORTED BABIES

Fathers of aborted babies can also feel intense grief. A teenage boy was in tears because his pregnant girlfriend had been taken to have an abortion. He had been thrilled about the baby, a little frightened, but had looked forward to accepting responsibility for his child and his child's mother. However unrealistic his plans, no other options were offered and he had to deal with his helplessness to protect his child, his grief at the loss, and a sense of betrayal. Helping him resolve the issues of grief, anger, and forgiveness can be done through grief counseling, acknowledgment of his loss, strategies such as writing out his anger, pain and sense of betrayal. Like other bereaved parents, he, too, has to find a place for his child.

One situation raised the question, "Do men have a need for replacement babies after abortions?" A bereaved mother came for help to grieve the death of her stillborn child. As we went through the grieving process together, she dealt with another grief, a previous abortion. Although her ex-husband had two children by a previous marriage, he and my client decided to have a child together. When she became pregnant he changed his mind, and wanted nothing to do with another child. He had also told her that prior to that marriage, he had persuaded two other women who were pregnant by him to abort. My client felt she could not manage the stepchildren and a baby without his support and so she had the abortion, reluctantly, hoping someone, especially the doctor, would suggest she not have it. Subsequently, the marriage broke up. He remarried and now has three children by his present wife. The question is, "Are these replacement babies for the three babies he asked to be aborted?" This illustrates the need for more information on the impact of abortion on men.

M.'s Story

Feelings of guilt and loss of self-esteem are common to many women suffering reproductive loss. These issues need to be addressed as part of good health care. It is especially important in the case of abortion. M., a lovely young woman in her mid-twenties, well to do, and studying here as a foreign student, presented for counseling in order to work out her feelings regarding an abortion she had six months prior to her initial contact with me. She came from a culture where out of wedlock sex for women is a serious taboo, and most of the women there marry at a very early age. M.'s peers pressured her because she was still a virgin. This worried her and she consented to sex with a young man whom her family approved of as a suitor. However, she was not ready to get married and wanted to continue her education. Her parents encouraged her in her studies. They were very proud of her, especially her father. She was very close to him, and felt it would break his heart if he ever found out about the pregnancy or the abortion. Adoption was not an option for her, because she said she could not send a child to live with people who were not of the same blood. She came to realize that she was trying to replace her lost baby by engaging in risky sexual behavior, and thereby punish herself. She was much clearer on what had happened with the abortion and understood her own behavior better. She believed that she had come to terms with the abortion. But she said sadly, "I always felt that I was special. Since the abortion, I just feel very ordinary." More work needed to be done to help her regain her sense of self-worth and self-respect.

B.'s Story

B., an attractive and pleasant 24-year-old woman, came for help in dealing with a recent abortion. A young woman working in her chosen profession, she was dating J., a 35-year-old professional man with whom she had fallen in love. They were not living together but saw each other frequently. She told me that on the night she conceived, they had unprotected intercourse, because J. found sex less enjoyable when he wore a condom. She believed that she was in a "safe" period of her cycle, although she was not actually following a recommended form of natural family planning. She remembered thinking afterward that it might be nice if pregnancy occurred. She was thrilled when she found that she was indeed pregnant. When she told this news to J., he did not share her enthusiasm. He said they were not ready, that it was not the time in his career to start a family. He did not tell her outright to get an abortion. Although he said it was her decision, she sensed that he wanted no part of this baby. In her hurt and disappointment, she made an appointment immediately at an abortion clinic and kept it. After the abortion, she found their relationship altered. B. believed that J. did not care as deeply for her, as she did for him. She tried not to show her feelings of anger and betrayal, as she believed that the relationship was tenuous and she was afraid to risk alienating him further. She was heartbroken about the loss of the baby and his distancing himself from her after the abortion.

As she talked about her grief, she came to realize that her decision to abort her baby was an impulsive one. She believed she acted somewhat rashly in her hurt, disappointment, and anger at J.'s reaction to the pregnancy. This young woman has suffered greatly, because she really did not want the abortion, was terribly hurt at J.'s reaction and did not believe that she had the resources to raise a child alone. Her relationship with J. was deteriorating. She realized that she had lost respect for him and was not sure that she still loved him, yet needed to cling to the relationship because she felt that she had sacrificed so much for it. She was grieving the baby and was experiencing remorse. Eventually, the relationship ended, thus adding to her burden of grief. In addition, her family did not know of the abortion or even the pregnancy. Nor has she discussed it with her friends, so she is isolated in her anguish. Clients have told us that knowing that they are free to call us helps to ease the loneliness even if they do not call.

H.'s Story

Some years ago, I received a phone call from a woman whom I will refer to as H. She had been given my name by an acquaintance who thought that I might be helpful to her.

H. explained that she had had an abortion a few years earlier. She and her husband had two children, and when she became pregnant with the third, they agreed to have an abortion because they felt that their family was complete. She was at 12 weeks gestation at the time of the abortion. H. and her husband had no formal religious background. Both were agnostic and they and their families of origin considered abortion to be an acceptable option. She was perplexed and concerned that with this background, she still could not forget the abortion; she thought of it frequently and had a persistent feeling of emptiness and sadness. She wanted to talk with her husband about her feelings, but he refused, saying that the abortion was a closed book. She could not speak with family or friends because of their easy acceptance of abortion. She felt they would not understand and might ostracize her. However, she still needed to talk about the abortion and her feelings and that was why she contacted me. As I listened to her, I had a sense that her grief needed to be expressed. I suggested this, and H. said, "That's it. This is unfinished business." In our discussion, she disclosed that she was sure the baby was a girl. I suggested that she name her, and gather some mementos of her child. She did not believe in God, as such, but had a spiritual reverence for and relationship with nature. I suggested a memorial service incorporating these ideas. She thanked me and said she would act on the suggestions. Two weeks later, I received a letter from her. It was on a note card beautifully depicting a nursing mother with her baby.

H. said, in essence, that she had named her baby Blossom and had put a picture of a 12 week fetus in a pretty little box along with some family souvenirs that she would have shared with Blossom had she lived. H. went on to say that she took the box and buried it by two pine trees on their naturally beautiful property in the country. There H. believed Blossom would be free to live in the wind, trees, and all of nature. H. felt that she had released Blossom and that a burden had been lifted. She concluded, "Sadly, we make decisions that seem right at the time, but really turn out to be painful mistakes. Thank you for helping me to realize that I was grieving and could still do something for Blossom."

SCHEDULING OF ELECTIVE ABORTIONS

In scheduling elective abortions it is of utmost importance to avoid dates that are significant to the woman. Christmas, New Year's, Valentine's Day, Easter, Passover, Mother's Day and Fathers' Day, birthdays, and wedding anniversaries are some of those important dates. Often these are family celebration days and, if the abortion is done on or near a significant day, that day becomes the sad anniversary of the loss of the baby. The woman should be asked at the time of scheduling if the date chosen has any special meaning for her or her family.

One young woman had an abortion on Valentine's Day. Each Valentine's Day is very difficult for her. Another woman had her abortion the day before Christmas Eve; hence Christmas to her became the anniversary of her loss, and took away the joy of the holiday for her.

ABORTION FOR GENETIC REASONS

Bereaved parents who came for help in dealing with their grief after an abortion for genetic problems were in much emotional pain. In most cases this was a child who was dearly wanted. For several couples, there had been fertility problems. In some cases the amniocentesis test was approached with trepidation. In others, the couple assured each other that everything was fine; the mother felt well, and "surely she would know if something were wrong!"

Whether the parents worried or not, when they received the news that the test showed positive for a congenital defect, they reported initial shock and numbness, as the news was difficult to assimilate. Some of the couples had discussed the possibility of a positive result, and had decided beforehand that they would elect abortion. Still it was a difficult time for them. For others who had expected good news, they had to come to terms with a baby with serious problems. They were confronted with a life and death decision of whether to abort or not. Still in shock, it was difficult to process information the physician offered.

One couple reported that the abortion itself was frightening and painful. After a strong saline solution was injected into the amniotic sac, the contractions were very strong and the baby was extremely active before its death. Another woman who had a saline abortion was horrified when the baby was placed in a cold, stainless steel basin. She insisted on having a blanket to wrap the baby. She held and sang to the baby and was grateful for the opportunity to mother this child. The baby of M. and C. was delivered barely alive. She was wrapped in a blanket and the parents held and cuddled her until she died.

The grief of these parents is profound. They have lost not only their real baby, but the ideal, dream child that they had envisioned.

Some one-on-one grief counseling was helpful to some of our clients who experienced this type of loss. All of them joined support groups which they found comforting. The opportunity to tell their stories to a group of people who understood and empathized brought a measure of peace. Some women experienced nightmares, which is not unusual in many kinds of reproductive loss. Even though they felt it was a necessity, they still expressed regret for the abortion. All participated in a memorial service at the end of the sessions. As they looked for meaning in these brief lives, one woman said, "The little girl I lost is a bridge to my other children. I have always loved them, but now I appreciate them even more." These parents went through a very painful ordeal. Having survived it, they would be the first to tell you it is a serious life-changing event.

IATROGENIC OUTCOMES IN REPRODUCTIVE LOSS

Iatrogenic outcomes are those "resulting from an attitude or activity of a physician. An iatrogenic disorder, is one produced inadvertently as a result of treatment by a physician for some other disorder" [17, p. 467].

Several clients have reported that their physicians offered abortion when they first met with them to verify a pregnancy and to receive pre-natal care. Most of these women had not even entertained the thought of abortion prior to this encounter. A number of young women over the years have complained bitterly that when they first presented for pre-natal care the first question the physician asked was along the lines of: "Are you going to keep this baby or do you want a termination?"; "Do you want this baby?"; "Do you want to abort this pregnancy?" The young women, who were thrilled at their pregnancy, found this type of question to be offensive and deflating. For some, the doctor's initial emphasis on abortion was disconcerting; the women wondered if such a doctor would do everything necessary to save the life of the baby if difficulties arose. Interestingly, this question was raised by women who professed a belief in the right of abortion on demand for others, but planned to bear their own babies.

One young woman had not thought much about abortion one way or the other, except that it was not an option for her. Her main concern was her own fertility. She was having difficulty in getting pregnant. When she finally did conceive, her baby was born prematurely. The obstetrician went to see the baby, then came to check the mother and said, musingly, "He's doing well. It's strange. Yesterday I aborted one his age." The mother was aghast! She said to me later, "How could she make such efforts to save my son and still do abortions?" This woman will always be grateful to this doctor for her skill and the efforts put forth for her and her family, yet unease entered the relationship because of the doctor's comments.

At a recent conference on perinatal loss, a 32-year-old woman shared her story. Married at eighteen years of age, she and her husband planned to have children but not immediately. However, she became pregnant shortly after her marriage and was distressed at having it happen so soon. She mentioned her distress to her doctor whom she sought out for pre-natal care. He offered abortion at once. She had not ever in her life considered abortion, but when the doctor suggested it, she agreed, thinking of him as the expert who considered her concerns serious enough to warrant an abortion.

This young woman and apparently her doctor were not aware that even women who have been trying to become pregnant have a transient sense of dismay when they do conceive. It may be due to a sudden recognition that a new era of their lives has begun. They face real adulthood with total responsibility for another being. The dismay nearly always passes fairly quickly and can be part of the maturing process.

This young woman did have the abortion. Later, she and her husband divorced. She married again, and in spite of efforts to become pregnant, did not conceive again. She may have aborted the only child she could have conceived, not because she requested the abortion or even considered it, but because the doctor suggested it. She is probably experiencing secondary infertility, a condition in which a woman conceives a child once and even carries a child to term, but then is unable to conceive again. She is grieving the loss of her child and the children she dreamed of having with her husband.

Fertility is a gift and a fragile one at that. An essential part of good health care is protecting it, particularly in young women who are in the process of planning their lives. One young woman had become pregnant while on the birth control pill. Her family doctor feared the baby would suffer from congenital defects because of it and so recommended that she consult with a doctor who did abortions. When she asked this doctor, "Would I be able to get pregnant again after the abortion?", she replied, "You might be able to conceive again, depending on the severity of the scarring of the uterus following the abortion." As a postscript, she kept her baby, regardless of the risks, as she did not want to lose her only possible chance of conception. Her supposed congenitally defective baby now runs circles around the house as a healthy, intact, five-year old about to enter kindergarten.

Abortion and other intrusive procedures presented as routine prenatal care can have serious iatrogenic outcomes. As mentioned previously (see Chapter 6), miscarriage can result after amniocentesis. Thus, a healthy child can suffer an iatrogenic death because of an intrusive procedure.

Whether it is in the form of medical pressures to have an abortion, an accident following intrusive procedures, or complications from abortion, it is a case of iatrogenic outcome. As one concerned health professional stated, "We have

have abortion rights, but we do *not* have pregnancy protection." A couple, married in their thirties, wanted children very much and were pleased when she became pregnant. She was offered amniocentesis but she and her husband refused, explaining that, whatever the outcome, they would keep the child. The doctor told them, "I could never live with a handicapped child." This appears to be a situation where the physician tried to influence a couple to have an intrusive procedure that they clearly did not want.

A bereaved parent wondered why it is considered necessary to urge abortion on couples when the baby is suffering from a fatal condition. I have recently heard of a program for pediatric palliative care where babies who are expected to die shortly after birth can be kept comfortable and the parents can spend this last and only precious time with them. The parents who participated in this program expressed gratitude for the opportunity. One woman, who had heard of it only after her fatally ill baby was aborted, fervently wished that she could have had the palliative care option and could have been encouraged or given the option to carry her baby to term. (See Resources, Appendix E.)

PREVENTIVE ASPECTS
OF REPRODUCTIVE LOSS

Reproductive loss is gradually (at last) being recognized as a source of grief as great as any other important loss in the human experience. Because of the slowness of society to see these as tragedies to grieve, the usual rituals and support after a death have not been available to mothers, fathers, and families experiencing these losses. With increasing awareness of the scope of the problem, we have developed strategies to help individuals to cope with their grief, to process it and to heal.

The losses we encounter in our clients are miscarriage, stillbirth, ectopic pregnancy, infertility, hysterectomy, elective abortion, and chosen childlessness. As health professionals, we are concerned with caring for those who grieve, but attempt also to look at what can be done to prevent so much pain.

Miscarriage

In most cases of miscarriage, there is no known cause. There have been some associations between alcohol use, smoking, marijuana use, and caffeine consumption [7, pp. 38-48]. Yet not every woman who uses the above substances miscarries, and women who have carefully abstained or have never used these substances have miscarried. Malnutrition can contribute to miscarriage but it would have to be very severe, unlikely significant in North America at this time. It could become a problem however, with the widening gap between rich and poor in North America. Basic prenatal care is recommended for all pregnant women. Yet, in spite of good prenatal care on the part of the physician and meticulous adherence to prescribed care on the part of the mother miscarriages do occur.

Stillbirth

Friedman and Gradstein tell us that little is known about what causes stillbirth [7, pp. 70-72]. The pregnancy can be normal and progressing well. Then the baby stops moving, bleeding occurs, or labor begins. There are 10.4 stillbirths for every 1000 births; 32 percent are from unknown causes. Most of the other causes are discovered after the fact [7, p. 70]. One exception could be toxemia of pregnancy (pre-eclampsia and eclampsia). In these cases, some, but not all, deaths of the baby can be avoided but only if the toxemia is discovered and treated in the early stages [7, p. 71].

Ectopic Pregnancy

With ectopic pregnancy, in half the cases no cause is found. The common causes are damage to the tube from pelvic inflammatory disease, other pelvic infections, post abortion infection and scarring, previous pelvic surgery, a prior ectopic pregnancy, or reconstructive surgery of the fallopian tube. Abnormalities of the tube may be a cause, as may some contraceptive pills (progestin only), and if pregnancy occurs while an IUD is in place, ectopic pregnancy can occur. But again, ectopic pregnancy also occurs when none of the above factors are in play [7, pp. 83-107].

Infertility

Infertility can be a long term grief, with a series of heartbreaking losses along the way. Assisted reproductive technologies (ART) can be used. Unfortunately, the pregnancy rate is low, and the miscarriage rate is high in ART. Pregnancy may never be achieved, and the couple is dealt a double blow. It is an emotionally and economically expensive project and stressful in other ways [7, pp. 138-144]. Women have told us that the mood changes due to the hormones they received during the cycles were disruptive to their families. Lovemaking lost joy and spontaneity, as it seemed to become a prescription rather than a choice. If the woman was working, her appointments at the ART clinic and coverage at work had to be arranged. Some of the women said that their own mood swings were difficult for their fellow workers.

While ART has brought great joy to some couples, disappointment has been the result for many others, adding grief upon grief. As the scientists involved increase their knowledge, it is hoped that more positive outcomes will result. In the meantime, ART are not a panacea for infertility. Some of our clients undergoing

ART did not become pregnant. For others, after several attempts, pregnancy occurred, but was followed by miscarriage. Of course, people do not come to us if the outcome is a happy one. However, the statistics for a successful delivery of a healthy baby are discouraging [7, pp. 142-143].

Abortion

One type of reproductive loss over which women can have some control is elective abortion. The number of elective abortions in Canada is steadily increasing to the expressed surprise of some groups and a sad sense of inevitability of others. Statistics Canada reported that 114,848 elective abortions were performed in Canada in 1997, an increase of 2.9 percent from 111,659 in 1996 [18]. There has been a steady rise in abortions since the Supreme Court of Canada struck down Canada's abortion law in 1988. In 1987 there were 70,023 abortions, or 19.4 per 100 live births [18]. In 1996, the rate of abortions had increased to 30.5 per 100 live births. In 1997, the rate was 33 per 100 live births. In the United States the rate has declined to 30.5 from 31.4 in 1996. The Canadian figures reported recently in the Montreal *Gazette* were 33.5 abortions for every 100 live births [19]. Even the executive director of Planned Parenthood stated that she was appalled. She reiterated the Planned Parenthood dictum that many women are forced to obtain abortions because they have not been provided with the means of birth control or the knowledge of how to use it. This statement is questionable, since sex education begins in the schools at an astonishingly early age, beginning in some schools as early as kindergarten. Students are given information regarding sex and contraception. In many schools, condoms are available. They are certainly available at any pharmacy. Many, if not most, physicians are ready to provide information on birth control and prescriptions. Perhaps schools, parents, and governments need to work with young people to support programs which encourage young teenagers to postpone sexual intercourse. These programs can be quite successful when initiated and carried out by young people, with appropriate assistance from educators and health professionals [20, p. A-18].

The American Academy of Pediatrics urges physicians to "encourage adolescents to postpone early coital activity and to promote chastity." Other medical resources suggest that the important factor in risky sexual behavior is lack of self esteem, and what sexually active girls need to learn is how to say "no" without hurting someone's feelings. Susan Martinuk makes the observation that North American teens are being groomed for sexual pleasure, while medical evidence is growing that sexually active teens are at a higher risk for depression and suicide than youngsters who retain their virginity. She points out that articles in the *Journal of the Society of Obstetricians and Gynecologists* of Canada in 1993–94 found that sex education programs being offered to teens did not help to lessen STDs and pregnancy [20, p. A-18].

One mother related that she was quite concerned because the mother of her 14-year-old son's girlfriend had taken her to the family doctor to obtain a prescription for the birth control pill. He told his mother, "I'm not ready for sex." His mother replied he should not engage in *any* activity in which he felt uncomfortable, and for which he did not feel ready. His rejoinder was, "Is something wrong with me? My girlfriend thinks I'm ready, her mother thinks I'm ready, and her doctor thinks I'm ready." His mother assured him that nothing was wrong with him, that sexual intercourse was inappropriate for him, and for 14-year-olds in general. Another parent taught sex education to his children with these words:

> A man never puts a girl in a situation where people will gossip about her. A man doesn't arrange things that will put a girl at odds with her family. A man doesn't steadily date a girl he isn't serious about because that just takes her out of circulation and she may not meet someone who is serious about her.

Coercion—Whose Choice?

In my work with bereaved women who have had abortions, I have been struck by the fact that in over half of the cases with clients who are grieving abortions, it has been someone else who had chosen the abortion: the husband or boyfriend, parent, a school counselor or nurse, a social worker or doctor, or someone else with power or perceived power over the pregnant mother.

The failure of our society in helping young people to understand and manage sex and relationships between the genders has ramifications. Several clients had relationships with men who had post secondary education and were fairly well established in their occupations. Each of the men I am speaking of did not want to use condoms, yet were, in varying degrees, astonished, panic stricken, angry, and some even cried "trick" and "trap" when pregnancy occurred and they insisted on aborting the child. Certain parts of our society have so effectively managed to separate sex from reproduction that we find adults of at least average intelligence, if not above, with some life experience reacting to the outcome of their sexual behavior as though they were very young teenagers, and like teenagers in a crisis, can have made a decision they may bitterly regret later.

One of our clients mentioned that choice has become almost synonymous with abortion. This appears to be borne out when one thinks of the deafening silence from society concerning the women who are coerced into having an abortion they do not want. The notion that a woman must have the total right to decide for abortion is based on the premise that men want children and will force women to become pregnant and have children the women do not want. Mary Parthun, social worker, points out that the concept "keep them barefoot and pregnant" is now for the most part an anachronism. She states:

Pride in fathering children as testimony to masculinity is often a pronounced cultural and ideological phenomenon in non-industrial, patriarchal societies with strong religious mores, but is certainly not a dominant sentiment in modern industrial society. On the contrary in a society in which masculinity is equated with material display and personal mobility, children are seen as a detraction from the expression of masculinity. Except within certain cultural sub-pockets in our society, support and pressure for abortion are institutionally strong among men. This is why liberalized abortion was achieved rather easily from the dominantly male legislative, judicial, and medical establishments, the lone "victory" for feminism which has seen most of its other issues hopelessly stonewalled [11, pp. 82-83].[1]

Parthun's comments were written in 1982 at the height of the feminist movement when many women believed that the sexual revolution would ensure their reproductive freedom. Twenty years later, a feminist career woman, Deborah Rankin, who lived through this era, offers a sobering social commentary on the consequences to both women and men of such reproductive freedom (see Appendix F for complete commentary).

For other major concerns such as women and poverty, pay equity, and research into women's health problems such as cancer and heart disease, support has been grudging, and progress slow. A quotation by Alan A. Stone, a lawyer and psychiatrist who is supportive of abortion, underlines the problems of male coercion. He says:

Decisions in society are made by those who have power and not necessarily by those who have rights. Husbands and boyfriends may in the end often wield the power and make the abortion decision. Many women may be forced to have an abortion, not because it is their right, but because they are forced by ego-centric men to submit to this procedure to avoid an unwanted inconvenience to men. To the extent this happens, . . . neither the dignity of life nor the dignity of women will be enhanced [21, p. 37].[2]

Theoretically, women make the choice for elective abortion. In actual fact, the men in women's lives have a great impact on the decision, according to T. Strahan [22, p. 7]. He cites a study of 110 women at the University of Nebraska, indicating that the most stressful events that occurred during pregnancy were out of wedlock pregnancy with no help from the baby's father, or in the case of a married woman, the husband does not want the baby she is carrying. Another study of 65 women at the Methodist Hospital of Indiana found that throughout pregnancy the need for emotional support and degree of satisfaction of the relationship with her partner consistently predicted the level of anxiety experienced. Even in societies

---

[1] Excerpt from *Care for the Dying and Bereaved,* by I. Gentles (editor). Copyright © 1982 Anglican Book Centre. Used with permission.

[2] Excerpted with permission from *Modern Medicine, 41*:9, April 30, 1973. Copyright © 2002 Advanstar Communications Inc., retains all rights to this material.

where children are greatly valued and fertile women highly esteemed, female attitudes toward motherhood are determined in a large part by the male attitude toward fatherhood, according to George Devereaux, an anthropologist who studied abortion in 400 pre-industrial societies [16, pp. 135-136].

What is troubling about the numbers of women who feel forced to have an abortion is that it puts them at greater risk for negative post abortion psychological sequelae. Mary Parthun identifies those women most at risk for the above sequelae:

1. Women who undergo abortion for genetic or physical reasons.
2. Women with serious psychiatric problems.
3. Teenagers, particularly where coercion and pressure by others are brought to bear on the decision to abort.
4. Women who feel strong ambivalence about the abortion, particularly where coercion and external pressures are factors.
5. Girls and women who lack personal and social support for the abortion and afterwards [23, p. 20].

Unfortunately, the most vulnerable women are the most likely to be pressured on many fronts to have an abortion. Violence by their partners toward women who want to carry a child to term has been documented. Parthun states:

> Assaultive male partners, considered the most controlling of males, frequently react violently to pregnancy and concentrate their violence on the unborn child, punching, and kicking the mother in the abdomen and otherwise designing the assault to threaten the infant. In situations where physical violence is not present, there is often considerable pressure from the male sexual partner to terminate the pregnancy, which represents interference with sexual access, a potential detraction from the woman's earning power and competition for her full attention [11, p. 83].

Indeed, pressure from the sexual partner seems to be the strongest force in leading a woman to seek a personally unwanted abortion and is a recurring theme in negative abortion aftermath. Emotional blackmail in the form of withdrawal of affection or threats to terminate the relationship are common manipulations. The impact of this pressure on the woman is shattering since it symbolizes a rejection of the relationship at a profound level. She feels devalued and rejected and these feelings both complicate and intensify the mourning process [11, p. 83]. I have found that some men who have hoped for a family and were happy when a pregnancy occurred, have felt the same overwhelming rejection and hurt when their partners chose to abort the child. Abortion even more than other reproductive losses takes its toll on relationships.

A survey of news reports across the United States demonstrates the scope of the problem of violent coercion of women to abort [24, pp. 5-6] (see Appendix G). The lengths to which some men will go to force their partners to have an abortion are horrifying. Women who refuse to have an abortion have been kidnaped, beaten, blackmailed, and forced to have abortions against their will.

The sheer injustice perpetrated on many women is outrageous. Abortion is obviously a much more complicated issue than the terms "freedom of choice" and "abortion on demand" would indicate. Dr. Christiane Northrup, M.D., is co-founder of the Women to Women Health Care Center in Yarmouth, Maine. Trained at Dartmouth Medical School and Tuft New England Medical Center, she is an Obstetrician, Gynecologist, and Assistant Clinical Professor of Obstetrics and Gynecology at the University of Vermont College of Medicine. Dr. Northrup is an internationally recognized speaker for women's health and healing. She states that if we lived in a culture that valued women's autonomy and where men and women controlled their fertility cooperatively, the abortion issue would be moot [25, p. 383]. She had performed abortions for years and tells us she will always advocate that women have the option of abortion. Through her experience, however, she has come to recognize the complexity of the issue and that there are no easy answers. She had run the gamut of doing a number of repeat abortions on women who did not use any other form of birth control, to doing abortions on women who reluctantly chose the procedure only because they felt they had no alternative.

Dr. Northrup is uncomfortable with "abortion on demand," because to her it implies that women need take no responsibility for their sexual behavior and its consequences. While some men have done this for ages, in women this attitude often is a symptom of low self-esteem. Many women who have had repeated abortions have told her that it was a form of self-destruction coming from their own self-loathing. She states firmly that women should resist any sexual contact with men who do not respect and value them. Dr. Northrup stopped doing abortions in the mid-1980s to work with women in helping them understand their sexuality and the need to value and respect themselves whether or not they have a male relationship. She anticipates a time when abortion is rare, when men and women will plan their families together and responsibly, leading to every child being loved and cared for [25, pp. 383-388].

One way to create this ideal may be through fertility awareness or natural family planning, which is also a highly effective method of fertility management [25, p. 387]. It involves learning how to determine the woman's time of ovulation. Dr. Northrup quotes Dr. Joseph Stanford, a family physician and expert in the fertility awareness method:

> Fertility is not a disease, even though it is often treated like one. It is part of who we are. When a couple uses this method, they often develop a deep respect for each other, for their fertility and for their sexuality. This enhances all aspects of the relationship. It is a spiritual thing [25, p. 401].

In my experiences with helping individuals and couples deal with reproductive loss, I have been impressed with the devotion, compassion, and understanding many men demonstrated toward their partners, even to the point of ignoring their own pain in order to support the mothers. With help to deal with their own grief while supporting their partners, the relationships of these couples go from good to better as they grow together. Unfortunately, I have also seen situations where the male's response to his partner's pregnancy is cold, callous, and self-serving. In many of these cases, the female partner does not choose abortion, but bends to the will of the man, either to attempt to save the relationship or because the prospect of single parenthood is too overwhelming.

Impact on Value System

Many women who obtain abortions are unprepared for the fact that the abortion violates their own value system. While this is seen to be related to women (or men) with a strong religious background, it often occurs in individuals who have no formal religious background, some of whom may characterize themselves as agnostic or atheists. This sense of having violated a value essential to their own perception of who they are is devastating. "I lost myself on that table," from a practicing Christian. "I used to feel that I was special, but since the abortion I just feel common and ordinary," Christian background, non-practicing. "The worst part is, I think, I killed someone. That's not me," from a non-religious, agnostic background. The violation of their own personal code was as painful to these women as the loss of their babies.

Margaret A. Somerville, Gale Professor of law and a professor of medicine at McGill University's Centre for Medicine, Ethics and Law tells us that the moral debate on abortion is not over. She warns us that a loss of the sense that abortion raises serious ethical questions is damaging to women and society [26, p. B-5]. The women earlier mentioned were certainly affected.

Another concern of our clients was the lack of information, which they felt they needed for informed consent. Some women said they were not told how much pain they would have. Others had no idea about the stage of development of the fetus. Women are assured that elective abortion is a safe procedure. It is, relatively, but there can be complications. Dr. Heather Morris reports on the physical complications of induced abortion. They include, among others, increases in ectopic pregnancies, spontaneous abortions, premature deliveries, and there are some indications that induced abortion in the absence of having a live birth shows increase in risk for breast cancer and increased difficulties at delivery. A rare but particularly tragic outcome is maternal death, usually from hemorrhage, embolism, or infection. Dr. Morris states, "It is difficult to think of any other medical procedure where the risks both short- and long-term are not generally shared with the patient" [27, p. 37]. Dahling [28, pp. 1584-1592] and Brind [29, pp. 12-15] are just two of a number of scientists who have discovered a link between elective abortion and breast cancer. This link is noted in young women under 18 years of age and women over 30 years of age who had an elective abortion before having a full term pregnancy. Women have a right to be aware of this link. Women contemplating abortion need to take the cancer link into consideration when making the decision whether or not to abort. Women who had elective abortions at the crucial time frame will require close medical follow up to detect possible cancer early.

It has been difficult to obtain information regarding legal abortion in Canada [30]. In 1998, the *National Post* requested abortion statistics in Ontario. The health ministry refused to release the information because they stated it would lead to violence. As far as is known, no riots occurred after the information was released: doctors in Ontario performed 44,002 abortions in 1998. Susan Martinuk reports on the other difficulties in obtaining information on abortion in Canada. She cites an independent research in depth analysis of Statistics Canada Hospital Morbidity file. The results showed that "one out of 13 women or 7.7 percent are hospitalized in a life and death situation after legally induced abortion in Canada." The statistics would be higher if admissions for complications that are not life threatening were included [30]. If women are not aware of risks to their health as well as their fertility, they are not making an informed choice. A 7.7 percent morbidity rate for a medical intervention required as a life saving measure can be acceptable. Is it acceptable risk in an elective procedure?

At a certain stage or circumstance in one's life, having children may not be feasible. Situations can change, a desire for children may emerge at a later date. Avoiding interventions which endanger fertility would certainly improve the chances of having children when desired. Of course many women who have had abortions have gone on to have children later. Even women who have never had an abortion can still have difficulty getting pregnant in their mid-thirties to menopause, as women's fertility begins to decline as early as age 27 [31]. If young women could be encouraged to cherish, respect, and manage their fertility without resorting to interventions which may have a permanent negative effect, it would make more sense for their overall health, even apart from possibly preventing the heartbreak of a future reproductive loss.

Coming to Terms with Childlessness

In the book *I Am A Woman Finding My Voice,* Janet Quinn shares her own experience with us, as a women childless by choice, still "keening for my unborn child." She has worked through her grief, and feels richly blessed in many ways, yet always "childless by choice" [32, p. 25].

Childlessness, whether chosen or not, can be a source of grief. "Listen to a successful woman discuss her failure to bear a child, and the grief comes in layers of bitterness and regret," writes Nancy Gibbs in *Time* [31, p. 36]. After interviewing a cross-section of highly successful women for her book, *Creating a*

Life: Professional Women and the Quest for Children [33], author and economist Sylvia Ann Hewlett found that a large number of these women who were childless experienced a profound sense of loss. Their responses, she said, pointed to a "motherlode of pain and yearning" [34, p. B4].

In the past 20 years, childlessness has doubled; today one in five women between ages 40 and 44 is childless [31]. However, for many women, Hewlett discovered that childlessness is not a choice or a "preferred outcome" [34, p. B4]. In fact, one of the women interviewed identified her childlessness as a "creeping non-choice" [31, p. 38]. Many factors can contribute to this "creeping non-choice": for example, building a career takes time and energy; finding a suitable partner can be difficult if not impossible; lacking knowledge about the early decline of fertility often leads to bitter disappointment.

As has been mentioned before, many women whose life situation or career path precluded having children find themselves grieving. Most of the women who have spoken to me about their regret at never experiencing parenthood and no prospects for grandchildren, have been very successful in many areas of their lives. They may have success in their careers, a comfortable life style, and interesting close friends, yet something is missing.

Some of these childless women may be grieving. Support in going through the grieving process can help them come to terms with their grief and disappointment. When they have done their grief work, some thoughts on motherhood can be shared. For example, a university professor spoke to a group of nurses about biological and spiritual motherhood. According to him, successful biological motherhood (conceiving and bearing a child) requires spiritual motherhood in nurturing, encouraging, loving, providing, and respecting the spirituality of the child. He told us how he had been privileged to observe this spiritual motherhood in the nurses, teachers, and other women who had never borne children, but brought their creative skills to bear for the welfare of individual children and children in general. Christiane Northrup quotes Alexis Deveaux, mother and sponsor of MADRE, a Latin American relief organization: "Motherhood is not simply the organic process of giving birth . . . it is understanding the needs of the world" [25, p. 462].

Janet Quinn writes on claiming her motherhood, ". . . I do not have to give birth to be a mother. There are children everywhere waiting for love and tenderness and nurturing. I am open to mothering them wherever I find them, with my touch, with my mind, with my heart, with my spirit, with my voice, with my vote, with my dollars. I am a woman claiming my motherhood" [32, p. 82].[3]

---

[3] Reprinted by permission of HarperCollins Publishers Inc.

REFERENCES

1. E. Gaskell, On Visiting the Grave of My Stillborn Little Girl, in *The Poetry of Childhood*, S. Carr (ed.), B. T. Batsford Ltd., London, 1981.
2. R. Stirtzinger and G. E. Robinson, The Psychological Effects of Spontaneous Abortion, *Canadian Medical Association Journal, 140*, pp. 799-801, 805, April 1, 1989.
3. A. Hager and O. M. Owens, Early Pregnancy Loss: Miscarriage and Ectopic Pregnancy, in *Pregnancy Loss: Medical Therapeutic and Practical Considerations*, J. R. Woods and J. Esposito (eds.), Williams and Wilkins, Baltimore, pp. 23-50, 1987.
4. P. A. Witzel and B. M. Chartier, The Unrecognized Psychological Impact of Miscarriage, *Canada's Mental Health*, pp. 17-21, March 1989.
5. *Webster's New World Dictionary of American English*, Third College Edition, Simon and Schuster, New York, 1992.
6. *Standards and Guidelines for Professional Nursing Practice in Care of Women and Newborns*, Association of Women's Health, Obstetrics and Neonatal Nurses, Washington, D.C., 1998.
7. R. Friedman and B. Gradstein, *Surviving Pregnancy Loss* (Revised), Little, Brown and Company, Boston, 1992.
8. J. W. Worden, *Grief Counseling & Grief Therapy* (2nd Edition), Springer, New York, 1991.
9. *There Was a Child*, Video, Canadian Learning Company, Toronto, 1991.
10. E. Robinson, *Adoption and Loss. The Hidden Grief*, paper presented for ASK, about reunion and the Canadian Council of Birthmothers, Toronto, May 2, 2001.
11. M. Parthun, Post Abortion Mourning: The Hidden Grief, in *Care for the Dying and Bereaved*, I. Gentles (ed.), Anglican Book Centre, Toronto, 1982.
12. J. D. Hunter, *Before the Shooting Begins: Searching for Democracy in America's Culture Wars*, The Free Press Division of Macmillan Inc., New York, 1994.
13. W. Rayburn and J. J. Laferla, Mid-Gestational Abortion for Medical or Genetic Reasons, *Clinical Obstetrics & Gynecology, 13*, pp. 71-82, 1986.
14. J. Lloyd and K. M. Laurence, Sequelae and Support after Termination of Pregnancy for Fetal Malformation, *British Medical Journal, 290*, pp. 907-909, 1985.
15. I. Kent, *Emotional Sequelae of Therapeutic Abortion, a Comparative Study*, paper presented before the Canadian Psychiatric Association, Saskatoon, Saskatchewan, September 30, 1977.
16. G. Devereaux, *A Study of Abortion in Primitive Societies* (Rev. Edition), International Universities Press, Inc., New York, 1976.
17. B. Miller and C. Keane, *Encyclopedia and Dictionary of Medicine and Nursing*, W. B. Saunders Company, Philadelphia, 1972.
18. Canadian Abortion Rate Climbs to 33 per Live Births While U.S. Rate Declines, *National Post*, April 8, 2000.
19. Abortion Rates on the Increase, Stats Can Says, *The Gazette*, Montreal, April 8, 2000.
20. S. Martinuk, Just Say 'Non,' *National Post*, p. A-18, January 31, 2000.
21. A. Stone, Abortion and the Supreme Court: What Now?, *Modern Medicine, 41*:9, pp. 32-37, April 30, 1973.
22. T. Strahan, Male Attitudes are Important in Abortion Decision Making, *Newsletter, 3*:1, Association for Interdisciplinary Research in Values and Social Change, Washington, D.C., Spring 1990.

23. M. Parthun, The Psychological Effects of Induced Abortion, in *Abortion's Aftermath,* Human Life Research Institute, Toronto, 1985, distributed by The de Veber Institute for Bioethics and Social Research.
24. The Many Faces of Coercion, *Post Abortion Review,* Elliot Institute, Springfield, Illinois, January-March 2000.
25. C. Northrup, *Women's Bodies, Women's Wisdom,* Bantam Books, New York, 1998.
26. M. Somerville, The Debate Isn't Over, *The Gazette,* Montreal, March 18, 2000.
27. H. Morris and L. Williams, Physical Complications of Abortion, in *Abortion's Aftermath,* Human Life Research Institute, Toronto, 1985, distributed by The de Veber Institute for Bioethics and Social Research.
28. J. R. Dahling, K. E. Malone, L. F. Voight, E. White, and N. S. Weiss, Risk of Breast Cancer among Young Women: Relationship to Induced Abortion, *Journal of the National Cancer Institute, 86,* pp. 1584-1592, 1994.
29. J. Brind, Abortion, Breast Cancer, and Ideology, *First Things, 73,* pp. 12-15, May 1997.
30. S. Martinuk, Can We Talk About Abortion? *National Post,* May 1, 2000.
31. N. Gibbs, Making Time for a Baby, *Time,* Canadian Edition, pp. 36-42, April 15, 2002.
32. J. Quinn, *I Am A Woman Finding My Voice,* William Morrow and Company, Inc., New York, 1999.
33. S. A. Hewlett, *Creating a Life: Professional Women and the Quest for Children,* Talk Miramax Books, New York, 2002.
34. S. A. Hewlett, Baby Blues, *National Post,* April 13, 2002.

CHAPTER 8

Reproductive Loss is
a Family Affair

> Separate from the other unnamed millions who walk the earth, each of these
> little groups of three or five or twelve brought together by the shuffle of
> chance, then welded by blood, sees in itself the whole of earth, or all that
> matters of it. What happens to one of the three or five or twelve will happen to
> them all. Whatever grief or triumph may touch *any* one of them will touch
> *everyone,* as they are carried forward into the unknowable.
>
> Belva Plain, *Evergreen* [1, p. 441]

The above quotation clearly describes an important fact of family life. What
affects one family member affects all the family members in varying degrees
[2]. Worden [3, pp. 117-118] describes this as he speaks of grief and the family
system, looking at the family as a system with boundaries with the community.
The family consists of one or more groups of individuals within the family system.
The individuals within each small group interact with one another. Each small
group interacts with the other groups. Groups can consist of parents, and children,
and other relatives. The groups usually consist of either two or three individuals.
There could be other groups including relatives living in the home.

There is interdependence between groups and if all groups are functioning
well there is a balance and calm within the family system. If a family member is
added or lost, the family may experience upset and imbalance. It affects the roles
and interrelationships of all the members of the family. In this chapter we will look
at the interaction of the various individuals in or connected to the family when
reproductive loss is experienced:

1. the single person, usually the mother;
2. the couple directly involved with the loss;
3. any present or future children of the couple;
4. parents of the single or couple (grandparents);
5. siblings of the single or couple;
6. friends and associates.

THE MOTHER ALONE

We are very aware that when a pregnancy occurs, it may not be in the context of a loving committed relationship. When a woman is pregnant, and has been abandoned by her partner, she may or may not have the support of her parents and/or her siblings. Even though offering support, they may view her reproductive loss, miscarriage, stillbirth, or abortion as a blessing. They might believe that she should consider it in that light, too, hence not permit her to grieve. The woman who has lost her lover, and is estranged from her family, has these losses to deal with as well as the loss of her baby. The practical problems of food, shelter, and clothing can be part of a very real sense of isolation. This woman is especially vulnerable and requires, and is entitled to, the best possible care in her grief. Her loss must be acknowledged and opportunity given for her to tell her story, to share what this loss means to her and to go through the process necessary for healing.

G., A Single Woman's Story

A young woman of 21 shared with me the joy she felt when she discovered that she was pregnant. Her relationship with the father of her baby was stormy. She described him as moody; he had difficulty holding a job and had been known to slap and push her if they had a disagreement. She had begun to realize that the relationship was not what she wanted when she became pregnant. He had become increasingly restless, especially since the company she was working for eliminated her job as part of restructuring. He resented the loss of income. When she told him of the pregnancy, he became very angry and ordered her to have an abortion. When she refused, he said "I'm outta here!," packed his belongings, and left. She had not heard from him for several weeks. She had not told her parents about the pregnancy or even that the baby's father had left. Her parents had never liked him, had wanted her to stop seeing him, and eventually visits to her parents' home stopped, as did phone calls and other communications. She told me she could not face an "I told you so" attitude on the part of her parents and her sibling, a brother two years older than she. Hence her family was unaware that she was even pregnant when she miscarried at 11 weeks gestation. She had verified her pregnancy with a home pregnancy test, and had not sought medical attention. She had some spotting for a day or two, and then experienced severe cramping accompanied by frank bleeding of a bright red color. She had just come home from job hunting when, in the foyer of her apartment building, she doubled over with the severity of the cramps. A neighbor whom she knew slightly came to her aid, and drove her to the emergency room of a nearby hospital. She miscarried there, was seen by a resident doctor from the obstetrical department, and a D & C was recommended. She was to be kept in overnight as the procedure was to be done the following morning and she would be released that evening if there were no complications. The neighbor had waited to see if further help was needed, and offered to drive her home the next day. There were no physical complications and she was discharged as planned. The neighbor drove her home, made tea and toast for her, but was in a hurry to return to her own family. She did offer to be available if further help was needed. G. was very grateful for the neighbor's kindness, but since she was a relative stranger, did not want to as she said "impose any more." She was home alone with her grief, in discomfort and felt completely isolated. A nurse in Day Surgery had given my number to G. as she was aware of my work with the Centre for Reproductive Loss. G. phoned me, to say that she had had a miscarriage, and was feeling "empty, confused, and very very sad." I told her that I was so sorry that she had lost her baby. This released a flood of tears. (She had not wept throughout the loss of job, partner, and miscarriage.) I waited quietly until she had no more tears, only interjecting when she apologized, telling her it was natural to weep and was part of healing. She was exhausted but stated she felt better, and we then made arrangements to speak again. She felt too tired to come in for an interview. I checked with her as to any physical symptoms she might have, her plans for follow up medical care, and her rest and nutrition. I also told her that she could call me whenever she felt the need, and then we set up regular appointments for telephone conferences until, if she wished, we could meet together. Over time in our talks, we discussed naming the baby, journaling, and writing letters to the baby. We also talked of her writing letters to the baby's father, and to her parents and brother. These letters did not need to be sent but were tools to work through the hurt and anger with the goal of arriving at forgiveness and peace. I suggested a memory box. She liked the idea, and put in a picture of herself when she was pregnant, a picture of her parents, a baby ring she had received from her godmother when she was a baby herself. I contributed a small toy, because we agreed every baby deserves a present. She had named her baby "Precious." Lightner and Hathaway have stressed the importance of naming the child and saving mementos to treasure in later years [4, pp. 151-152].

While G. did not attend church services, she did believe in God and hoped for the possibility of life after death. I referred her to a clergyman who is understanding of the grief of reproductive loss and cooperates with memorial rituals which G. wanted to plan for her child. She had decided to send the letter to her parents. To her surprise and delight, they contacted her immediately. At first they did not understand her grief concerning the baby. Their dislike of the father and the thought of her struggling with the pressures of being a single mother gave them a sense of relief over the miscarriage. However, their genuine love for their daughter and her openness about her grief helped them to understand and to realize for the first time that they had lost their first grandchild, and this was a source of pain for them. The parents and brother attended a small memorial service arranged with the clergyman mentioned above. As they worked through their grief together, they were able to work through other differences and their bonds became stronger than they had ever been. With their support she returned to school, and found a part time job.

This story had a happy ending. Not all do. The estrangements may not always be healed and isolation may continue. This occurs where even those who care are unable to recognize miscarriage, stillbirth, abortion, or infertility as events to grieve. If we are to help, we must enable the bereaved who experience these losses to tell to significant others what such a loss means to them, so that it is dealt with from the mother's viewpoint, not someone else's.

THE COUPLE

The couple who is committed to the relationship has the potential for great mutual support, but there is a danger of emotional distancing. A number of factors can influence how each partner and the couple together deal with reproductive loss. Some of the factors I have found to have an impact on how a couple deals with such a loss are:

1. The length and stability of the relationship and the emotional closeness of the two people involved.
2. Their age and their experience with previous loss. This may be the first serious loss that one or both of them have encountered. If they have had previous losses, have they done their grief work, or have they not been able to work it through?
3. Their understanding that people grieve differently, that men and women grieve differently and that people manifest their grief in different ways.
4. The effectiveness of communication between the two partners.
5. The cultural backgrounds of the two partners. Are they from the same background or differing ones? Could there be a conflict in the perception of appropriate ways of dealing with loss? Can these differences be negotiated?
6. The meaning or importance of this pregnancy to each partner and their desire for children.
7. Other stresses in their lives, health, economic, familial, political problems. Reproductive loss can be superimposed on a couple whose energies are already overtaxed in dealing with other issues which can also be life and death.
8. The type of reproductive loss—miscarriage, stillbirth, abortion, infertility, giving a child up for adoption—can cause stress in differing ways. Every grief has common components, and every grief has its own distinct stresses.
9. In the case of miscarriage and stillbirth, when and where the loss took place, health care workers involved, and the kind of care, support, and understanding the couple felt they received can greatly affect the healing process.

10. The support or non-support received from extended family, friends, and community at large. This will be discussed more fully in succeeding sections.

It is essential that we recognize that reproductive loss can have serious implications for the couple's relationship. Worden reminds us the death of a child puts strain on this relationship [3, p. 122]. On the other hand, if they can share their grief, support each other and work it out together, they can emerge stronger as individuals and as partners.

K. and B.

K. and B. were happily expecting their first child and the pregnancy was progressing well. At six and a half months gestation, a mishap occurred and the amniotic sac was torn. K. developed a severe infection, and despite the efforts of the medical personnel, the baby died and K.'s life was seriously threatened. After several days in the hospital the infection was brought under control. When K. was released from the hospital she felt very weak, was still experiencing pain, and had little appetite.

When a mother's life is threatened, the bonding process is complicated with delivery of a live baby. However, when the infant is lost, the mother must deal with her own brush with death as she begins grieving for her deceased child. K. felt emotionally and physically ravaged.

B. had lost his child and nearly lost his wife. K. and B. found it difficult to talk about the loss because it was so painful and they tried to spare each other. He did not talk about his own feelings and was alarmed at the depth of his wife's grief and was still worried about her physical health.

K. held very high standards for herself in her work and in her personal life. She valued emotional control and calmness when confronted with crises. Hence, the roller coaster of emotions usual in reproductive loss plus her own illness was quite upsetting to her.

She went back to work in an attempt to put the tragic event behind her, but she was not physically or emotionally ready for the return as she was totally exhausted. She found the well-meant inquiries about the baby too distressing and consequently took further leave of absence.

She was upset that she was not able to function at work and this she experienced as failure, with accompanying loss of self-esteem and identity. She did not realize that difficulty in functioning at work soon after a loss is not uncommon. It was very important for her to be helped to realize that what she was going through was normal in view of her ordeal. As she did her grief work and regained her physical strength, she would find her skills and sense of competence returning.

Meanwhile, K. and B. were not talking very much or spending time together. It was important to help this couple realize that men and women often grieve differently, as discussed by Vogel [5, pp. 12-15], Gray [6, pp. 325-327], and Lang and Gottlieb [7, pp. 233-255].

B. was so concerned about his wife that the loss of the baby, though painful, was secondary to him. Also, he was not sure what to say to her as he was afraid to upset her. She had withdrawn as she felt buffeted with grief while dealing with physical recovery and lack of energy. They had little or no social life since the loss, because K. found it hard to be with their friends and did not like being in crowds. She also was concerned that her sadness would spoil others' good time.

After I discussed these issues with her, K. agreed that she and her husband, with his agreement, would set aside time to talk about their loss. He was pleased to try to reestablish their former companionable and affectionate relationship. They would also find some quiet recreation that they could enjoy together, but not in a crowd. As a couple they could go for walks, have a meal out, go for a ride or find a non-strenuous sport at this time that they could do together. Although she had always enjoyed church services and derived a sense of peace and strength there, she felt she was not ready to return to services and face the questions and concern of her fellow parishioners. B. believed in prayer but was not a church-attender. They decided to make brief visits to church outside of services, for quiet prayer and rest.

K. and B. felt their marriage was stronger as they worked through their grief and concerns. K. slowly came to terms with the fact that accepting help is not a sign of weakness. She realized that nearly everyone needs help in times of severe crises, and seeking and accepting assistance is a healthy response.

Importance of Couple Communication

D. contacted me concerning her miscarriage. D. had a teenage daughter by her former husband and was now happily married to H. They had a little girl and were looking forward to the birth of their baby. In spite of long hours and hard work, H.'s business failed. D. continued her own job, but money was tight. Then she miscarried at home. It was traumatic for them both. D. had hoped to have a son for her husband, and was fearful that she could not get pregnant again, as she was in her early 40s. They were in danger of losing their home. H. was desperately searching for work. They were both heartbroken over the miscarriage. D. was on leave for six weeks; her work involved working with babies. Her immediate supervisor was very understanding. She was in such distress that the doctor recommended that she remain off work for at least three months and her supervisor agreed. In the meantime, H. found a job with a modest salary, but things were still tight financially. D. tried to put up a brave front, but still wept easily, had trouble sleeping, and lost her appetite. H. was from a different culture, very family centered. His father was greatly concerned for D. and kept trying to cheer her. Finally, he made arrangements to help D. and H. in their financial difficulties. "There," he said, "Now my dear daughter can be her sunny self again. I've missed her!" D. appreciated his generosity, but felt pressure to put on a happy face when her sadness was overwhelming. Her mother was sympathetic, but she was working full time. We continued to talk by phone on a weekly basis. D. went to work but in a different area, as she was still not prepared to be with babies every day. H., who came from an emotionally expressive culture, was able to weep openly and often. He appeared to recover sooner than D. but was understanding of her continuing grief. His new job requires much attention as he learns new skills and he has received positive feedback regarding his work, which lessens his anxiety about supporting his family. D. and H. have been able to sustain a warm and loving relationship. D. was having some difficulty with nutrition and rest. She wasn't hungry and had trouble sleeping. We decided together that she should continue taking her vitamins, and devised easy high nutrient snacks. She and her husband have different religious faiths, but there is mutual respect, and prayer is a source of comfort for them. She is more optimistic about their future, but is still grieving, seven months after the miscarriage which is not unusual.

Another young couple was grieving three miscarriages and fertility problems. They were very close and communicated well. He said, "It's hard for me, but so much harder on my wife. The babies are so real to a woman right from the start. It is not as real for the man." He was very perceptive. Even before she feels movement, the other symptoms of pregnancy keep the mother very aware of the baby. Once they share feeling the baby move, then the baby becomes more real to the father, but still to a lesser degree than to the mother.

Understanding this and communicating their feelings and concerns to each other is essential for the couple to resolve their grief and disappointment and move on. Men see their role as "fixer" and solver of problems [5, pp. 12-15]. Women share feelings but do not necessarily expect or want a solution. Unless this is clarified it can lead to hurt feelings and resentment. Men are more likely to get back to work quickly, and often can find an escape from the pain by throwing themselves into their work. Livelihood is a reality factor here also. The mother, on the other hand, may take longer to be able to return to work, and her grieving often takes longer. There is a potential for misunderstanding in such a situation. She may feel he doesn't care, and he may become impatient because she does not seem to make an effort to move past her grief. Here again, communication is important. Grief work cannot be rushed, and getting back into a regular routine does not mean indifference. Interpretation of these facts by a counselor and/or support groups has been shown to be helpful. This is an opportunity to gain or improve communication skills within the marriage. If the relationship is weak, the reproductive loss may lead to the break-up of the marriage. In strong relationships the couple may develop the skills they need [8, p. 113]. Difficulties in the sexual life of a couple may arise after a loss. There can be a loss of interest on the part of one or both persons. They may lack the energy to engage in sex.

Several couples had struggled with fertility problems for years. When finally confronted with the fact that they could not have children, they were in deep mourning. One aspect of their reaction often reported was a lack of interest in sex. For a number of years the sexual act had been primarily directed toward pregnancy. This goal vanished with their hopes for pregnancy. At this point, one or both of the partners could not make the transition to engaging in sexual activity as a communication of love, or a source of pleasure and comfort.

These couples were concerned for their marriages. Patience and gentleness are required as the couple moves toward resuming the sexual part of their relationship. Revisiting activities of a non-sexual nature that they enjoyed together can be a start. Setting an environment, such as a special place, a quiet dinner, candle light can help recapture memories of happy times. At first just demonstrating affection without undue pressure can generate feelings of warmth, closeness, and safety. This can encourage them to approach lovemaking for its own sake and not as a chore or obligation. Sometimes additional help may be needed, such as sex therapy [8, p. 112].

CHILDREN

When a couple experiences reproductive loss this can affect the children they already have in a variety of ways. If the loss is an early miscarriage, the children may not even know of the pregnancy. Depending on where the miscarriage takes place they may be directly involved. If it happens at home, they may see their mother in distress and may see blood. They may be bundled off to a neighbor's or a relative. Mommy is gone to the hospital. What's wrong? Whatever the loss, children need the truth. The late Dr. Hyman Caplan, former Director of Child Psychiatry at McGill University, stated "Children should always be told the truth, but not necessarily all the truth." We may tend to shield children from all information or give them more information than they can manage.

In the case of stillbirth, the children were probably aware of the baby, had maybe even felt the baby move when holding their hand against mommy's tummy.

When there is an ectopic pregnancy, and the mother goes to the hospital, there is a great deal of tension on the part of the other significant adults because the mother's life is endangered. No matter how carefully the adults try to mask their fears, children pick up on the tension.

As soon as the father or adult looking after the children has the information, the children need to be told. There was a little baby, but he died. He was not able to live. If the mother is doing well say so. If there are complications with the mother, they can be told that she needs to stay at the hospital for now and the doctors and nurses are taking good care of her. If the mother sent a loving message, it should be passed on to the children. The children may worry that they may die too. They can be assured that the cause of the baby's death was different and will not affect these children. If they knew about the pregnancy before the death, they may feel guilty if they did not want a little brother or sister. If they were looking forward to the new baby, they may express anger at their parents. The entire family, parents and children, have to be reassured that no one is to blame. Opportunity must be provided for children to ask questions. Care should be used in the choice of words we use with children. He was "sick and died" can unduly frighten a child if he or she has a minor illness. "The baby is sleeping" can make a child afraid to go to sleep. "'God' and 'the angels' came and took him" can frighten a child. Will they come and take me? [5, pp. 18-19]. Bereavement educator Dawn Cruchet advises using correct terms, "dead, died, and death," and avoid euphemisms [9]. She gives a useful outline of children's perceptions of death:

> **0-2 years**—Loss is realized as absence. These children sense the anxiety and sadness of those around them. They need familiar routines and extra physical contact.
> **3-5 years**—Death is viewed as temporary and reversible. As they try to understand they may repeat the same questions over and over. They require patience and honesty.
> **6-9 years**—Children begin to understand that death is final. Death is perceived as a person, a monster, bogeyman or ghost. They are curious and want to know the causes of dying.
> **10+ years**—At this time children start to realize that death is permanent, universal, irreversible, and has a cause [9].

Children's need for love and security increases when a perinatal death occurs. At the same time, parents are deeply involved with their own grief. Energy levels are low, they may have less patience just when children are becoming more demanding, acting out their own apprehension and anxiety. Instead of hiding their grief, parents can explain "Mommy and Daddy are sad because our baby isn't with us." Letting the children see your tears can release theirs. Physical contact, hugs, a hand on the shoulder are very important. Relatives and friends who share the family's values can be helpful to children and parents, taking on some of the household tasks and helping with meals. Taking the children out for a treat gives the parents some respite. Allowing the child to participate in memorial services can be beneficial. Drawing a picture or making a little present for the baby can be therapeutic.

Most of us as parents want to shield our children from unhappiness and the tragedies of life. It cannot be done. What can be done is to deal with these issues simply and honestly; adults can act as buffers rather than shields, mediating the impact of painful events.

Not telling the children in order to protect them can be counter-productive. The children know something is not right. Comments children have made to me following their mothers' miscarriages, stillbirth, or other losses illustrate the point. "Mommy cries a lot when she thinks I'm not looking." "Mommy is always so sad." "Daddy is always working. He doesn't laugh anymore." "It's no fun at home anymore." These children had not been told about the specific loss affecting their parents. A very simple explanation without undue detail could have helped them to better understand the changes in their parents and in the home environment.

It can be very hard to talk to children about death. A good rule is to keep it simple. Answer questions honestly. Don't give them more information than they need. When their questions are answered honestly and they feel free to ask, they will obtain the information they need in the amount and content they can manage.

GRANDPARENTS

The parents of the couple suffering reproductive loss may be a source of comfort and strength or may add to the stress. They may recognize the grief and respond appropriately or may be unhelpful [5, pp. 15-16].

D.'s father-in-law was a good example of a kindly loving parent who wanted to help, but also could not tolerate D.'s and H.'s pain. Without understanding, he did not allow them to grieve. Financial assistance was fine, but insisting on constant cheerfulness added to the pressure. I hasten to say that his very real affection and concern still was appreciated.

One young couple lost their little girl, who was stillborn. This couple was very close and devoted. Both sets of parents lived overseas but kept in touch by phone. If the newly bereaved mother wept on the phone, her mother sharply reprimanded her, and told her she should take more interest in her mother and an aging uncle, so she could think about someone else for a while instead of being so selfish and self-centered. The young woman was so hurt and outraged at what she perceived as her mother's cold indifference that she refused to take phone calls from her. The husband took all the phone calls. He fully supported his wife, yet his culture obliged him to treat his elders with deference. He handled the situation with great tact. A year later, they had a healthy baby. The young mother was still resentful and was working slowly toward forgiveness of her mother with her husband's help.

Another couple who suffered the loss of their son were astonished and hurt at her mother's reaction. She, too, had lost a child, but she could not relate to her daughter's grief. She believed that her loss was much greater than her daughter's. Also I suspect that her daughter's loss reawakened some of her own grief feelings. Many times parents cannot bear their children's pain, so tend to ignore or trivialize a loss as a coping mechanism. The younger couple must be helped to deal with their own grief and then work toward understanding their parents' lack of empathy. Honest disclosure of their own needs and feelings to their parents may help to mend rifts in the relationship. Usually the grandparents are very concerned for their children. In their own grief they may not be able to reach out, and sometimes they just feel helpless.

A grandmother called me to say that her daughter had a little girl who was stillborn. Her daughter E. was inconsolable. The stillbirth had occurred three months earlier and E. was still weeping every day, was not eating well, and did not seem interested in activities that she used to enjoy. E.'s mother wanted to know how she could help. First I acknowledged the loss of her grandchild, and encouraged her to voice her own grief. We discussed ways of dealing with grief, and that grieving takes longer than we once thought. The important point here is that this woman cared deeply for her daughter and sought help and information to respond effectively to her in her grief. She was very concerned and was determined to find out how to help her daughter. Having help with her own grief and some guidelines to follow, she felt better equipped to assist her daughter.

SIBLINGS OF BEREAVED PARENTS

We have encountered some dramatic contrasts in how siblings have responded to parents experiencing reproductive loss. Some show a total lack of understanding. One woman was very offended when her sister who had just lost a baby could not bring herself to go to the christening of her baby.

Two other women who had suffered reproductive losses were expected to go and help their sisters who had new babies. There was outrage when one of the women explained that it was too difficult and she couldn't do it. The other woman did go but found it so painful that she had to leave early. Again resentment was voiced. There was no recognition of the suffering these women were enduring and of how particularly painful it was to be around babies.

It often happens that the grieving mother has been the sibling who always cared for and supported the other; in such a case, her sisters could not adjust to the role of giving support.

Another common problem is a long-standing sibling rivalry that makes understanding very difficult; the bereaved mother is then surprised and hurt at her sisters' indifference.

Many of our clients did receive much support from siblings and in-laws, ranging from visiting in the hospital, phoning every day, outings for their children, lawn mowing, grocery shopping and, most important of all, expressing real sorrow at the loss of the infant.

One family of sisters was particularly impressive. When one of them lost her baby, the others all rallied around her. One contacted the Centre for Reproductive Loss for her; two came in from out of town to be with her and her husband. The event was given the importance it merited and the loving concern of her sisters helped the bereaved woman in her healing process.

FRIENDS AND ASSOCIATES

While family members can be healing or wounding in how they deal with the bereaved couple, the same is true for friends, neighbors, and colleagues. Because many people do not know what to say, they either say the wrong thing or appear to ignore the event entirely [5, pp. 16-17].

D. had a long-time friend visiting from out of town. When she heard of the miscarriage she said, "It's a good thing you lost the baby. You were in no financial condition to have a child." When another friend objected to her comment, this "friend" told her, "It had to be said." One wonders why? Needless to say, the friendship came to an end.

Without a knowledge of what grief entails, some people are quite free with their criticisms and the time limits they put on grieving. In *Working through Your Grief,* Ronald Sunderland relates an experience of a friend of his. Her daughter, Betty, had died at the age of 13. Three months after her death, her mother, a school teacher, was sitting in the staff room in tears. She realized that Betty would not graduate with her class and that she would never know her as an adult. When a second teacher entered the room and saw the tears she said, "Oh, for goodness sake, Pat. It's been three months!" [10, p. 12].

We now know that, especially in that first year after a death, each holiday, anniversary, or any other important day may bring a realization of another aspect of the loss and a welling up of grief. This is normal.

Many friends and neighbors of our bereaved clients were most sensitive, generous and helpful. Cards and letters were deeply appreciated. Food and flowers dropped off at the home indicated concern and care. Often the bereaved cannot respond immediately to these gestures in their pain and lack of energy. Yet they do appreciate them.

What everyone can do is acknowledge the loss, and extend condolences. If you don't know what to say, admit it. "I don't know what to say to help, but I am so sorry!" The other need the bereaved have is to tell their story. A listening friend is a pearl beyond price. Friends should not hesitate to suggest a way to help, leaving the bereaved free to accept or reject the offer. It might be hard for them to be aware of their own needs.

In reproductive loss, a child has died. This is a momentous event, deserving of respect, compassion, and appreciation for the gift of life.

REFERENCES

1. B. Plain, *Evergreen,* Dell, New York, 1979.
2. J. Winchester-Nadeau, *Families Making Sense of Death,* Sage, Thousand Oaks, California, 1998.
3. J. W. Worden, *Grief Counseling & Grief Therapy* (2nd Edition), Springer, New York, 1991.
4. C. Lightner and N. Hathaway, *Giving Sorrow Words,* Warner Books, New York, 1990.
5. G. L. Vogel, *A Caregiver's Handbook to Perinatal Loss,* de Ruyter-Nelson, St. Paul, Minnesota, 1996.

6. K. Gray, Grieving Reproductive Loss: The Bereaved Male, in *Men Coping With Grief,* D. A. Lund (ed.), Baywood, Amityville, New York, 2001.

7. A. Lang and L. Gottlieb, Parental Grief Reactions and Marital Intimacy Following Infant Death, *Death Studies, 17,* pp. 233-255, 1993.

8. D. H. Ewy and R. F. Ewy, *Death of a Dream,* E. P. Dutton Inc., New York, 1984.

9. D. Cruchet, *Helping Children Deal With Death—Growing Through Grief Aftercare Program,* Mount Royal Commemorative Services, Outremont, Quebec, 1998.

10. R. Sunderland, *Working Through Your Grief,* Service Corporation International, 1989.

CHAPTER 9
Support Groups

The Assembly of Care

They must have heard a calling—those who came
Together—not knowing each other's name
Or how their spirits, stricken, came to be
As they assembled with uncertainty.

They came in need of life beyond their night
Of anguish endless. How common was their need
To dry their eyes; to see a morning's light;
To till their hearts; to plant another seed.

Around the room they'd listen and they'd share.
I wonder if they have become aware
How they were first for healing; how they are—
Simply by being here—the first to care for one another.

Nursed through their Night of Scars,
They have become each other's Morning Stars.
By need they came. They leave to go on living.
They came in Need, but leave behind their Giving.

Vincent Marquis [1]

A support group is often one of the few places where bereaved individuals can speak freely of their pain, grief, and loss and share with others who understand their loss. Group sharing has been found helpful for parents suffering from a variety of losses: miscarriage, stillbirth, abortion, infertility, and giving a child up for adoption.

This chapter offers suggestions for the formation of a support group (placement of participants, selection of meeting place, provision of information for the leading of the group meetings and for follow-up). It also presents what we as facilitators have learned and what participants have recommended.

PURPOSE

The purpose of the support group is to provide a "safe place" for people who have had a reproductive loss and are grieving. The group provides support, increased understanding of grief and the grieving process, and an opportunity for sharing experiences and feelings with others who can understand the depth of their suffering because of similar experience. Tools such as grief education materials are provided to help them deal with their pain and effectively work through grief.

PARTICIPANTS

Applicants are screened to assess their readiness in doing group work and to refer those who would benefit more from individual counseling. Those individuals who are dealing with serious issues other than grief and reproductive loss are referred to the appropriate services because such issues might not be relevant and could affect the group negatively.

Both parents are encouraged to attend the sessions. However, if parents cannot attend together, one parent is not only acceptable but is more than welcome. The one who does attend benefits directly and, because of the insights gained, helps the other to benefit indirectly from the group.

Members are grouped according to their loss. For example, a woman who has had a hysterectomy may not find it helpful to be in a group of parents who have lost babies. She would probably be more comfortable with participants whose losses are similar to her own.

The ideal number of participants is between 8 and 12. In case of the absence of one or two members, fewer than 6 may not allow enough interaction. On the other hand, more than 12 participants does not give sufficient time for everyone to participate.

SETTINGS FOR MEETINGS

It is advisable for group meetings to be held in comfortable, pleasant surroundings. This helps to provide a therapeutic environment where the participants can relax. For people experiencing reproductive loss, hospitals and clinical settings have unhappy associations. Such settings are often where the loss occurred. Therefore, a meeting place away from such areas should be arranged if at all possible.

FACILITATORS

The facilitators for our groups are health professionals who are familiar with group process. We have found that co-facilitating has worked well. Non-verbal communication is more easily observed; observations can be shared and adjustments made to meet emerging needs of the group. While we have found co-facilitating to be valuable, one facilitator can certainly work effectively with the group.

MECHANICS OF THE GROUP

Some of our groups met for an hour and a half on a weekly basis for a total of 10 meetings. Although such a timeframe is quite intense, it has been effective. After this period, some participants found that they still needed the group, but not so intensely. We would suggest continuing to meet every two weeks or once a month until the group members no longer felt the need to meet. Frequency and duration of the meetings can be negotiated with the group.

Additional support was provided by encouraging the participants to phone the facilitators between meetings. The participants were followed up after the sessions were completed. Contact on or near the anniversary of the loss was greatly appreciated. This contact can be made by telephoning or sending a card. A reunion of the entire group, held 3-6 months after the sessions had ended, was very well received.

CONTENT OF THE MEETING

1. Each member is asked to *tell her/his own story*. The story may need to be told more than once. Telling the story is essential to healing.

2. Everyone is given the *opportunity to speak* at each meeting. However, he/she speaks only when ready. A participant may pass if he/she is too overcome to speak at a particular time. We have found that those who pass at first, usually respond later so such an opportunity must be provided. Often periods of silence are necessary to process thoughts and emotions.

3. The importance of *shedding tears* in healing the pain of grief is emphasized. We encourage the group members to be free to cry and not to apologize for tears. Often friends and family try to discourage weeping and "talking about it," thinking erroneously that "it is better to get your mind on something else." However, not being free to weep and to talk about the pain can hinder the grieving process. Having a box of tissues available demonstrates that weeping is not only allowed but expected; this helps avoid embarrassment.

4. Written materials are provided in *handouts* at each meeting. We recommend reading on grief and loss. Participants can borrow books on reproductive loss from our library. Handouts can include information on grief and personal stories of people dealing with their own grief and loss. Art forms such as music, poetry, painting, and sculpture which depict grief and loss can help in the participants' expression of grief. We found that group members were resourceful and generous in locating and sharing valuable information on grief-related topics.

5. Strategies we suggest for dealing with grief are as follows:
   a. *Keep a journal.* Writing out thoughts and feelings is an outlet for pain and grief which can give insight into the writer's own feelings. Progress in grief work can also be recognized.
   b. *Write letters.* Letters can be written to the person lost (babies) expressing what the loss has meant, any anger, regrets, and wishes for the deceased. Other letters can be addressed to health care professionals and/or the family members, describing the pain, disappointment, resentment for lack of support, appreciation if appropriate, or any other issues that were important to the experience. These letters may or may not be sent.

6. A simple *memorial service* is planned together and held toward the end of the sessions. This provides an opportunity to "do" for the lost one, to bring closure to the group, and to assist in the grief work.

7. A *written evaluation* at the last session by each participant is important. It gives feedback to the facilitators as to what was helpful, what could be added, or what could be taken away. It provides opportunity for the group members to bring together and process the group experience and to see their own progress.

SUPPORT GROUP GUIDELINES

In order to provide an environment that is safe, secure, and stable, participants are asked to respect the following guidelines:

1. *Commitment.* Each member is asked to commit to the entire number of sessions, since it is difficult to note progress if they attend only one or two sessions. We ask them to notify the facilitators if they cannot attend a meeting. Some couples leave the group when they become pregnant because they do not want to focus on the grief and sadness of their previous loss. Sometimes, they do come back later to complete their grief work.

2. *Punctuality.* While starting on time and ending on time is ideal, facilitators find that flexibility is advisable and is appreciated by grieving people.

3. *Acceptance.* There are no right or wrong feelings. Avoid judging or correcting comments and contributions by members.

4. *Confidentiality.* Participants must know that what is shared in the group remains in the group. This is stated at the outset and participants are reminded again at the middle session and at the last one.

5. *Avoid comparisons.* Whether there was one loss or several losses, comparisons are not useful. We have often stated that everybody's pain is 100 percent. Each member is entitled to grieve. It has been noted in the groups that participants with many losses understand this very well. Participants with one loss may feel apologetic about their grief as they hear of multiple losses from other group members.

WHAT WE LEARNED FROM OUR
GROUP PARTICIPANTS

1. Buried grief can seriously affect the individual's life for years. It is not unusual for a woman to begin to grieve her loss five, ten, twenty years or longer after such an experience.

2. Even with support and intervention, grieving takes longer than expected.

3. Being near pregnant women, babies, and small children, even months after the group support, is still difficult for some of our participants.

4. Reproductive loss triggers grieving over other loss issues.

5. Often several losses occur in quick succession (e.g., baby, parent, job). This causes great stress as each loss must be grieved.

6. Family members may not be helpful to the bereaved couple. They may be grieving themselves and cannot tolerate the parent's pain.

7. All of the participants in our groups experienced great insensitivity at times from family, friends, co-workers, and health care professionals.

8. Parents who have lost children through miscarriage, stillbirth, and/or abortion find reproductive loss support groups helpful.

RECOMMENDATIONS FOR ALL
HEALTH CAREGIVERS

We are grateful for the concern and careful thought that went into the recommendations from the group members who have taught us so much. The following recommendations have come from the parents themselves:

1. Parents have told us how angry they were, especially after a miscarriage, that the terms "products of conception" and "fetal tissue" were used to describe the loss of their baby. Therefore, such terms should be avoided.

2. Parents would like to have the reality of this loss acknowledged by the health care professionals who see them at this critical time since acknowledgment of the loss, especially by hospital personnel, can start the healing process.

3. Training for all health care workers in helping parents with their grief in reproductive loss is essential.

4. When a problem with the pregnancy/baby is discovered, prompt and honest sharing of this information with parents is important. This should be done with compassion and recognition of the significance of this baby and the grief such a loss would entail.

5. Train and involve ultrasound technicians. They are often present when a problem with the baby is discovered.

6. The place where the tragic news is given should be in a private area, possibly in a location away from pregnant women or babies.

7. Follow-up health care should be scheduled at a time when other pregnant women are not present. It is very difficult for bereaved parents to be in a waiting room with pregnant women.

CONCLUSION

The support group for individuals suffering reproductive loss can contribute to healing. As parents have stated, "The members of this group are the only people to whom I can talk about our lost children."

REFERENCE

1. V. Marquis, The Assembly of Care, in *Journey,* 4:4, p. 6, Fall 1994, Newsletter of the National Catholic Ministry to the Bereaved, with permission from the author.

CHAPTER 10
Caring for the Caregiver

Primum non nocere—Above all, do no harm

Hippocrates

*   *   *

Do not believe that he who seeks to comfort you lives untroubled among the simple and quiet words that sometimes do you good. His life has much difficulty and sorrow. Were it otherwise, he would never have been able to find those words.

Rainer Maria Rilke [1, p. 72][1]

Although it has been said that a little knowledge is a dangerous thing, in my experience working with caregivers—professional, lay, or volunteer—I have found that a little knowledge about grief care can be a very beneficial thing, one which can go a long way in "doing no harm" or at least preventing additional harm.

The benefits of imparting a little grief care knowledge became quite apparent through the seminars that I gave in Montreal beginning in 1994, with co-founder of the Centre for Reproductive Loss, Anne Lassance. At that time there was a need for professional training in grief care which was not being addressed, especially in the area of reproductive loss. When I approached several colleagues asking for their assistance in counseling clients who had experienced reproductive loss, they agreed to help but only with some training in this area. Thus, the seed was planted for developing the seminars on "Grieving Reproductive Loss." Initially intended for health professionals only, our seminar format worked well for non-professional volunteers also. The original outline of the seminar evolved and expanded to become this book. That outline included the nature of grief, grief reactions, the body, mind, spirit connection, the healing process (at that time, in its infancy and only partially developed), facilitating the healing process, obstacles to grieving, what to say and do, and what not to say or do to help the bereaved, men

---

[1] Reprinted by permission of John Wiley & Sons, Inc.

and grief, other family members and grief. The day-long seminar also included an excellent video, "There Was a Child," role modeling of healing interventions by the leaders of the seminar followed by simultaneous role playing in groups of two or three, "lecturettes," much fruitful group discussion and ample time allotted for sharing of grief and healing experiences. One of the outcomes of the seminar which we had not anticipated was the healing of grief experiences of the participants. By a strange coincidence (Dr. Bernie Siegel believes that coincidence is God's way of remaining anonymous [2, p. 239]), one health professional had randomly selected a role play scenario as "counselee" that matched her own experience of a miscarriage she had suffered 14 years earlier. Although her loss was not a recent bereavement, but one that she thought she had grieved fully and resolved, it had not been adequately acknowledged at that time nor had she named the baby. After several minutes of her role play as a "counselee" during which she told her story, she had her loss acknowledged by the "counselor" who encouraged her to name the baby and place the baby on the family tree. In the post role-playing discussions, as she related her healing experience, she was visibly moved and relieved by what took place in those few minutes of role playing. These group discussions in some ways functioned like a support group as people told their stories, had their experiences validated and received support and encouragement from one another; they also provided the occasion to learn from each other, leaders included. The evaluations of the seminars by the participants were overwhelmingly positive and provided helpful feedback regarding the structure and content of the format for future seminars.'

GRIEF CARE EDUCATION THEN—
TOO LITTLE, TOO LATE

Most health practitioners have never received much in the way of grief care education in their training. Before the widespread acceptance of palliative care/hospice model of care, not much was known about the care of the dying, the nature of loss and grief, how to deal with the dying patient and the grieving client, and, least of all, how to deal with the caregivers'/health professionals' own grief. For the most part, until the 1950s and 1960s, caring for the patients' physical needs was uppermost in the minds of health care providers, with hardly a thought given to their spiritual needs, except perhaps to pray that the patient would not die on one's shift and thus avoid having to actually deal with loss, face the grieving family, or, worst of all, deliver the "bad news." When one is ill-equipped to deal with loss and grief, mistakes are made, perhaps in saying the wrong thing or not saying the right thing. It is difficult to comfort the sorrowful when one is so uncomfortable with sorrow and death. "The word 'care' has its roots in the Gothic *kara,* meaning to grieve, experience sorrow, cry out with. The person who truly cares must join with the person in pain. Sometimes that is all that can be done, which is hard for anyone to accept . . ." [2, p. 228].[2] Rather than joining with the person in pain, some health care providers may have put on the armor of "professional detachment" and become emotionally distant and withdrawn. As for taking care of our own needs at such times, no one ever told us how important it was to look after them or, indeed, that the counselor/care giver even had needs at all. And so we may have buried our frustration and anger, denying that we ever had needs or feelings and, in spite of all that, we carried on the best we could, albeit unsatisfactorily at times. We, too, were grieving and did not know how to comfort one another in our pain and grief.

As a nurse, I remember vividly an instance of not knowing how to comfort each other in the work place. I was working the evening shift on a surgical unit when one of our patients, a 19-year-old male, suddenly died. Because the staff had become very attached to him, we were all affected by his death. One of the nurses brought coffee to the grieving family as her way of caring, of joining in their pain. The next morning when the head nurse learned of his death, she also was grief-stricken but her response at that time was very puzzling. She was upset that the used coffee cups were left in his room and were not picked up by the previous shift. Instead of expressing her sorrow over his death, she responded with anger that the coffee cups were not removed. Looking back on that event, it is evident that her grief and anger over his death were displaced onto the coffee cups. Of course, no one realized the dynamic of her reaction at the time or offered comfort and support to her or to each other after his death.

The education of students in the health professions in the area of grief and reproductive loss has been woefully inadequate and may have been responsible for passing on some information that was misguided, inaccurate, or incomplete. A few examples: 1) A prestigious psychiatric reference book published over 40 years ago, once considered grief to be pathological and not a normal reaction to loss; 2) Prior to 1970, some researchers, wishing to study the effects of abortion upon women in the first trimester, selected for their control group women who had suffered a first trimester miscarriage; at that time, they did not realize that miscarriage was such a grief issue for women. And from Deutsch:

A 1945 reference textbook regarded stillbirth as the nonfulfillment of a "wish fantasy" [3].

Given some of the errors about grief and reproductive loss that were passed on, it is easy to understand how grief became disenfranchised and why health professionals were not adequately prepared to deal with grief and loss, especially reproductive loss. Fortunately, in recent years, that picture is changing, as the education of health professionals has taken on a more humane approach and educators have gained more accurate knowledge in the care of the dying through

---

[2] Reprinted by permission of HarperCollins Publishers, Inc.

the development of training programs in grief care education and conferences about death and bereavement.

GRIEF CARE EDUCATION NOW

Educational programs involving care of the dying and the bereaved should address the counselors'/caregivers' sense of their own mortality or personal death awareness, as well as issues related to existential anxiety. Worden also suggests other areas that should be included:

1. encourage participants to explore their own history of losses; (Worden suggests a series of questions for reflection on the caregiver's own history of losses.);
2. provide sufficient information so that they get a sense of what is helpful and what is not helpful for the bereaved;
3. provide the opportunity to identify unfinished business of prior losses and identify currently unresolved losses;
4. help caregivers/counselors to know their own limitations and when they need to refer [4, pp. 134-136].

This last point of knowing one's own limitations and knowing when to refer is perhaps one of the most difficult for health professionals to put into practice because it requires acknowledging which grieving persons the counselor cannot work effectively with, and also knowing which life stressors affect their ability to cope. Worden's comment is illuminating: "One of the subtle seductions in the mental health professions is the notion that one is capable of handling all situations" [4, p. 135]. Elsewhere he states:

Counselors are well known for their inability to negotiate their own help and support systems. Therefore, those of you doing grief counseling and grief therapy need to know (1) where you get emotional support, (2) what your limitations are, and (3) how to reach out for help when you need it [4, p. 138].

In addition to the above, I would add that counselors need to know where their *spiritual* support and strength comes from since they will be helping the bereaved deal with the spiritual aspects of grief in the body, mind, spirit connection. Just as the bereaved need to know how to care for themselves in body, mind, and spirit, so also counselors and other caregivers must be aware of how to care for themselves in body, mind, and spirit. Caring for oneself can go a long way in heeding Hippocrates' warning to physicians, "do no harm."

THE CAREGIVERS' OWN GRIEF

The death of a baby can be especially difficult for caregivers who work in newborn nurseries or labor and delivery units where the expectation is for a joyful, positive outcome, the birth of a baby. Yet, sadly, babies do die and health care providers are affected by these losses and may need help with their own grieving. In the article "Care of the Health Providers," the author, a nurse and support group facilitator, suggests several ways for caregivers to care for themselves as well as to maximize their coping skills following the death of a baby:

1. Accept your own feelings.
2. Ask for help from co-workers. Consider work teams, e.g., one person does the paper work and one person interacts with the parents.
3. Staff meetings to review the case and allow staff to share their feelings.
4. Attendance at funeral and/or letter to the parents.
5. Attend support group for perinatal loss.
6. Keep a journal of feelings.
7. Share your feelings with co-workers or others who understand confidentiality and the grief process.
8. Tell yourself you did the best you could with the information you had at the time.
9. Seek professional help if you get stuck at any stage in the grief process or you feel unable to carry out the duties of your job over time [5, p. 12].

While attending the funeral is not always possible, there is an alternative way for the caregiver to find closure. Some hospitals have in recent years initiated commemorative services, ceremonies, or rituals for bereaved parents who had suffered a reproductive or perinatal loss. Recognizing the need for caregivers to grieve the loss of their patients, pastoral care and bereavement committee staff have encouraged them to attend as well. These services are usually held annually or every three months on-site in the hospital chapel, and they afford the opportunity for caregivers and bereaved parents to grieve these losses together and to experience their shared humanity. Attending such services is another way for caregivers to care for their work-related grief issues. Outside of the hospital setting, many funeral homes offer after-care programs for the bereaved. In Montreal, for example, the Mount Royal Cemetery Funeral complex offers support groups and workshops on grief and loss. Also, in October 1999, they initiated a memorial service for deceased children to be held annually. This service, which was coordinated by their bereavement educator, Dawn Cruchet, allows bereaved parents and caregivers alike to grieve and remember those babies and children who are gone but not forgotten.

Caregivers will find most helpful a book by Gary Vogel, titled *A Caregiver's Handbook to Perinatal Loss*. In it, the author addresses those aspects of grief and perinatal loss that are most pertinent to a wide range of caregivers, such as physicians, nurses, therapists, counselors, clergy, funeral directors, clerical staff, genetic counselors, hospital social workers, and the pastoral care team. He emphasizes the need for caregiver renewal and replenishment and offers helpful advice that is applicable to all caregivers including nonprofessional ones. He suggests that caregivers:

- know your limitations
- do your own (grief) work
- learn to receive as well as you give
- learn to set boundaries [6, pp. 79-80].

Know Your Limitations

Many caregivers mistakenly believe that they can handle any situation, as Worden has already pointed out. Part of the difficulty in not knowing one's limitations is the fact that caregivers have not had much practice at assessing themselves objectively vis-à-vis their limitations. Vogel believes that "the key is to know yourself well enough to know when you need to not be giving of yourself" [6, p. 80]. One example of this is the neonatal nurse who spoke up for herself in refusing a difficult assignment after she had experienced several patient deaths quite close together: "I just can't do it. I can't take another death. I spent *months* with this patient and I just can't do it" [7, p. 98].

Do Your Own (Grief) Work

Caregivers must be aware of their own grief issues and deal with them before helping others with similar losses. This would entail exploring their own "loss history," identifying "unfinished business of prior losses," and identifying "currently unresolved losses."

Learn to Receive as Well as You Give

Caregivers who continually give of themselves without having their needs met or taking sufficient time out for renewal, replenishment, and rest may be at risk for burnout. The comments of this caregiver attest to such a possibility: "I think I have given and given and given, and I just can't have anyone else ask me for one more thing. I'm tapped out" [7, p. 100]. Another caregiver stated: "If you feel like your needs are met, you're not going to be continually asking for more, asking for reaffirmation" [7, p. 62].

Learn to Set Boundaries

While this last point is related to knowing one's limitations, it is still difficult to say "no" when the demands of caregiving exceed the supply of energy, abilities, capabilities, and resources of the caregiver. Knowing one's limitations will help the caregiver in learning to set boundaries, in knowing what one can do and what one cannot do, and in knowing when to refer or even ask for help. Caregivers need to let others know that they are not omnipotent, that they can't fix everything, and that they are human. Sometimes caregivers forget to share their humanity with those in their care.

The Healing Process Model©—A Guide for Caregivers

The Healing Process Model© itself, with a few modifications, can be used as a guide to help caregivers with their own grief issues, particularly work related ones.

ACKNOWLEDGE THE EFFECTS OF THE REALITY OF THE LOSS

Caregivers, just as bereaved individuals, need to acknowledge their feelings about the loss of a patient or client; they may need to have their feelings about the loss validated by co-workers so that they themselves will have permission to experience those feelings and not deny that they are there. By accepting that those feelings are present, caregivers can more readily begin the healing process of their own grief.

In describing her first experience with a baby who had died, one nurse recalled, "I've never discussed feelings of pain and grief. I didn't know there was something to process" [7, p. 110].

Other caregivers are aware that they go through an emotional grief period themselves when doing grief care assignments: "There's no way you could witness that and not feel some emotional grief for those people" [7, p. 43].

Upon completion of an emotionally heavy case load involving the deaths of two patients, a neonatal nurse described her response: ". . . you cannot think when you come back after an episode like that; you can't even think straight. At least I can't. I would just like to be given the option to go home. Well, first have my debriefing session with a professional and then go home" [7, p. 18].

Caregivers can benefit from peer support in their acknowledgment of the effects of patient loss as well as personal loss. Staff members should be encouraged to console one another at the time of loss, and not dismiss or explain away feelings of grief. After her miscarriage had devastated her, a health professional upon returning to work was told by a colleague that perhaps subconsciously she did not want the baby and that this probably brought about the miscarriage. Despite great strides in knowledge about the bereaved's reactions to reproductive losses, there still remains a great deal that needs to be done in grief care education for health professionals, even in the 21st century.

Because their own grieving could affect their work with others, caregivers should inform their supervisors of a personal loss, especially if they might be caring for a patient with a similar loss. One should not assume that a nurse who had recently experienced a pregnancy loss would be the best one to care for a patient who also had had a pregnancy loss. She may not be emotionally ready to do so.

The person making patient assignments could first listen sympathetically about the meaning that the pregnancy loss has for her and then give her the choice to care for that patient or not. Ideally, the caregiver should be able to speak up for herself regarding a difficult assignment. However, that may not always be possible, as this particular caregiver realized how she had been affected upon returning to work: "I realized after I got here and couldn't speak up for any assignment or anything. I don't know how much more I can take. I mean, how many deaths do you have to have before nurses get bereavement leave?" [7, p. 97].

Caregivers may need to be reminded that tears are not a sign of weakness. Commenting on this, Colin Murray Parkes, the well known psychiatrist and bereavement authority, has observed:

> It is a strange paradox that experienced senior nurses and doctors, who understand well the healing value of tears following bereavement are likely to interpret similar behaviour on the part of another nurse or doctor as a sign of weakness, "burn-up,"[3] or incipient psychiatric illness. Yet there are many occasions when grief is just as normal a reaction for staff as it is for patients and relatives [8, p. 5].

One caregiver who did feel comfortable with tears commented, "My tears are part of my humanity" [7, p. 191]. Tears in the eyes of the caregiver are a way of acknowledging the loss and can thus be comforting to the family that has lost a baby. A nurse remembered the man who was touched by her tears after the death of his grandchild: "He knew that I really cared about them" [7, p. 68].

Because abortion loss and grief may not be readily apparent in abortion clinics and pregnancy termination units, those who work there need to be reminded of their effects. Since they encounter death on a regular basis, the personal lives of the staff could be affected by so many death experiences. They, too, may need to debrief and acknowledge the reality of abortion loss and grief. Even the wife of a doctor who had formerly performed abortions said she was affected. She realized this when she found herself sinking into a depression which she attributed to her husband's work.

TELLING THE STORY

Caregivers will need to de-brief and tell their story of grief and loss to understanding staff members if they are working in the hospital setting. The Perinatal Loss and/or Bereavement Committee members should be available to allow caregivers to de-brief anytime after the death of a baby; they can also encourage and facilitate staff meetings to provide the opportunity for caregivers to review and discuss patient losses. Meetings can be tape recorded for those who cannot attend so that they can feel that they are part of the healing process and are not alone or isolated in their grief. The importance of de-briefing after a difficult loss is reflected in this caregiver's comments: ". . . I guess I'd have felt better

---

[3] North American readers should note that the author is using the term "burn up" in a sense similar to the familiar "burnout." The term "grief" is being used in a very broad sense to cover various kinds of stress, not only the stress of loss due to death of a cherished person [8, p. 5].

if I could have come in and talked with somebody, if I could have found some staff nurses that understood, or had been there. Because I felt almost like I was going crazy. And this wasn't even my baby. I kept thinking, I feel this great sense of loss but it isn't even my baby" [7, p. 15].

When caregivers work alone apart from an institutional setting, they may need to seek out some other sympathetic listener who understands the nature of grief and loss and the importance of telling one's story. They can also attend a support group for reproductive/perinatal loss as well as telling their story by writing in a journal to record the facts of the loss and their feelings about it.

The documentation of storytelling by caregivers working on the front lines and dealing with death and bereavement on an everyday basis was the objective of a project undertaken by the Vanderbilt University Medical Center in November 1993. This initiative, called the Tandem Access Project (TAP), was developed in order to gather stories from nurses who work in the NICU (Neonatal Intensive Care Unit) and was concerned about what the telling of stories of grief does for the nurses as storytellers and as readers of those stories by other nurses [7, p. 267]. Many of these nurses who were interviewed found great relief and comfort in telling their stories of grief in response to the question, "Can you remember any event involving grief on the job that has stayed with you, any story you couldn't shake loose?" [7, p. 5]. Telling stories of grief in the manner of a peer-narrative format, as was done for this project, has allowed the nurses "the time and intimate attention that is deserved when one encounters grief" [7, p. 4]. After her interview, one of the nurses replied, "Thank you for allowing me to grieve" [7, p. 4].

EXPLORE HISTORY
OF REPRODUCTIVE LOSS

Caregivers who have suffered reproductive loss need to explore those losses, examine the kind of grief work that they did or did not do, and identify any "unfinished business" related to the loss. This is especially important for caregivers working with newborn babies or coming into contact with pregnant co-workers. They may put themselves at risk for experiencing an intensified grief reaction in those situations if they have not adequately mourned previous reproductive losses. When making grief care assignments, co-workers need to be sensitive to one another and be pro-actively supportive towards those who may have recently experienced a reproductive loss. C. M. Parkes, speaking about the caregiver's own grief, made this observation:

> Colleagues are often aware when one of their number is getting out of his or her depth. They should reach out in support before the other needs to cry out for help. Staff who insist on returning to the ward when they are off duty or who possessively take over a particular patient may need help to get out of a situation that is threatening to harm them [8, p. 7].

EXPLORE HISTORY OF OTHER LOSSES
AND STRESS FACTORS

Just as with reproductive loss, caregivers need to be aware that their own losses, death related or non-death related, as well as other stressors, can affect their work and their personal well-being. They need to examine those factors which would impede their caregiver role and identify any "unfinished business of prior losses" and "currently unresolved losses." Once again, this involves knowing their own limitations, what their needs are, when to ask for help or when to refer. Regarding caregiver needs and grief, Parkes has stated:

> . . . there are times when our needs must not be ignored; we may have lost our ability to remain in control of a situation—become "*over involved.*" This is particularly likely to occur if a patient's sufferings trigger off like feelings in ourselves. Perhaps we are of the same age, or our life situation may be similar. The patient's grief touches a raw spot in us. We may have experienced losses or disappointments in our own life and we suddenly find ourselves overwhelmed. In such cases it is wise to step back from the situation, to recognize our limitations and to *draw in others who can share in the support* of this person [8, p. 7].

INTERPRET GRIEF REACTIONS
AS NORMAL

Caregivers need to be familiar with what constitutes normal grief reactions and be able to recognize them not only in their clients and patients *but also in themselves.* Using the body, mind, spirit connection format is one way to assess easily and quickly those thoughts, feelings, and behaviors which manifest themselves as normal grief reactions (see Chapter 1).

Caregivers are not immune to experiencing grief reactions. One neonatal nurse spoke of the difficulty dealing with babies that die and described the nurses who told their stories of grief for the book *Journey of the Heart:*

> After seven years at this job, I continue to be struck by the sheer weight of grief, and by the innumerable ways it bends and shapes us. No one is immune—we just react in different ways.
> We just happen to spend a lot of time in a place where the forces of death and suffering become commonplace. The voices of the storytellers here attest to the equally enduring forces of the heart and show us persons who refuse to let their reactions to death and suffering become commonplace. These are people who don't choose whether or not to feel the pain, the anger, or the love that goes with grief. They can't help but feel it. None of us can [7, p. 3].

While caregivers know what these reactions are ("head knowledge") and can normalize them for everyone else, they sometimes fail to normalize them for themselves. This can happen when they have unrealistic expectations of themselves, and mistakenly believe that they are immune to such reactions or that they can "think" and "reason" their way out of grief. It is not unusual to hear such a comment as the following myth which gives rise to unrealistic expectations: "I'm not supposed to feel this way. After all, I'm a nurse (doctor, minister, etc.) and I should be able to handle this better." Caregivers have to know what is happening to them in a grief situation, so that they can act on it, seeking out someone with whom they can de-brief and who can validate their reactions, if not immediately then at some other more appropriate time. They need to acknowledge those feelings and intuitive promptings ("heart knowledge") which demand attention and should not be dismissed. Listening to such intuitive promptings alerts the caregiver to recognize their feelings, and to reach out to others who can help to shoulder their pain.

CONTINUE RELATIONSHIP WITH THE DECEASED

Although the features of this component of the healing process do not appear on the surface to have the same meaning for the caregiver as for the bereaved, nevertheless some aspects do apply.

Because they have engaged in a similar grieving process, caregivers forge a bond not only with their patients/clients but also with the family members who become part of their larger circle of care and concern. Caregivers assist family members to cope with the transition of their loved one from life to death and to prepare them for continuing the relationship with the deceased. They participate as facilitators for continuing that relationship in the after-care aspects of bereavement. These would include making follow-up telephone calls, home visits, and sending cards or letters to the bereaved shortly after and on the anniversary of the death.

Bereaved parents themselves have fostered the continuance of that relationship for the caregiver by staying in touch with a caregiver for several months or in some cases years after their baby's death. A few other parents have remembered the anniversary of the baby's death by sending flowers or some other token of recognition and gratitude to the caregiver who cared for their baby. For them, the caregiver represented a tangible link to their beloved baby and staying in touch facilitated continuing the relationship with the deceased.

At another level, these painful experiences of grief become part and parcel of the caregiver's being, as each patient/client finds a place in their memory and on the "family tree" of their professional life. As this nurse said about one of her patients, "I will certainly always remember him" [7, p. 44]. Another caregiver recalled the memory of a deceased baby she had cared for as "a little gem that sparkled in my memory bank and demanded to be treasured and not forgotten" [7, p. 47].

HONOR THE ULTIMATE QUESTIONS ABOUT LIFE, DEATH, AND SPIRITUALITY

Caregivers who have first addressed their own issues related to existential anxiety and who have a sense of their own mortality or personal death awareness will be more *grounded* when confronted with life and death events, the meaning of suffering and questions about spirituality. Their grounding will enable them to be more supportive of bereaved parents who struggle with the inevitable "why" questions that they raise, as they look for answers to events that seem to make no sense at all. In the face of such questions with no answers, caregivers also can feel sad, angry, hurt, powerless, and helpless in not being able to fix something that can't be fixed. Challenged by these issues, caregivers could seize the opportunity to examine and explore their own spirituality and reflect upon their relationship to the Cosmos, Creator or God. To guide them in their practice, caregivers must develop a personal philosophy of care, a set of values, attitudes, and beliefs about the meaning of life, death, and suffering. The Chinese symbol for crisis contains the pictogram for opportunity and, depending upon how one deals with crisis, its outcome can lead either to disaster or growth. One caregiver's story about the healing intervention of a compassionate physician for the bereaved family of a dying baby illustrates not only the growth aspect of crisis but also that physician's philosophy of care:

It was such a beautiful thing that he did. He let them think they had those precious last hours with her. He let them have the prayer service, and he let them cry over her. . . .

I thought about how we rush death sometimes, and how he really gave them that extra time. After the two-and-a-half hour period, he gently and quietly stood up, and went over and listened to her, and I think he said, "Her heart rate's slowing down." Ten minutes after that he got up and said, "She's gone." Then the tears, the wailing, the family just totally lost it. I thought, they have no idea this baby's been gone for two-and-a-half hours.

. . . what happened is not important, but what you make out of it is what is important. The quality of death that we gave that family was so much more important than the knowledge that their baby had already died. Their last moments with their baby meant so much more than anything else that we could have ever done [7, p. 26].

EXAMINE THE MEANING OF "GUILT WORK" WITHIN "GRIEF WORK"

Caregivers sometimes experience guilt feelings within the context of their caregiving and their own grief. They could feel guilty when they cannot "fix" everything, especially in situations where they can only be present to the bereaved in their grief and sorrow, where they must learn to listen without fixing and to resist the temptation to withdraw or run away when things can't be fixed. Just as with the bereaved, caregivers might blame themselves and feel guilty for any number of interventions they may have done or not done in their caregiving. "I guess it's the guilt that is really the most damaging to me as a career nurse," acknowledged one caregiver [7, p. 32].

Dr. James E. Miller offers sound advice for caregivers who often feel guilty and helpless when they felt they were unable to do more for the bereaved. "No matter how much you do to help, there is so much you cannot do to help. The more you come to know what your caregiving can accomplish, the more you come to know what it cannot accomplish" [9]. Because caregivers sometimes try to do too much and because sometimes there are elements in caregiving that are beyond the control and ability of caregivers, Miller believes that caregivers must accept and affirm that there are ways one cannot help. Setting realistic expectations can help prevent some of the guilt, especially imagined guilt.

Just as with the bereaved, guilt can be real or imagined; it can be an obstacle to grief work; it may need to be reality tested; finally, the guilt may need to be resolved through the "seeking and granting of forgiveness."

AWARENESS OF ANGER AND NEED FOR FORGIVENESS

In their caregiving, caregivers can experience anger associated with grief and loss similar to what the bereaved experience. "Grief and anger are partners," is something I have often said to reassure my grieving clients when feelings of anger catch them by surprise.

"Because the experience of grief makes it difficult for us to be or feel helpful to the person experiencing bereavement, the counselor can easily feel frustration and anger," states Worden [4, p. 133]. There are many instances when caregivers experience anger in their work with the dying and the bereaved. Some of the most common ones that I have seen are the following: Caregivers could be angry at the situation itself, at their co-workers for lack of grief support, and even angry at themselves. One caregiver commented on her anger at the situation :

> I used to have so much anger, at first, working with bereaving families. I would be so angry if a patient died. I think it was because I couldn't direct it right. . . . Maybe I just wanted the control, even just the control over my own feelings, instead of just letting it go.

I have gotten used to the fact that the feelings are going to be there. Sometimes I feel a little strange about it. What's wrong? Did I get too involved, did I do something wrong. But, you know, looking back on the last few, they come and they go through me at their own speed [7, p. 114].

Part of the anger that arises from the situation could be attributed to the expectation that the caregiver has of being in control of a situation, especially one involving grief care which often has different "rules" and which follow the different needs and the uniqueness of each of their patients/clients. Frustration can easily turn to anger when the caregiver, wanting to make things perfect, follows rigid rules of protocol rather than taking cues from the bereaved. Flexibility in caregiving may even be the key to preventing frustration and anger from taking hold. James E. Miller believes that the caregiver's strength lies in their ability to be flexible and that authentic caregiving requires that caregivers respond to the person's uniqueness and situation, learn what works best, and even be willing to be inexact [9]. The comments of this caregiver reflect such flexibility in bereavement and grief care:

. . . when it comes to families, it just works better for me to take my cues from them. There's no set of rules of what to say, of what to do and what not to do. Let them give you the direction that they need, what they're comfortable with. What's their fondest desire [7, p. 41].

Caregivers themselves need grief support in their work and when it is not there, they can experience feelings of frustration, distress, and eventually anger. This nurse experienced a lack of support from her co-workers during her particularly difficult grief care assignment:

It was a terrible thing. And I never really had that many people come by and help, or really say anything to me during that or after. It's almost like they wanted to pretend it didn't happen. Everybody just stayed in their own little corner. And then when I left I ended up crying all the way home, I felt so terrible [7, p. 14].

Sometimes caregivers can become angry at themselves for not being able to do all that they wanted to do in their caregiving; they may berate themselves for things they said or did to the bereaved that were not helpful, or even things they did not say or do that they might have said or done. At such times, caregivers need to tell themselves that they did the best they could have done given the circumstances and the information they had at the time; they must also come to realize their need to forgive themselves for their failures or mistakes (real or imagined), forgive their co-workers and colleagues for their lack of support at critical times, and finally ask others to forgive them for their own mistakes, indifference, and lack of support.

They can also dispel their anger through letter writing or directing their concerns to their supervisors or other administrators, seeking concrete resolutions to actions which may have brought about an angry reaction in the first place.

Certainly, the need for grief support of one another in the workplace, especially through Employee Assistance Programs (EAP), is one of those areas deserving of awareness and attention.

FACILITATE CLOSURE

Caregivers, too, have the need for closure, for letting go of the pain of grief and for achieving a sense of peace, while at the same time cherishing the memory of those who had been in their care. Closure can also mean letting go of any remnant of guilt and anger associated with the caregiving; it can mean being grateful for having had the privilege of helping at such a critical time and being thankful for what the bereaved have to teach all of us about grieving and healing.

The caregiver must learn to "clean yourself up," that is, not ignore the need for closure and not carry the grief around either consciously or unconsciously. I remember the summer I cared for a woman who was dying at home. For me, closure came through gardening, and being surrounded by growing living things, where I found peace and comfort in working the earth with my bare hands.

Caregivers can also achieve closure through de-briefing of losses on a regular basis, attending funeral/commemorative services and writing cards or letters to the bereaved, to mention a few. Follow up telephone calls to the bereaved facilitate closure for the caregiver who also has a need to say goodbye and to know that the bereaved are going to be alright and are able to cope:

> It's for our benefit as well, so we'll feel okay about it. . . . for some reason we seem to feel responsible for these people when they leave the institution. You just want to know that they're going to be okay when they go home, and that they're going to be able to go on. You want them to know that somebody cared [7, p. 19].

Another caregiver expressed the need for closure: "I realized what an intimate thing we had shared, and we had no closure. She was gone without being able to say good-bye. There was no closure and I felt very strange" [7, p. 18].

CARE FOR SELF IN BODY, MIND, AND SPIRIT

Caregivers must be just as attentive to caring for their own physical, emotional, and spiritual needs as they are for those in their care. Caregivers who consistently neglect their own well-being will soon deplete themselves and will have little left over to give to others. Caregivers can take a lesson from the body's own wisdom in caring for itself; for example, oxygenated blood from the lungs travels first to feed the coronary arteries of the heart enabling it in turn to pump blood to the rest of the body. In recent years, the fact that more emphasis has been placed upon the topic of caring for the caregiver is an indication that caregivers still need to be reminded of this aspect of their caregiving. Journal articles, books, conference presentations, workshops, and videos stress the importance of caring for the caregiver and offer concrete, practical suggestions for their professional and personal well-being. Dr. James E. Miller has produced just such a work, a video, that caregivers will find helpful. This video, "The Grit & Grace of Being a Caregiver—Maintaining Balance as You Care for Others," is an artistic and meditative presentation which allows caregivers the opportunity to step back and reflect upon ways to care for themselves while caring for others [9]. It lends itself readily to group discussion and is suitable for both lay and professional caregivers. There are seven guiding principles which are presented in this video:

1. The healthiest way to care for another is to care for yourself.
2. By focusing on your feelings you can focus *beyond* your feelings.
3. To be close, you must establish boundaries.
4. In accepting the helplessness of your helping, you become a better helper.
5. Caregiving is more than giving care. It is also *receiving* care.
6. As a caregiver, your strength is in your flexibility.
7. In the everydayness of your caregiving lies something more: sacredness [9].

These principles go beyond addressing the usual aspects of caring for oneself (sleep, rest, nutrition, exercise, etc.); they give a broader dimension of care by urging the caregiver to "be among people who support, affirm, lift"; "open yourself to the healing touch of nature"; "allow opportunities to experience joy"; "pamper yourself from time to time"; "love yourself all the time" [9].

In caring for themselves, caregivers may need to exercise some form of "selfishness" in demonstrating their love and respect for themselves, especially in regard to protecting their time and energy from toxic people or situations, or other non-fulfilling activities and pursuits which deplete rather than restore or renew their body, mind, and spirit.

ASSESSMENT FOR BURNOUT PREVENTION

This component is concerned about preparation and prevention; it is concerned about how well prepared caregivers are in their ability to identify stress factors and to prevent burnout while caring for others. Such caregiver preparation or readiness begins with assessment and an honest appraisal of identifying what is stressful for that particular caregiver. Stress identification includes personal and environmental stress factors in the workplace and caregivers need to acknowledge to themselves that they may be vulnerable to such stress.

For caregivers to acknowledge *to others* their vulnerability to stress requires that their peers be open and non-judgmental. Unfortunately, some health professionals have expressed fear of reprisals and being judged unfavorably should they disclose to their peers their own vulnerability to stress. "Establishing this human element that enables self-disclosure also heightens insights and sensitivity to patients, their families, and work peers" [10, p. 31], states Janet A. Simone, a medical social worker. Since the well-being of the caregiver is linked to the well-being of the one receiving care, caregivers must develop an awareness of those signs and signals which indicate when they are stressed. Simone has identified several stress indicators:

> "Listening" to one's body involves awareness of physiological cues like tight muscles, headache, a diminished or insatiable appetite. Irritability, inability to concentrate, lethargy, insomnia, overuse of alcohol, and urges to cry or run and hide are other warning signals of stress. . . . Indicators that the entire group is stressed include frequent arguments, scapegoating, defensiveness, absenteeism and rapid turnover [10, p. 31].

It is interesting to note that the signs of stress or stress indicators are similar to what has already been described as normal grief reactions; it is hardly surprising that stress and grief manifestations would share common ground since it is now acknowledged that grief, loss, and bereavement are stressful experiences. Those caregivers who are working in grief related areas will need to tease out those factors which give rise to normal grief reactions from those factors which produce stress.

Caregivers who have unrealistic expectations of themselves are likely candidates for burnout. Simone describes burnout:

> Essentially burnout refers to physical, emotional, and behavioral symptoms that signal the depletion of energies. One may consciously acknowledge that one hasn't any more to give, but frequently the burnout process involves a less conscious, gradual detaching from patients and peers. As one reaches minimal quality caregiving and involvement, feelings of guilt may surface, and this guilt frequently sparks frenzied, overcompensatory efforts that lead to the exhaustion of burnout [10, p. 28].

In order to prevent or reverse burnout, caregivers must be prepared to identify stress factors in their work environment so that they can plan strategies to cope with them and bring about the necessary changes that will alleviate the stress. For example, creating a supportive working environment is one way to reduce stress. Simone offers some suggestions for achieving a creative environment:

- showing mutual respect and support among staff;
- taking lunch breaks and adequate time off from work;
- planning timeout from stressful patients;
- scheduling meetings at "protected" times for debriefing;
- venting feelings and obtaining feedback;
- contributing to a spirit of camaraderie;
- acknowledging colleagues by name;
- recognizing when a job is well done;
- making one's own needs known [10, pp. 33-34].[4]

---

[4] Reprinted by permission of Neonatal Network®.

Speaking at a conference in Montreal, pediatrician Dr. Robert Hutcheon, drawing upon the wisdom of his own experience as a physician, offered several helpful suggestions for health practitioners in his talk on "The Wounded Healer: Spiritual Self-Care for Harried Practitioners" [11]. In acknowledging that his suggestions are not all inclusive, he recommended that practitioners:

- Acknowledge their problems of woundedness to self, God and others, as well as the need for God's help;
- Find the courage to seek help;
- Learn to apologize and ask for forgiveness, especially to patients;
- Become part of a team;
- Change their medical practice if need be;
- Become part of a self help group or establish one;
- Seek out a mentor or supervisor in order to get a "reality check" as a human person;
- Cultivate a healthy and realistic spiritual life, one that fits into the demands of life, and learn to cherish solitude;
- Balance a well rounded life style with sufficient "R & R" which includes physical activity; also learn to cherish friendships;
- Rediscover a sense of vocation and altruism in giving loving service; practice receiving as well as giving;
- Begin to meditate on our own mortality and attend to "unfinished business" [11].

Heeding Dr. Hutcheon's advice could have a definite impact upon the prevention of burnout for health practitioners and other caregivers.

Above all, caregivers need to review the ways they take care of themselves and ways they do not. Are they able to say no when they have reached a limit, when they are "tapped out"? Have they developed a sense of self-worth beyond the job which would enable them to weather the inevitable "bad day" at work? [10, p. 34]. Do they "define themselves in terms of who they are rather than what they do to earn a living"? Can they achieve satisfaction outside of work in recreational pursuits such as sports, hobbies, music, contact with nature? Finally, do caregivers who encounter a great deal of death related losses in their work know how to achieve healthy grieving?

Reviewing the components of the Healing Process Model© can be instrumental in bringing about constructive healthy grieving for the caregiver, thereby coping with the stress of grief and loss and circumventing the path to burnout.

Acknowledge the Effects of the Reality of the Loss

- validate feelings of pain and grief
- peer support for patient loss and personal loss
- console one another at time of loss
- inform superiors about nature of personal loss which could affect work
- being allowed to refuse difficult assignments

- speaking up for choice of assignment
- taking bereavement leave
- recognize healing value of tears

Telling the Story

- debrief and tell story of loss and grief
- review and discuss patient losses
- seek out a sympathetic listener who understands the grieving process
- join a support group
- tell story by writing in a journal

Explore History of Reproductive Loss

- examine the kind of grief work that they did or did not do
- identify any "unfinished business" related to the loss
- be sensitive and pro-actively supportive when making grief care assignments

Explore History of Other Losses and Stress Factors

- examine those factors which would impede caregiver role
- identify "currently" unresolved losses
- know one's limitations, when to ask for help, when to refer
- do not ignore caregiver's own needs

Interpret Grief Reactions as Normal

- recognize normal grief reactions in clients and in themselves
- assess thoughts, feelings, and behaviors using the body, mind, spirit connection format
- have realistic expectations of themselves
- acknowledge intuitive promptings
- reach out to others for help

Continue Relationship with the Deceased

- caregiver is a tangible link between parents and deceased baby
- each client/patient finds a place in the caregiver's memory bank

Honor the Ultimate Questions About Life, Death, and Spirituality

- address their own issues related to existential anxiety
- have a sense of their own mortality or personal death awareness
- be spiritually grounded
- examine and explore their own spirituality
- reflect upon their relationship to the Cosmos, Creator, God
- develop a personal philosophy of care

- develop a set of values, attitudes, and beliefs about the meaning of life, death, and suffering

Examine the Meaning of "Guilt Work" within "Grief Work"

- realize they cannot fix everything
- accept and affirm that there are ways one cannot help
- setting realistic expectations can ward off guilt
- reality test guilt
- resolve guilt through the "seeking and granting of forgiveness"

Awareness of Anger and Need for Forgiveness

- realize that "grief and anger are partners"
- flexibility in caregiving is key to preventing frustration and burnout
- strive for authentic caregiving by responding to the person's uniqueness and situation
- take cues from patients/clients
- realize their need to forgive themselves for their failures or mistakes (real or imagined)
- forgive their co-workers and colleagues for their lack of support at critical times
- ask others to forgive them for their own mistakes, indifference, and lack of support
- dispel anger through letter writing

Facilitate Closure

- let go of pain of grief
- cherish the memory of those who had been in their care
- let go of any remnant of guilt and anger associated with loss and grief
- be grateful for the privilege of helping at such a crucial time
- be thankful for what the bereaved have to teach us about grieving and healing
- learn to "clean yourself up" emotionally
- do not ignore need for closure
- debrief losses on a regular basis
- attend funeral/commemorative services
- make follow-up telephone calls and send cards or letters to bereaved
- achieve a sense of peace

Care for Self in Body, Mind, and Sprit

- be attentive to physical, emotional, and spiritual needs
- do not neglect their own well-being
- learn about ways caregivers can care for themselves
- exercise some form of "selfishness" in demonstrating their love and respect for themselves

- protect their time and energy from toxic people, situations or non-fulfilling activities
- seek activities which restore, renew and replenish their body, mind and spirit

Assessment for Burnout Prevention

- facilitate caregiver preparation in order to enhance their ability to identify stress factors and to prevent burnout while caring for others
- identify what is stressful for that particular caregiver
- identify personal and environmental stress factors
- acknowledge to themselves and to others that they may be vulnerable to stress and be allowed to do so without fear of reprisals or being judged unfavorably as being weak
- appreciate the fact that the well being of the caregiver is linked to the one receiving care
- develop an awareness of those signs and signals which indicate when caregivers are stressed
- tease out factors which give rise to normal grief reactions from those factors which produce stress
- be aware that stress and grief manifestations share common ground since grief, loss, and bereavement are stressful experiences
- have realistic caregiving expectations
- plan strategies to cope with stress
- create a supportive working environment
- review ways caregivers take care of themselves and ways they do not
- know how to achieve healthy grieving
- review the components of the Healing Process Model©

CONCLUSION

Jeffrey A. Kottler, author of *The Compleat Therapist,* believes that both reason and intuition are essential components in successful therapeutic encounters:

> Reason and intuition are complementary in the effective therapist's mind. They feed off one another. They validate the truth of what the other infers. One encourages and supports the expansiveness of the narrow belief of the other. And when applied together, they provide the high degree of flexibility that is so important to therapeutic work [12, p. 127].

Anyone who uses the Healing Process Model© as a guide to grieving reproductive loss must remember that the key to its effectiveness lies in its flexibility in being able to take cues from the bereaved, to utilize the holistic approach of the body, mind, spirit connection and to apply both "head knowledge" (reason) and "heart knowledge" (intuition) together in the grief work of bringing comfort to those who mourn.

REFERENCES

1. R. M. Rilke, *Letters to a Young Poet* (Rev. Edition), M. D. Herter Norton (trans.), W. W. Norton & Company, Inc., New York, 1954.
2. B. Siegel, *Peace, Love & Healing,* Harper, New York, 1989.
3. H. Deutsch, *The Psychology of Women: A Psychoanalytic Interpretation* (Vol. 2), *Motherhood,* Grune & Stratton, 1945.
4. J. W. Worden, *Grief Counseling & Grief Therapy,* Springer, New York, 1991.
5. P. Poetsch, Care of the Health Providers, *Health Provider's Manual for Helping After Perinatal Death,* H.A.N.D. of Santa Clara County, Los Gatos, California, 1987.
6. G. E. Vogel, *A Caregiver's Handbook to Perinatal Loss,* de Ruyter-Nelson, Saint Paul, Minnesota, 1996.
7. A. Todd (ed.), *Journey of the Heart: Stories of Grief As Told by Nurses in the NICU,* Vanderbilt University Medical Center, Nashville, Tennessee, 1995.
8. C. M. Parkes, The Caregiver's Griefs, *Journal of Palliative Care, 1*:2, pp. 5-7, 1986.
9. J. E. Miller, *The Grit & Grace of Being a Caregiver; Maintaining Balance as You Care for Others,* video, Willowgreen Productions, Fort Wayne, Indiana, 1993.
10. J. A. Simone, The Intensity of Newborn Intensive Care: Caring for the Caregivers, *Neonatal Network,* pp. 27-35, April 1984.
11. R. Hutcheon, *The Wounded Healer: Spiritual Self-Care for Harried Practitioners,* paper presented at the Isaiah 40 Foundation Conference on "Christian Clinical Practice in Medicine and Psychotherapy: Healing the Whole Person," Montreal, December 2000.
12. J. A. Kottler, *The Compleat Therapist,* Jossey-Bass, San Francisco & Oxford, 1991.

Appendices

List of Grief Symptoms

Symptom   **Description**

Affective

Depression   Feelings of sadness, mournfulness, and dysphoria, accompanied by intense subjective distress and "mental pain." Episodes (waves) of depression may be severe and are sometimes (but not always) precipitated by external events (locale, receiving sympathy, reminders of shared activities, anniversaries, meetings, etc.). Feelings of despair, lamentation, sorrow, and dejection predominate.

Anxiety   Fears, dreads, and forebodings such as fear of breaking down, of losing one's mind or going mad, of dying, fear of being unable to cope without spouse, separation anxiety, fear about living alone, financial worries, and worries about other matters previously dealt with by spouse.

Guilt   Self-blame and self-accusation about events in the past, notably about events leading up to death (feeling that more could have been done to prevent death). Guilt feelings about behavior toward partner (should have treated differently, made different decisions).

Anger and   Irritability toward family, in child rearing, with friends (feeling they
hostility   lacked understanding for and appreciation of the deceased, and about the bereaved's grief). Anger about fate, that death has occurred, anger toward the deceased spouse (e.g., about being left alone, not provided for), toward the doctors, nurses of spouse.

APPENDIX A (Cont'd.)

Symptom	Description
Anhedonia	Loss of enjoyment of food, hobbies, social and family events, and other activities which had previously been pleasurable even if the spouse was not actually present. Feeling that nothing can be pleasurable without spouse.
Loneliness	Feeling alone even in the presence of others, and periodic bouts of intense loneliness, notably at the times when spouse would have been present (evenings, weekends), and during special events that they would have shared.

Behavioral manifestations

Agitation	Tenseness, restlessness (atypical), jitteryness, over-activity often without completing tasks (doing things for the sake of the activity), searching behavior (looking for spouse, even though they "know" this is useless).
Fatigue	Reduction in general activity level (sometimes interrupted by bouts of agitation mentioned above); retardation of speech and thought (slowed speech, long latencies); general lassitude.
Crying	Tears and/or watery eyes, general expression one of sadness (drooping of sides of mouth, sad gaze).

Attitudes toward self, the deceased, and environment

Self-reproach	See A: Guilt.
Low self-esteem	Feelings of inadequacy, failure, and incompetence on one's own, without spouse; worthlessness.
Helplessness, hopelessness	Pessimism about present circumstances and future, loss of purpose in life, thoughts of death and suicide (desire not to go on living without spouse).

APPENDIX A (Cont'd.)

Symptom	Description

Sense of unreality — Feeling of "not being there," of "watching from outside," that events in the present are happening to someone else.

Suspiciousness — Doubting the motives of those who offer help or advice.

Interpersonal problems — Difficulty in maintaining social relationships, rejection of friendship, withdrawal from social functions.

Attitudes toward the deceased — *Yearning* for deceased, waves of longing, calling out for him/her, intense pining.

Imitation of deceased's behavior (e.g., manner of speaking, walking), following deceased's interests, pursuits.

Idealization of deceased: the tendency to ignore any faults, exaggerate positive characteristics of spouse.

Ambivalence: alternation of feeling about deceased.

Images of deceased, often very vivid, almost hallucinatory; firm conviction of having seen/heard spouse.

Preoccupation with the memory of the deceased (both with sad and happy memories) and need to talk, sometimes incessantly, about deceased, to the exclusion of interest in any other topic.

Cognitive impairment

Retardation of thought and concentration — Slowed thinking and poor memory; see also B: Fatigue.

Physiological changes and bodily complaints

Loss of appetite — (Occasionally, overeating) accompanied by changes in body weight: sometimes, a considerable loss of weight.

Sleep disturbances — Mostly insomnia, occasionally oversleeping; disturbances of day/night rhythm.

Energy loss — See B: Fatigue.

APPENDIX A (Cont'd.)

Symptom	Description
Bodily complaints	These include headaches, neckache, back pain, muscle cramp, nausea, vomiting, lump in throat, sour taste in mouth, dry mouth, constipation, heartburn, indigestion, flatulence, blurred vision, pain on urination, tightness in throat, choking with shortness of breath, need for sighing, empty feeling in abdomen, lack of muscular power, palpitations, tremors, hair loss.
Physical complaints of deceased	Appearance of symptoms similar to those of the deceased, particularly of those symptoms of the terminal illness (e.g., heart fluttering if loss were from heart attack): the bereaved may be convinced of having the same illness that afflicted the deceased.
Changes in drug taking	Increase in the use of psychotropic medicines (tranquilizers, etc.), in alcohol intake, in smoking.
Susceptibility to illness and disease	Particularly infections (lowering of immunity), also those relating to lack of health care (cancer, tuberculosis, etc.), and stress-related diseases (e.g., heart conditions).

Reproduced from: Wolfgang Stroebe and Margaret S. Stroebe, *Bereavement and Health; The Psychological and Physical Consequences of Partner Loss,* Cambridge University Press, 1987, Chapter 2, "The Symptomatology of Grief," Table 2.1, pages 10-12. Reprinted with the permission of Cambridge University Press.

APPENDIX B

Elizabeth Ann, our child, has breathed her last,
   this long moment will not stay in the past.
For me, her proud Daddy, and my dear wife,
   this precious child has changed our life.
                (Jim Zoland, "A Child I Can No Longer Hold")

No footprint remains before or behind
Sand and salt have no memory
We have entrusted her name to the blind illiterate wind
She who was taken and given at the same moment.
                (Michael Dilts, "A Walk on the Beach")

Allison—you were so young
You gave us so much and your life had just begun.

You were with us ten days which wasn't enough
but you gave us a lifetime of strength,
just showing how you fought.
                (David Maxwell, "Allison Clare's Poem")

From "The Eloquence of Pain: Poetry of Bereaved Fathers Following a Perinatal Loss," by Michael Dilts in *Men Coping with Grief,* Dale A. Lund (ed.), Chapter 19, pp. 349-363, Baywood, Amityville, New York, 2001. With permission.

APPENDIX C
. Letter to Sandi

Dear Sandi,

Just recently I decided to let you be born. When I first knew that you were inside me I was delighted that you would be my baby and I would be able to be your mummy. When my body started to reject you I was worried and very frightened. It felt like a nightmare I had had earlier was coming true. I became afraid to love you because I was worried you would be taken away. I decided to pretend you weren't real and maybe you weren't inside me after all. I tried to but I couldn't because I wanted you so much. I saw a doctor to see if he could help me keep you and he told me you weren't real and gave me some pills to fix my empty body . . . but you were there like I had thought. I saw another doctor hoping that he would tell me you were alright and he said he hoped so but that night my pains started and you broke into pieces and came out of me instead of growing into the beautiful baby I knew you had been. I was devastated. As they made me ready for surgery I felt raped and split wide open and my doctor was cracking jokes to make me feel better but I didn't. I eventually "bought in" to the world trying to tell me not to hurt and I shouldn't have. I was in agony. My baby, my precious baby had been taken away from me and I needed to cry, and scream at the ignorant doctor, at God, at whoever would be there. I needed to feel my pain because it was real and *it was there,* just like you were. Instead I went on living believing you "fetal material" like they called you on my chart (at a level) but knowing you were my baby (in my heart). I wanted to cuddle you and hold you and sing to you and I never had that chance to do those things. I wanted to be your mummy and the doctor took you away. I'm sorry I trusted him sweetie and I'm sorry that I let them bury my pain so I couldn't let you live in my mind anymore. You deserve better. Now I remember you and cherish the time we spent. I love you Sandi and wish we could have had more, more time, more memories, more loving. I can't change that now though and I just pray to God that we will sometime. Remember that I love you and wish I could have shown you. Maybe sometime we will.

Love Mummy

*   *   *

This letter was written fourteen years after the miscarriage occurred. Sandi's mother gave permission to publish this letter so that others (especially health professionals) would become aware of the profound impact that miscarriage can have. This mother of three children presented for counseling of general life issues and not for the miscarriage, which was made known when I took her reproductive loss history. She had been "in therapy" 14 years ago for over a year in order to deal with the miscarriage. This therapy had focused primarily on forgetting the miscarriage and "talking about my childhood instead." When I asked her if she had named the baby, she suddenly burst into tears and uttered the name "Sandi." With this naming of her miscarried baby, she felt that a weight had been lifted and that she finally had been given permission to grieve. She reported that this healing experience of grieving her loss had a positive effect upon her life, her personality, her world view, and her subsequent career choice of wanting to help others who were grieving reproductive loss.

APPENDIX D
On Visiting the Grave of My Stillborn Little Girl
Sunday, July 4th, 1836

I made a vow within my soul, O child,
When thou wert laid beside my weary heart,
With marks of death on every tender part,
That, if in time a living infant smiled,
Winning my ear with gentle sounds of love
In sunshine of such joy, I still would save
A green rest for thy memory, O Dove!
And oft times visit thy small, nameless grave.
Thee have I not forgot, my firstborn, thou
Whose eyes ne'er opened to my wistful gaze,
Whose sufferings stamped with pain thy little brow;
I think of thee in these far happier days,
And thou, my child, from thy bright heaven see
How well I keep my faithful vow to thee.

Elizabeth Gaskell (1810-1865)

On an Infant Dying as Soon as Born

I saw where in the shroud did lurk
A curious frame of Nature's work;
A floweret crush'd in the bud,
A nameless piece of Babyhood,
Was in her cradle-coffin lying;
Extinct, with scarce the sense of dying:
So soon to exchange the imprisoning womb
For darker closets of the tomb!
She did but ope an eye, and put
A clear beam forth, then straight up shut
For the long dark: ne'er more to see
Through glasses of mortality.
    Riddle of destiny, who can show
What thy short visit meant, or know
What thy errand here below?
Shall we say that Nature blind
Check'd her hand, and changed her mind,
Just when she had exactly wrought
A finish'd pattern without fault?
Could she flag, or could she tire,
Or lack'd she the Promethean fire

(With her nine moon's long workings sicken'd)
That should thy little limbs have quicken'd?
Limbs so firm, they seem'd to assure
Life of health, and days mature:
Woman's self in miniature!
Limbs so fair, they might supply
(Themselves now but cold imagery)
The sculptor to make Beauty by.
Or did the stern-eyed Fate descry
That babe or mother, one must die;
So in mercy left the stock
And cut the branch; to save the shock
Of young years widow'd, and the pain
When single state comes back again
To the lone man who, reft of wife,
Thenceforward drags a maimèd life?
The economy of Heaven is dark,
And wisest clerks have miss'd the mark,
Why human buds, like this, should fall,
More brief than fly ephemeral
That has his day; while shrivell'd crones
Stiffen with age to stock and stones;
And crabbèd use the conscience sears
In sinners of a hundred years.
    Mother's prattle, mother's kiss,
Baby fond, thou ne'er wilt miss:
Rites, which custom does impose,
Silver bells, and baby clothes;
Coral redder than those lips
Which pale death did late eclipse;
Music framed for infants' glee,
Whistle never tuned for thee;
Though thou want'st not, thou shalt have them,
Loving hearts were they which gave them.
Let not one be missing; nurse,
See them laid upon the hearse
Of infant slain by doom perverse.
Why should kings and nobles have
Pictured trophies to their grave,
And we, churls, to thee deny
Thy pretty toys with thee to lie -
A more harmless vanity?

                Charles Lamb (1775-1834)

On My First Son

Farewell, thou child of my right hand, and joy;
My sin was too much hope of thee, loved boy:
Seven years thou wert lent to me, and I thee pay,
Exacted by thy fate, on the first day.
O, could I lose all father, now! For why
Will man lament the state he should envy?
To have so soon 'scaped world's, and flesh's rage,
And, if no other misery, yet age!
Rest in soft peace, and, ask'd, say here doth lie
BEN JONSON his best piece of Poetry:
For whose sake, henceforth, all his vows be such,
As what he loves may never like too much.

Ben Jonson (1573?-1637)

All poems from *The Poetry of Childhood,* S. Carr (ed.), B. T. Batsford, Ltd, reprinted with permission.

APPENDIX E
Resources

- A Place to Remember
  1885 University Ave. #110
  St. Paul, Minnesota 55104
  http://www.aplacetoremember.com

- The Baby's Breath Newsletter
  The Canadian Foundation for the Study of Infant Deaths
  586 Eglinton Avenue East
  Suite 308
  Toronto, Ontario M4P 1P2

- C.L.I.M.B.
  Center for Loss in Multiple Birth
  c/o Jean Kollantai
  P. O. Box 91377
  Anchorage, Alaska 99509 (U.S.A.)

- Centre for Reproductive Loss
  c/o Kathleen Gray, Director
  P. O. Box 282
  Station Côte St. Luc
  Montreal, Quebec H4V 2Y4
  Tel. (514) 486-6708; Fax (514) 486-7226

- IAAC-ACST
  The Infertility Awareness Association of Canada
  L'association canadienne de sensibilisation à l'infertilité inc.
  406 – One Nicholas Street
  Ottawa, Ontario K1N 7B7
  Tel. (613) 244-7222; Fax (613) 244-8908
  1-800-263-2929
  iaac@fox.mstn.ca
  www.iaac.ca

- The Nurturing Network
  Mary Cunningham Agee, Director
  P.O. Box 1489
  White Salmon, Washington 98672
  Tel. (509) 473-4026; Fax (509) 493-4027
  1-800-TNN-4MOM
  tnnc@nurturingnetwork.org
  www.nurturing network.org

- Pen Parents of Canada Newsletter
  52548 RPO Coquitlam Centre
  Coquitlam, BC V3B 7J4

- The Post-Abortion Review
  Elliot Institute
  P. O. Box 7348
  Springfield, Illinois 62791 (U.S.A.)

- HAND
  Helping After Neonatal Death
  Helping Hands Newsletter
  P.O. Box 341
  Los Gatos, California 95031-0341
  Tel. (408) 995-6102; (888) 908-HAND
  www.handonline.org

- Infertility Network
  160 Pickering St.
  Toronto, Ontario M4E 3J7
  Tel. (416) 691-3611; Fax (416) 690-8015
  E-mail: 102137.3465@compuserve.com
  Web site: www.infertilitynetwork.org

- Willowgreen
  10351 Dawson's Creek Blvd, Suite B
  Fort Wayne, Indiana 46825-9323
  Tel. (219) 490-2222; Fax (219) 497-9622

- AGAST, International
  Alliance of Grandparents, A Support in Tragedy
  353 East Verde Lane
  Phoenix, Arizona 85012
      Or
  P.O.Box 17281
  Phoenix, AZ 85011-0281
  Tel. (602) 604-8462; Fax (602) 604-8461
  Toll Free: 888/774-7437
  E-mail: GRANMASIDS@aol.com

- National Catholic Ministry to the Bereaved
  28700 Euclid Avenue
  Cleveland, Ohio 44092-2527
  Tel. (440) 943-3480; Fax (440) 943-3500
  NCMBereave@aol.com
  www.griefwork.org

- Rachel's Vineyard Ministries
  Weekend retreats for healing after abortion:
  Manual available
  National Hotline 1-877-HOPE4Me
  www.rachelsvineyard.org

- National Office of Post-Abortion Reconciliation and Healing
  3501 South Lake Drive
  P.O. Box 0-7477
  Milwaukee, Wisconsin 53207-0477
  1-800-5WECARE
  http://www.marquette.edu/rachel

- SHARE Pregnancy and Infant Loss Support Inc.
  National Office, St. Joseph Health Center
  300 Capitol Drive
  St. Charles, Missouri 63301-2893
  Tel. 1-800-821-6819

- Morning Light Ministry
  c/o St. Mary Star of the Sea Church
  11 Peter St. South
  Mississauga, Ontario, Canada L5H 2G1
  Tel. (905) 278-2058; Fax (905) 278-0961
  Internet: http://www.myna.com/~stmary/bereave.htm

- Abiding Hearts (for support to carry your baby to full term)
  P.O. Box 904
  Libby, Montana 59923 U.S.A.
  Fax: (406) 587-7197
  E-mail: hearts @ lclink.com
  Internet: abidinghearts.com

- Anencephaly Support Foundation
  30827 Sifton
  Spring, Texas 77386 U.S.A.
  Tel. (281) 290-8383
  Toll Free (In U.S. only): 1-888-206-7526
  Internet: http://www.asfhelp.com/asftoc.htm

- SOFT (for Trisomy 13, Trisomy 18 and other related conditions)
  c/o Barb Van Herreweghe
  2982 S. Union St.
  Rochester, N.Y. 14624
  Toll Free in Canada and U.S.: 1-800-716-7638
  E-mail: BARBSOFT@aqol.com
  Internet: http://www.trisomy.org

- National Potter Syndrome Support Group
  c/o Evy Wright
  225 Louisian
  Dyess AFB, Texas 79607
  Tel. (915) 692-0831
  E-mail: Potter_Syndrome@hotmail.com

- Cherubs (for Congenital Diaphragmatic Hernia)
  c/o Dawn Torrence
  P.O. Box 1150
  Creedmoor, North Carolina 27522 U.S.A.
  Internet: www.gloryroad.net/~cherubs
  E-mail: cherubs@gloryroad.net

- Canadian Down Syndrome Society
  811 – 14 Street N.W.
  Calgary, Alberta T2N 2A4
  Toll Free : 1-800-883-5608
  Tel. (403) 270-8500
  Fax (403) 270-8291
  E-mail: cdss@ican.net
  Web site: http://home.ican.net/~cdss

- The Spina Bifida and Hydrocephalus Association of Canada
  220-388 Donald Street
  Winnipeg, Manitoba R3B 2J4
  Toll Free: 1-800-565-9488
  Fax (204) 925-3654
  E-mail: spinab@mts.net

- Easter Seal Society
  1185 Eglinton Ave. East Suite 706
  Toronto, Ont. M3C 3C6
  Tel. (416) 421-8377
  Toll free: 1-800-668-6252
  Fax (416) 696-1035
  E-mail: infoaeasterseals.org
  Internet: http://www.easterseals.org

- Ontario Association for Infant Development (O.A.I.D.)
  c/o Peel Infant Development
  6660 Kennedy Rd., Suite 200
  Mississauga, Ontario, Canada L5T 2M9
  Tel. (905) 564-7485

- Centennial Infant and Child Centre
  (An Infant Development Programme for Children with Special Needs)
  1580 Yonge St.
  Toronto, Ontario M4T 1Z8
  Tel. (416) 935-0200
  Fax (416) 935-0300

- The Shrine of the Holy Innocents
  (In Memory of Children Who Have Died Unborn)
  128 W. 37th St.
  New York, N.Y. 10018
  Tel. (212) 279-5861 ext. 224
  Fax (212) 868-2501
  Email: shrine@innocents.com

- Centering Corporation
  1531 N. Saddle Creek Rd.
  Omaha, Nebraska 68104
  Tel. (402) 553-1200

- London Interfaith Counselling Centre
  442 William Street
  London, Ontario N6B 3E2
  Tel. (519) 434-0077

- ARENA (Adoption Resource Exchange of North America)
  67 Irving Place
  New York, N.Y. 10003
  Tel. (212) 254-7410

- National Adoption Information Clearinghouse
  5640 Nicholsen Place, Suite 300
  Rockville, Maryland 20852
  Tel. (301) 231-6512
  Fax (301) 984-8527
  E-mail: naicinfo@erols.com
  Web site: http://www.naicinfo.com

- Group B Strep Association
  P.O. Box 16515
  Chapel Hill, North Carolina 27516
  Web site: http://www.groupbstrep.org

- King's College Centre for Education about Death and Bereavement
  266 Epworth Avenue
  London, Ontario, Canada N6A 2M3
  Tel. (519) 433-3491 ext. 4374
  Fax (519) 432-0200
  E-mail: jmorgan@julian.uwo.ca
  Web site: http://www.wwdc.com.death

- The Natural Family Planning Association
  3050 Yonge St. Suite 205
  Toronto, Ontario M4N 2K4
  Tel. (416) 481-5465

- WOOMB (World Organization of Ovulation Method Billings)
  1506 Dansey Ave.
  Coquitlam, British Columbia V3K 3J1
  Tel. (604) 936-4472

- BOMA – U.S.A. (Billings Ovulation Method Association)
  316 North 7th Street
  St. Cloud, Minnesota 56303
  Tel. (320) 252-2100
  Fax (320) 252-2877
  Toll Free Tel. 1-888-637-6371
  E-mail: nfpstc@cloudnet.com

- SERENA Canada (Service for the Regulation of Natality)
  151 Holland Avenue
  Ottawa, Ontario K1Y 0Y2
  Tel. (613) 728-6536
  Fax (613) 724-1116
  E-mail: serena@on.aibn.com

- The Couple to Couple League (CCL)
  P.O. Box 111184
  Cincinnati, Ohio 45211
  Tel. 1-800-745-8252 or 513-471-2000
  Fax (513) 557-2449

- Hannah's Prayer Ministries
  Christian Support for Fertility Challenges
  P.O. Box 168
  Hanford, CA 93232-0168
  Voicemail/fax (775) 852-9202
  E-mail: hallahs@hannah.org
  Web site: www.Hannah.org

- Angels in Heaven Ministries
  Founders: Doug and Debbie Heydrick
  Web site: www.angelsinheaven.org

- Wintergreen Press
  3630 Eileen Street
  Maple Plain, Minnesota 55359
  Tel. and Fax (952) 476-1303

- The deVeber Institute for Bioethics and Social Research
  3089 Bathurst St., Suite 316
  Toronto, Ontario M6A 2A4
  E-mail: bioethics@deveber.org
  www:deveber.org

- Bereavement Services
  Gunderson Lutheran Medical Foundation
  1910 South Avenue
  LaCrosse, Wisconsin 54601
  E-mail: berservs@gundluth.org

- Marguerite Bourgeoys Family Centre
  Fertility Care™ Programme
  Coxwell Medical Building
  Suite 100, 688 Coxwell Avenue
  Toronto, Ontario M4C 3B7
  Tel. (416) 465-2868
  Fax (416) 465-3538
  E-mail: fertilitycare@sympatico.ca

- National Down Syndrome Congress
  7000 Peachtree Dunwoody Rd., Bldg. 5, Suite 100
  Atlanta, Georgia 30328
  Wed site: www.ndsccenter.org

- National Down Syndrome Society
  666 Broadway, 8th floor
  New York, New York 10012-2317
  Web site: www.ndss.org

- M.E.N.D.
  (Mommies Enduring Neonatal Death)
  P.O. Box 1007
  Coppell, Texas 75109
  972-459-2396
  Web site: www.mend.org

- Hannah's Prayer (help for women who have experienced pregnancy loss)
  P.O. Box 5016
  Auburn, California 95604-5016
  Web site: www.hannah.org

- Sarah's Sadness
  http://www.geocities.com/Heartland/Hills/6042/
  A Web site especially for Jewish women who have suffered a miscarriage, a stillbirth, or the death of a child younger than 30 days old, designed by a woman who has shared that experience; site includes a collection of prayers, prose and poems (can be used to create a ceremony or to add to the suggestions already given for one), a discussion board, a memorial area, links to religious, spiritual, medical, and emotional support groups (especially in the Montreal area), and information about healing aromatherapy and herbal treatments for grief and mourning.

APPENDIX F
Commentary on Reproductive Freedom

Deborah Rankin

One of the most pervasive myths of the post-feminist era is the belief that reproductive freedom has improved women's lives. Contraception and abortion ostensibly empower women to choose the timing and circumstances of pregnancy, even as society has discarded the outmoded notion of illegitimacy. Post-modern democracies pride themselves on being tolerant and inclusive and to all outward appearances, women are free to choose motherhood on their own terms. But the smiling facade of feminism masks the painful contradictions of women's real lives.

The advent of the birth-control pill ushered in sweeping social changes and allowed women, for the first time in history, to choose a life path other than automatic childbearing. However, the pill had an unforeseen down side. It jump started the sexual revolution and slammed the door on male commitment. The 1960s playboy staked out his claim to pregnancy-free sexual entitlement and left the newly emancipated woman wondering how to make him tie the knot.

The most contested social change affecting women's reproductive lives has been the legalization of abortion. Abortion supporters view access to abortion as a sine qua non of women's freedom and progress, whereas opponents view it as the epitome of moral decline. Yet despite decades of public sparring, there has rarely been any discussion about the impacts of abortion on women's lives.

Growing studies highlight the Pyrrhic victory of abortion rights. The World Conference on Breast Cancer cited abortion as a risk factor for breast cancer in its 1998 Global Action Report. Increasingly, studies link abortion to infertility and chronic reproductive health problems. In stress studies conducted by Dr. Georgia Witkin, a leading expert on gender-specific stress differences, women identified abortion as the third-highest-rated grief and loss stressor, outranking even death of a family member.

For years, social studies have documented the twin realities of male coercion in abortion decisions and father absenteeism. Legal, funded access to abortion has created a context of no legitimate right of refusal, according to U.S. sociologist James Davison Hunter. Women who resist male pressure to abort pay for their transgressions. When deadbeat dads are asked why they don't support their children, one of the most frequently cited reasons is that the mother of the child could have had an abortion. Unwilling fathers are not the only culprits. Young, poor, marginalized women are all too often pressured to abort by family members, employers, and the professionals who broker their existence.

Single mothers have become just about everybody's favourite punching bags. Conservatives accuse them of welfare abuse and insinuate blame for crime and juvenile delinquency, even as liberals castigate them for not using birth control. These criticisms are not entirely without merit. Studies do link single motherhood to poverty and the social pathologies that ensue from it. Contraceptive studies, such as the 1998 Canadian Contraceptive Study, show that nearly 40 per cent of all women are not using birth control or family planning, or use it inconsistently.

What is objectionable about these arguments is their blaming rhetoric. Critics fail to grasp the significance of the trend toward single female-headed households. Women rarely choose to go it alone. Their single-parent status is typically a reflection of male abandonment.

The fact that so many women are spurned by their male partners says something about the credulity of supposedly liberated women. Women are becoming pregnant in situations that are too casual to reasonably justify any expectation of male support.

Male exploitation is the flip side of female romanticization. Men are groomed from childhood onward to pursue the path of least resistance. The goof-off boy culture, followed by boozing and cruising in young adulthood, all conspire to inculcate in men an attitude of selfish irresponsibility.

The paradox is that when men assume the role of protector and provider, they aren't socially validated. In today's marketplace of ideas, there is zero tolerance for gender differences and no room for men to carve out a positive, proactive role for themselves.

The problem with the feminist critique is that it plays to male pathology by typecasting all men as villains. Years of disparaging marriage and hokey family values have taken their toll. The sad fact is that for too many men, the role of bad guy is the only one they know. In the end it all works out as self-fulfilling prophecy.

Marches and sloganeering will not end female misery. Women need to take a long hard look at the kind of life choices they are making and ask themselves where their best interests really lie. Anything less is incompatible with true equality.

Deborah Rankin is a longtime community activist in Montreal.

Reprinted from *The Gazette,* p. B-3, "Reproductive Freedom Hasn't Helped Women," April 1, 2002, Montreal, with permission.

APPENDIX G

- A twenty-one year old legal receptionist, Lorena Rivera, disappeared on her way to work in Oklahoma City in April 1997. More than a month later, her body was found in a shallow grave. Twenty-one weeks pregnant, this young mother of a three-year old son had been shot twice and beaten to death. According to police, her boyfriend, Nathaniel Dee Smith, murdered Rivera because she refused to get an abortion [*The Oklahoman*, 6/2/99].
- Women who resist the pressure of others to abort often face violent reprisals. It is not uncommon for attacks on reluctant women to take place at the door of an abortion clinic. An example, a man began to beat his girlfriend when she refused to enter the door of an abortion clinic [*Washington Times*, 8/18/97]. According to the sworn testimony of Richard Seron, a security guard wounded during an abortion clinic shooting in 1994, the greatest threat to women near abortion clinics is not from pro-life protestors, but rather from the men who are accompanying their wives or girlfriends to the clinic [*Boston Globe*, 4/16/99].
- When Sonya Hayes of Toledo, Ohio, refused to abort because of her religious convictions, her boyfriend, Terrance Davis, 27, allegedly shot her in the stomach, killing her and her unborn son. Prosecutors have said it was obvious that the gunman was aiming for the unborn child when he fired the gun [*Associated Press*, 2/8/00].
- Alfred Smith was convicted of second degree murder for killing his pregnant girlfriend, Deborah Moody, in 1997. He burned her car in an attempt to hide the body. Prosecutors said Smith killed Ms. Moody for refusing to have an abortion because of her religious beliefs [*Los Angeles Times*, 5/21/98].
- Thirty-eight year old Kevin Robinson was convicted of killing 15-year-old Daphne Sulk because she refused to get an abortion. The defense his lawyers put forth was that Robinson and the victim did not know each other well [*Village Voice*, 10/3/98].
- In Arkansas, four men have been charged with murder under the state's new Fetal Protection Act. They are accused of beating Shawana Pace, due to give birth, resulting in the death of her baby daughter. According to the police, one of the men, Eric Bullock, was the woman's boyfriend who hired the other men to attack her after she refused to have an abortion. Ms. Pace told the police that she pleaded for her baby's life as she was beaten. The men told her, "Your baby is dying tonight" [*Arkansas Democrat Gazette*, 11/9/99].
- Nicolas Griffin, a Florida law school graduate, was sentenced to five years probation and 250 hours of community service for trying to get his girlfriend to abort their daughter. Griffin had hired friends to blackmail his girlfriend by threatening to mail copies of a videotape the couple had made of themselves having sex to the woman's family, friends, and employer unless she had the abortion [*Miami Herald*, 2/7/99].

- A female inmate is suing the Hawaii state corrections system after a nurse injected the drug Depo-Provera into her abdomen when she was processed into prison, causing the death of her unborn child. The lawsuit alleges that the nurse knew of the pregnancy and that the inmate was told she would be put in solitary confinement if the intake process did not go smoothly [*Honolulu Star Bulletin,* 8/3/99].
- Shontrese Otrey won a $25,000 settlement from Emergency Shelters, Inc., Richmond, VA, after she was pressured by staff members to get an abortion. Ms. Otrey said she was told that the shelter did not provide services for pregnant homeless women. She stated that a staff member drove her to the bank to withdraw money for the abortion, then took her to the abortion clinic [*Richmond Times Dispatch,* 10/29/99].
- A federal judge in Florida has dismissed a lawsuit against an abortion clinic brought by a woman who says she was held down by staff members when she tried to leave in the middle of an abortion. The woman said she experienced severe pain during the abortion and made repeated requests to be taken to the emergency room. The lawsuit contended that actions by staff members at Aware Woman Center for Choice violated the Freedom of Access to Clinic Entrances (FACE) Act, but the judge disagreed and dismissed the case. He also ruled the woman could not pursue the case under an alias [*Associated Press,* 1/8/00].

Reprinted from "The Many Faces of Coercion," *The Post-Abortion Review,* 8:1, pp. 5-6, January-March 2000, with permission.

Bibliography

Allen, M., and Marks, S., *Miscarriage: Women Sharing from the Heart,* John Wiley & Sons, Inc., New York, 1993.

Anonymous, Who Counsels the Counselor?, *Journal of Nurse-Midwifery, 36*:3, p. 151, May/June 1991.

Attig, T., Relearning the World: On the Phenomenology of Grieving, *Journal of the British Society for Phenomenology, 21*:1, pp. 53-66, January 1990.

Bal, M., *Narratology: Introduction to the Theory of Narrative,* University of Toronto Press, Toronto, 1992.

Bartrop, R. W., Depressed Lymphocyte Function After Bereavement, *Lancet, 16,* pp. 834-836, 1977.

Basen, G., Eichler, M., and Lippman, A. (eds.), *Misconceptions: The Social Construction of Choice & the New Reproductive and Genetic Technologies,* Voyageur, Hull, Quebec, 1993.

Becvar, D. S., and Becvar, R. J., Storytelling and Family Therapy, *The American Journal of Family Therapy, 21*:2, pp. 145-160, 1993.

Belkin, L., Born Too Soon, *Redbook,* March 1993.

Benfield, D. G., Leib, S. A., and Vollman, J. H., Grief Response of Parents to Neonatal Death and Parent Participation in Deciding Care, *Pediatrics, 62*:2, pp. 171-177, 1978.

Bennet, G., *The Wound and the Doctor,* Secker and Warburg, London, 1987.

Best, E. K., Grief in Response to Perinatal Loss: An Argument for the Earliest Prenatal Attachment, *Dissertation Abstracts International, 42*:6, December 1981.

Billings, E., and Westmore, A., *The Billings Method: Controlling Fertility Without Drugs or Devices,* Random House, New York, 1980.

Bishop, A., and Scudder, J..R., Jr., *The Practical, Moral, and Personal Sense of Nursing: A Phenomenological Philosophy of Practice,* State University of New York Press, Albany, New York, 1990.

Blankfield, A., Grief and Alcohol, *American Journal of Drug and Alcohol Abuse, 9,* pp. 435-436, 1982-1983.

Bockelman, W., Stories to Tell, *Guideposts,* pp. 30-32, March 1994.

Bolman, L. G., and Deal, T. E., *Leading With Soul: An Uncommon Journey of Spirit,* Jossey-Bass, San Francisco, 1995.

Bolton, C., and Camp, D. J., Funeral Rituals and the Facilitation of Grief Work, *Omega, 17,* pp. 343-352, 1986-1987.

197

Borg, S., and Lasker, J., *When Pregnancy Fails*, Beacon Press, Boston, 1981.

Bornstein, P. E., and Clayton, P. J., The Anniversary Reaction, *Diseases of the Nervous System, 33*, pp. 470-472, 1972.

Bourne, S., and Lewis, E., Pregnancy After Stillbirth or Neonatal Death, *Lancet, 2*, pp. 31-33, 1984.

Bourne, S., and Lewis, E., Delayed Psychological Effects of Perinatal Deaths: The Next Pregnancy and the Next Generation, *British Medical Journal, 289*, pp. 147-148, 1984.

Bowlby, J., *Child Care and the Growth of Love*, Pelican Books, London, 1957.

Brodzinsky, D., Schechter, D., and Henig, R. M., *Being Adopted: The Lifelong Search for Self*, Doubleday, New York, 1992.

Brost, L., and Kenney, J. W., Pregnancy After Perinatal Loss: Parental Reactions and Nursing Interventions, *Journal of Obstetrical, Gynecologic and Neonatal Nursing, 21*:6, pp. 457-463, 1992.

Brown, M., *Nurses: The Human Touch*, Ballantine Books, New York, 1992.

Bruner, J. S., *Acts of Meaning*, Harvard University Press, Cambridge, Massachusetts, 1990.

Bryant, P. L. (ed.), *The Pen-Parents of Canada Newsletter*, P.O. Box 52548 RPO Coquitlam Centre, Coquitlam, BC, V3B 7J4.

Buckman, R., *How to Break Bad News: A Guide for Health Care Professionals*, University of Toronto Press, Toronto, 1992.

Burke, T., *Rachel's Vineyard, A Psychological and Spiritual Journey of Post Abortion Healing*, Alba House, New York, 1994.

Burke, T., and Reardon, D. C., *Forbidden Grief—The Hidden Pain of Abortion*, Acorn Books, Springfield, Illinois, 2002.

Cain, A. C., Erikson, M., and Fast, I., Children's Disturbed Reactions to their Mother's Miscarriage, *Psychosomatic Medicine, 24*, pp. 58-66, 1964.

Cain, A., Fast, I., and Erickson, M. Children's Disturbed Reactions to the Death of a Sibling, *American Journal of Orthopsychiatry, 34*:4, pp. 741-752, July 1964.

Caplan, S., and Lang, G., *Grief: The Courageous Journey* (a step-by-step process for surviving the death of a loved one), Cor Age Books, London, Ontario, 1993.

Carnahan, B., *A Gentle Touch: Massage Therapy for People in Painful Times*, Boulder County Hospice, Boulder, Colorado.

Carter, J. W., and Carter, M., *Sweet Grapes: How to Stop Being Infertile & Start Living Again*, Perspectives Press, Indianapolis, Indiana, 1989.

Cassell, E., *The Nature of Suffering*, Oxford University Press, New York, 1991.

Chez, R. A., Helping Patients and Doctors Cope with Perinatal Death, *Contemporary OB/GYN, 20*, pp. 98-102, August 1982.

Chez, R. A., and Flood, B., *Acute Grief and Mourning* (ACOG Self-Learning Package), ACOG, Washington, D.C., 1983.

Clayton, J., *Women in Mourning: Stories of Grieving Women*, Centering Corporation, Omaha, Nebraska, 1996.

Cochran, L., and Claspell, E., *The Meaning of Grief: A Dramaturgical Approach to Understanding Emotion*, Greenwood Press Inc., New York, 1987.

Cohen, M., *She Was Born, She Died: A Collection of Poetry Following the Death of an Infant*, Centering Corporation, Omaha, Nebraska, 1983.

Colborn, T., Dumanoski, D., and Myers, J. P., *Our Stolen Future: Are We Threatening Our Fertility, Intelligence, and Survival?—A Scientific Detective Story*, A Plume Book, Penguin Books, New York, 1996.

Colman, A., and Colman, L., *Earth Father, Sky Father: The Changing Concept of Fathering,* Prentice-Hall, Englewood Cliffs, 1981 (re bereavement counseling for men involved in abortion)

Colt, G. H., The Silent Partner, *Parenting,* pp. 100-103, February 1995.

Connelly, M., *Given In Love: Releasing a Child For Adoption,* Centering Corporation, Omaha, Nebraska, 1990.

Corney, R. J., and Horton, F. T., Pathological Grief Following Spontaneous Abortion, *American Journal of Psychiatry, 131,* pp. 825-827, 1974.

Coyle, C. T., *Men and Abortion: A Path to Healing,* Life Cycle Books Ltd., Toronto, 1999.

Davidson, G. W., *Understanding Death of the Wished-for Child,* OGR Service Corporation, Springfield, Illinois, 1979.

Davies, B., Family Responses to the Death of a Child: The Meaning of Memories, *Journal of Palliative Care, 3,* pp. 9-15, 1987.

Davis, D. L., *Empty Cradle, Broken Heart: Surviving the Death of Your Baby,* Fulcrum, Golden, Colorado, 1991.

Davis, P. (ed.), *When the Bough Breaks II* (2nd Edition), The San Diego Guild for Infant Survival Inc., Poway, California, 1994.

Dean, A. E., *Letters to My Birthmother: An Adoptee's Diary of Her Search for Her Identity,* Pharos Books, New York, 1991.

Deits, B., *Life After Loss: A Personal Guide Dealing with Death, Divorce, Job Change & Relocation,* Fisher Books, Tucson, Arizona, 1992.

Dewey, D., When a Congregation Cares: Organizing Ministry to the Bereaved, *Death Education, 12,* pp. 123-135, 1988.

Diagnostic and Statistical Manual of Mental Disorders (2nd Edition, Revised), American Psychiatric Association, Washington, D.C., 1968.

Diemler, R., *Starting or Expanding a Post-Abortion Outreach,* H.E.A.R.T., Inc., Cincinnati, Ohio, 1998.

Dilts, M., The Eloquence of Pain: Poetry of Bereaved Fathers Following a Perinatal Loss, in *Men Coping With Grief,* D. A. Lund (ed.), Baywood, Amityville, New York, pp. 349-363, 2001.

Doerr, H., *Stones for Ibarra,* Penguin Books, New York, 1978.

Doka, K. J., *Disenfranchised Grief,* Lexington, Toronto, 1989.

Doka, K. J., *Death and Spirituality,* Baywood, Amityville, New York, 1993.

Downey, V., Bengiamin, M., Heuer, L., and Juhl, N., Dying Babies and Associated Stress in NICU Nurses, *Neonatal Network, 14*:1, pp. 41-46, February 1995.

Eastham, K., Dealing With Bereavement in Critical Care, *Intensive Care Nursing, 6,* pp. 185-191, 1990.

Elder, S., *Pathways Through Grief: A Tool for Healing and Growth,* Conference at King's College, London, Ontario, Canada, May 1996.

Eneroth, C. V., *"If There's Anything I Can Do . . ." A Practical Guide for Helping Others Cope with Grief,* Classic, Spokane, Washington, 1988.

Engel, F., *Taming the Beast: Getting Violence Out of the Workplace,* Ashwell, Montreal, 1998.

Erikson, E., *Childhood and Society* (2nd Edition), W. W. Norton & Company, New York, 1963.

Erling, J., and Martinez, S. (eds.), *Our Baby Died. Why?: Journal and Workbook for Children* (Rev. Edition), de Ruyter-Nelson, Saint Paul, Minnesota, 1994.

Estok, P., and Lehman, A., Perinatal Death: Grief Support for Families, *Birth* *10*:1, pp. 17-25, 1983.

Fabricant, S., Linn, M., and Linn, D., *Healing Relationships: With Miscarried, Aborted and Stillborn Babies,* Sheed & Ward, Kansas City, Missouri, 1985.

Fallaci, O., *Letter to a Child Never Born,* Simon & Schuster, New York, 1975.

Feely, N., and Gottlieb, L. N., Parents' Coping and Communication Following Their Infant's Death, *Omega, 19,* pp. 51-67, 1988-1989.

Feifel, H., *New Meanings of Death,* McGraw-Hill, New York, 1977.

Ferguson, D., *Little Footprints: A Special Baby's Memory Book,* Centering Corporation, Omaha, Nebraska, 1989.

Finkle, D., Marilyn in the Rockies, *Saturday Night,* pp. 25-29, June 3, 2000.

Frey, W. H., Not-So-Idle-Tears, *Psychology Today, 13,* pp. 91-92, 1980.

Friedman, M., *Family Nursing, Theory and Assessment,* Appleton Century Crofts, New York, 1981.

Fritsch, J., with Ilse, S., *The Anguish of Loss: Visual Expressions of Grief and Sorrow,* Wintergreen Press, Maple Plain, Minnesota, 1992.

Garland, K. R., Unresolved Grief, *Neonatal Network, 5,* pp. 29-37, 1986.

Garner, C. H., and Patton, Jr., G. W., *Devenir parents,* version française, Serono Canada Inc., Toronto.

Garner, C. H., and Patton, Jr., G. W., *Pathways to Parenthood,* Serono Canada Inc., Toronto.

Gilbert, R. B., *Heartpeace: Healing Help for Grieving Folks,* Abbey Press, St. Meinrad, Indiana, 1996.

Golden, T. R., and Miller, J. E., *When a Man Faces Grief, 12 Practical Ideas to Help You Heal from Loss,* Willowgreen Publishing, Fort Wayne, Indiana, 1998.

Gore, P., From the Other Side of the Atlantic Part 1: The Social Evolution of the Foetus, *The Dodge Magazine, 3*:97, pp. 9, 22, 23, 1997.

Greer, B., Dear NICU . . . , *Neonatal Network, 14*:1, pp. 69-70, February 1995.

Grief Related to Perinatal Death, *ACOG Technical Bulletin,* Number 86, pp. 1-4, April 1985.

Gryte, M., *Inner Healing After Abortion,* Centering Corporation, Omaha, Nebraska, 1995.

Gunderson, J. M., and Harris, D. E., *Quietus: A Story of a Stillbirth,* Centering Corporation, Omaha, Nebraska, 1990.

Haasl, B., and Marnocha, J., *Bereavement Support Group Program for Children—Leader Manual,* Accelerated Development Inc., Muncie, Indiana, 1990.

Hafner, R. J., and Roder, M. J., Agoraphobia and Parental Bereavement, *Australian and New England Journal of Psychiatry, 21,* pp. 340-344, 1987.

Hager, L. Pregnancy After Miscarriage, *Parenting,* pp. 97-103, February 1995.

Hardgrove, C., and Warrick, L. H., How Shall We Tell the Children? *American Journal of Nursing, 74*:3, pp. 448-450, 1974.

Hase, S., The Stress of Grief, *New Zealand Nursing Journal, 82*:5, pp. 21-22, June 1989.

Hauerwas, S., *Naming the Silences: God, Medicine, and the Problem of Suffering,* William B. Eermans, Grand Rapids, Michigan, 1990.

Health Provider's Manual for Helping After Perinatal Death: A Resource Network for Information on Perinatal Loss, H.A.N.D. of Santa Clara County, California, Los Gatos, California, 1987.

Helmrath, T. A., and Steinitz, G. M., Parental Grieving and the Failure of Social Support, *Journal of Family Practice, 6,* pp. 785-790, 1978.

Hewlett, S. A., *Creating a Life: Professional Women and the Quest for Children,* Talk Miramax Books, New York, 2002.

Hickman, M. W., *Last Week My Brother Anthony Died,* Abingdon Press, Nashville, Tennessee, 1984.

Hilgers, T. W., *Creighton Model Fertility Care™ System and NaPro Technology®: A Contemporary Approach to Women's Health Care,* Pope Paul VI Institute Education Department, Omaha, Nebraska, 2001.

Hodge, D. S., and Graham, P. L., Supporting Bereaved Parents: A Program for the NICU, *Neonatal Network, 4*:3, December 1985.

Hodge, D. S., and Graham, P. L., A Hospital-Based NICU Bereavement Program, *Journal of Perinatology, 3,* pp. 11-18, 1989.

Horowitz, M. H., Adolescent Mourning Reactions to Infant and Fetal Loss, *Social Casework,* pp. 551-559, 1978.

Ilse, S., *Single Parent Grief,* de Ruyter-Nelson, Saint Paul, Minnesota, 1994.

Ilse, S., *Unsupported Losses: Ectopic Pregnancy, Molar Pregnancy, and Blighted Ovum,* de Ruyter-Nelson, Saint Paul, Minnesota, 1994.

Ilse, S., *Coping with Holidays and Celebrations: After Miscarriage, Stillbirth, SIDS, Infant Death or the Death of an Older Child,* A Place to Remember, Saint Paul, Minnesota, 1995.

Ilse, S., *Giving Care Taking Care,* Wintergreen Press, Maple Plain, Minnesota, 1996.

Ilse, S., and Burns, L. H., *Miscarriage: A Shattered Dream,* Wintergreen Press, Maple Plain, Minnesota, 1989.

Ilse, S., and Doerr, M. W., *Another Baby? Maybe . . . Thirty Questions on Pregnancy After Loss,* Wintergreen Press, Maple Plain, Minnesota, 1996.

Ilse, S., and Leininger, L., *Grieving Grandparents,* Wintergreen Press, Inc., Maple Plain, Minnesota, 1985.

James, J., and Cherry, F., *The Grief Recovery Handbook,* Harper & Row, New York, 1988.

James, P. D., *The Children of Men—A Novel,* Alfred A. Knopf, New York, 1992.

Janoff-Bulman, R., *Shattered Assumptions: Towards a New Psychology of Trauma,* Free Press, New York, 1992.

Janson, M. H., The Prescription to Grieve, *Hospice Journal, 1*:1, pp. 103-109, Spring 1985.

Johnson, J., Sexual Intimacy and Replacement Children After the Death of a Child, *Omega, 15,* pp. 109-118, 1984-1985.

Johnson, J., and Johnson, M., *Grief—What It Is and What You Can Do,* Centering Corporation, Omaha, Nebraska, 1995.

Johnson, J., Johnson, M., et al., *Miscarriage: A Book for Parents Experiencing Fetal Death,* Centering Corporation, Omaha, Nebraska, 1983.

Jones, D. R., Goldblatt, P. O., and Leon, D. A., Bereavement and Cancer, *British Medical Journal, 289,* pp. 461-464, 1984.

Kahn, D. L., and Steeves, R. J., Witnesses to Suffering: Nursing Knowledge, Voice, and Vision, *Nursing Outlook, 42,* pp. 260-264, 1994.

Kennell, J. H., Slyter, H., and Klaus, M. H., The Mourning Response of Parents to the Death of a Newborn Infant, *New England Journal of Medicine, 283*:7, pp. 344-349, 1970.

Kent, I., and Nicholls, W., Bereavement in Post-Abortive Women: A Clinical Report, *World Journal of Psychosynthesis, 13*:4, pp. 14-17, Autumn-Winter 1981. (Reprints available from Ian Kent M.D., 925 W. Georgia St., No. 1321, Vancouver, B.C. V6C 1R5.)

Kesselman, I., Grief & Loss Issues for Abortion, *Omega, 21*:3, pp. 241-247, 1990.

Kirkley-Best, E., and Kellner, K., The Forgotten Grief: A Review of the Psychology of Stillbirth, *American Journal of Orthopsychiatry, 52*, pp. 420-429, 1982.

Klass, D., *Parental Grief: Solace and Resolution,* Springer, New York, 1988.

Kluger-Bell, K., *Unspeakable Losses: Understanding the Experience of Pregnancy, Loss, Miscarriage and Abortion,* W. W. Norton & Co. Inc., New York, 1998.

Knapp, R. J., and Peppers, L. G., Doctor-Patient Relationships in Fetal/Infant Death Encounters, *Journal of Medical Education, 54*, pp. 775-780, October 1979.

Kohn, I., and Moffitt, P. L., *A Silent Sorrow,* Dell, New York, 1992.

Kohn, I., and Moffitt, P. L., *A Silent Sorrow—Pregnancy Loss: Guidance and Support for You and Your Family* (2nd Edition), Routledge, New York and London, 2000.

Kohner, N., and Henley, A., *When a Baby Dies,* Pandora Press, London, 1992.

Kolf, J. C., *How Can I Help?: Reaching Out to Someone Who is Grieving,* Baker Books, Grand Rapids, Michigan, 1989.

Krauthammer, C., Who's Sorry Now? *National Post,* May 12, 2000.

Kroen, W. C., *Helping Children Cope with the Loss of a Loved One: A Guide for Grownups,* Free Spirit, Minneapolis, Minnesota, 1996.

Kuebelbeck, J., and O'Connor, V., *Caregiver Therapy,* Abbey Press, St. Meinrad, Indiana, 1995.

Kuenning, D., *Helping People Through Grief: A Sensitive Guide to Help You Know How and When to Share Your Concern with People in Crisis and Pain,* Bethany House, Minneapolis, Minnesota, 1987.

Kuntz, B. B., I Didn't Think His Death Would Hit Me So Hard, *RN,* p. 30, February 1984.

Larson, D. G., *The Helper's Journey: Working With People Facing Grief, Loss, and Life-Threatening Illness,* Research Press, Champaign, Illinois, 1993.

Lattanzi, M., and Coiffelt, D., *Bereavement Care Manual,* Boulder County Hospice, Boulder, Colorado, 1979.

Lattanzi, M., and Hale, M. E., Giving Grief Words: Writing During Bereavement, *Omega, 15*, pp. 45-52, 1984-1985.

Laudenslager, M. L., The Psychobiology of Loss: Lessons from Human and Nonhuman Primates, *Journal of Social Issues, 44*, pp. 19-36, 1988.

Laudenslager, M. L., and Reite, M. L., Losses and Separations: Immunological Consequences and Health Implications, *Review of Personality and Social Psychology, 5*, pp. 285-312, 1984.

Laurensen, N. H., and Bouchez, C., *Getting Pregnant: What Couples Need to Know Right Now,* Fawcett Columbine, New York, 1991.

Leon, I., Short-Term Psychotherapy for Perinatal Loss, *Psychotherapy, 24*, pp. 186-195, 1987.

Leon, I. G., The Invisible Loss: The Impact of Perinatal Death on Siblings, *Journal of Psychosomatic Obstetrics and Gynaecology, 5*, pp. 1-14, 1986.

Leppart, P. C., and Pahlka, B. S., Grieving Characteristics After Spontaneous Abortion: A Management Approach, *Obstetrics Gynaecology, 64*, pp. 119-122, 1984.

Levang, L., and Ilse, S., *Remembering with Love: Messages of Hope for the First Year of Grieving and Beyond,* Fairview Press, Minneapolis, Minnesota, 1992, distributed by Wintergreen Press, Maple Plain, Minnesota.

Lewis, E., and Casement, P., The Inhibition of Mourning by Pregnancy: A Case Study, *Psychoanalytic Psychotherapy, 2,* pp. 45-52, 1986.

Linn, D., Linn, M., and Fabricant, S., *Healing the Greatest Hurt,* Paulist Press, Mahwah, New Jersey, 1985.

Linn, E., *I Know Just How You Feel . . .: Avoiding the Clichés of Grief,* The Publisher's Mark, Incline Village, Nevada, 1986.

Littlefield, C. H., and Rushton, J. P., When a Child Dies: The Sociobiology of Bereavement, *·Journal of Personality and Social Psychology, 51,* pp. 797-802, 1986.

Lothrop, H., *Help, Comfort & Hope after Losing Your Baby in Pregnancy or the First Year,* Fisher Books, Tucson, Arizona, 1997.

Lowman, J., Grief Intervention and Sudden Death Syndrome, *American Journal of Community Psychology, 7,* pp. 665-677, 1979.

Ludwig, D., Flintrop, T., Wolf, M., Pirkl, V., and Sundwall, D., *Heavenly Creations: Garment Patterns for Premature Infants that Will Be Lovingly Remembered,* Infants Remembered In Silence, Inc., Faribault, Minnesota, 1995.

Luebbermann, M., *Coping with Miscarriage: A Simple, Reassuring Guide to Emotional and Physical Healing,* Prima Publishing, Rocklin, California, 1995.

Lund, D.A. (ed.), *Men Coping With Grief,* Baywood, Amityville, New York, 2001.

Mahan, C. K. et al., Bibliotherapy: A Tool to Help Parents Mourn Their Infant's Death, *Health and Social Work, 8,* pp. 126-132, 1983.

Malacrida, C., *Mourning the Dreams (How Parents Create Meaning from Miscarriage, Stillbirth & Early Infant Death),* Qual Institute Press, Edmonton, Alberta, 1998.

Malacrida, C. A., Perinatal Death: Helping Parents Find Their Way, *Journal of Family Nursing, 3:2,* pp. 130-148, 1997.

Manning, M., *All Seasons Pass—Grieving a Miscarriage,* Sorin Books, Notre Dame, Indiana, 2000.

Martinez, S. E., *A Place to Remember: Memories of Our Baby,* de Ruyter-Nelson, Saint Paul, Minnesota, 1994.

Martinez, S. E., *Sacred Healing: A Metaphysical Approach to Prayer, Meditation and Dreams After the Death of a Baby,* de Ruyter-Nelson, Saint Paul, Minnesota, 1994.

Martinson, I. M., Davies, E. B., and McClowry, S. G., The Long-Term Effects of Sibling Death on Self-Concept, *Journal of Pediatric Nursing, 2,* pp. 227-235, 1987.

Massé, S., and Phillips, J., *Her Choice to Heal: Finding Spiritual and Emotional Peace After Abortion,* Ramah International, Colorado Springs, Colorado, 1998.

Matsakis, A., *I Can't Get Over It: A Handbook for Trauma Survivors* (2nd Edition), New Harbinger, Oakland, California, 1996.

McDonald-Grandin, M., *Will I Ever Be a Mother?* Celeste Books, Portland, Oregon, 1983.

McAll, K., and Wilson, W. P., Ritual Mourning for Unresolved Grief After Abortion, *Southern Medical Journal, 80,* pp. 817-821, 1987.

Melges, F. T., and Demaso, D. R., Grief-Resolution Therapy: Reliving, Revising and Revisiting, *American Journal of Psychotherapy, 34,* pp. 51-61, 1980.

Menning, B. E., Wenta, A. C., and Garner, C. H., *Aperçu sur l'infertilité,* Édition révisée, Serono Canada Inc., Toronto.

Menning, B. E., Wentz, A. C., and Garner, C. H., *Insights into Infertility* (Rev. Edition), Serono Canada Inc., Toronto, 1990.

Michaels, D. R., Too Much in Need of Support to Give Any? *American Journal of Nursing, 71*:10, pp. 1932-1935, 1971.

Michaels, N., *Helping Women Recover from Abortion,* Bethany House, Minneapolis, Minnesota, 1988.

Miles, M. S., Helping Adults Mourn the Death of a Child, *Issues in Comprehensive Pediatric Nursing, 8,* pp. 219-241, 1985.

Miller, J. E., *Helping the Bereaved Celebrate the Holidays: A Sourcebook for Planning Instructional and Remembrance Events,* Willowgreen, Fort Wayne, Indiana, 1992.

Miller, J. E., *How Will I Get Through the Holidays? (Thoughts for Those Whose Loved One Has Died),* Willowgreen, Fort Wayne, Indiana, 1992.

Miller, J. E., *A Pilgrimage Through Grief: Healing the Soul's Hurt After Loss,* Abbey Press, St. Meinrad, Indiana, 1995.

Miller, J. E., *The Caregiver's Book: Caring for Another, Caring for Yourself,* Augsburg Fortress, Minneapolis, Minnesota, 1996.

Miller, J. E., *The Rewarding Practice of Journal Writing,* Willowgreen, Fort Wayne, Indiana, 1998.

Miller, J. E., and Golden, T. R., *A Man You Know is Grieving, 12 Ideas for Helping Him Heal from Loss,* Willowgreen, Fort Wayne, Indiana, 1998.

Miller, R. J., and Hrycyniak, S. J., *Grief Quest—Men Coping with Loss,* Saint Mary's Press, Winona, Minnesota, 1996.

Mitford, J., *The American Way of Birth,* Dutton, New York, 1992.

Mogenson, G., *Greeting the Angels: An Imaginal View of the Mourning Process,* Baywood, Amityville, New York, 1992.

Morgan, J. H., and Goering, R., Caring for Parents Who Have Lost an Infant, *Journal of Religion and Health, 17,* pp. 290-298, 1978.

Moroe, B., and Williams, D., *Being a Friend to Someone Who Is Grieving . . . What You Can Do and Say,* Grief Encounters, Inc., Edina, Minnesota, 1996.

Moulder, C., *Miscarriage: Women's Experiences and Needs,* Pandora Press, London, 1990.

Mount, B. M., *Sightings: In the Valley of the Shadow,* Inter Varsity Press, Downers Grove, Illinois, 1983.

Mullen, K., Gold, R., Belcastro, P., and McDermott, R., *Connections for Health,* Wm. C. Brown, Dubuque, Iowa, 1986.

Mundy, L., *Grief Therapy for Men,* Abbey Press, St. Meinrad, Indiana, 1997.

Mundy, L., *Grief-Walking—Four Prayerful Steps to Healing After Loss,* Abbey Press, St. Meinrad, Indiana, 1998.

Murray, N. P., *Living Beyond Your Losses: The Healing Journey Through Grief,* Morehouse, Harrisburg, Pennsylvania, 1997.

Newman, L. R., and Willms, J., The Family Physician's Role Following a Neonatal Death, *Journal of Family Practice, 29,* pp. 521-525, 1989.

Nouwen, H. J. M., *With Open Hands,* Ave Maria Press, Notre Dame, Indiana, 1995.

Nykiel, C., *No One Told Me I Could Cry. A Teen's Guide to Hope & Healing after Abortion,* Young Family Press, Frankfort, Illinois, 1997.

O'Keeffe Lafser, C., *An Empty Cradle, A Full Heart,* Loyola Press, Chicago, 1998.

O'Toole, D., *Healing and Growing Through Grief*, Compassion Books, Burnsville, North Carolina, 1993.

Oakley, A., McPherson, A., and Roberts, H., *Miscarriage*, Penguin, New York, 1990. (Revised from 1984 Fontana edition)

Our Children Live Forever in Our Hearts: Memory and Comfort Book, The Children's Mercy Hospital, Kansas City, Missouri, 1992.

Panuthos, S. C., and Romeo, C., *Ended Beginnings: Healing Childbearing Losses*, Bergin & Garvey, South Haley, Massachusetts, 1984.

Parker, L., and O'Leary, J. M., Impact of Prior Loss Upon Subsequent Pregnancy: The Function of the Childbirth Class, *International Journal of Childbirth Educators, 4*:3, pp. 7-9, 1989.

Parrott, C., *Parents' Grief: Help and Understanding After the Death of a Baby*, Medic, Redmond, Washington, 1992.

Pasnau, R. O., Fawzy, F. L., and Fawzy, N., Role of the Physician in Bereavement, *Psychiatric Clinics of North America, 10*, pp. 109-120, 1987.

Paulley, J. W., Pathological Mourning: A Key Factor in the Psychopathogenesis of Autoimmune Disorders, *Psychotherapy and Psychosomatics, 40*, pp. 181-190, 1983.

Pennells, M., and Smith, S. C., *The Forgotten Mourners: Guidelines for Working with Bereaved Children*, Jessica Kingsley, London and Bristol, Pennsylvania, 1995.

Phipps, S., The Subsequent Pregnancy After Stillbirth: Anticipatory Parenthood in the Face of Uncertainty, *International Journal of Psychiatry in Medicine, 15*:3, pp. 243-263, 1985.

Poletti, R., and Dobbs, B., *Vivre son deuil et croître*, Éditions Jouvence, Genève, 1993.

Polkinghorne, D., *Narrative Knowing and the Human Sciences*, State University of New York Press, Albany, New York, 1988.

Pollock, G. J., The Mourning Liberation Process in Health and Disease, *Psychiatric Clinics of North America, 10*, pp. 345-354, 1987.

Pregnancy After a Loss, Abbott Northwestern Hospital, Minneapolis, Minnesota, 1991.

Radetsky, M., Sudden Intimacies, *Journal of the American Medical Association, 254*:10, p. 1361, September 1985.

Random House Dictionary of the English Language, J. Stein (ed.), Random House, Inc., New York, 1966.

Raphael, B., Grieving Over the Loss of a Baby, *Medical Journal of Australia, 17*, pp. 281-282, 1986.

Rawlings, M. K., *The Yearling*, Charles Scribner's Sons, New York, 1961.

Reclaiming the Future: Accepting Loss, Resolving Grief, in *Unsung Lullabies: A Parents' Guide to Healing After Childbearing Loss*, H.A.N.D. of Santa Clara County, Los Gatos, California, p. 24, 1992.

Recurrent Miscarriage: A Guide for Patients, The American Fertility Society, Birmingham, Alabama, 1991.

Régnier, R., *La perte d'un être cher*, Éditions Québecor, Montréal, 1993.

Régnier, R., and Saint-Pierre, L., *Surmonter l'épreuve du deuil*, Éditions Québecor, Montréal, 1995.

Reich, E. J., *Waiting: A Diary of Loss and Hope in Pregnancy*, Harrington Park Press, Binghamton, New York, 1992.

Ring-Cassidy, E., and Gentles, I., *Women's Health After Abortion: The Medical and Psychological Evidence*, The de Veber Institute for Bioethics and Social Research, Toronto, 2002.

Robinson, E., *Adoption and Loss: The Hidden Grief*, Clova, Christie's Beach, South Australia, 2000.

Rogers, M. P., and Reich, P., On the Health Consequences of Bereavement, *New England Journal of Medicine, 319*, pp. 510-512, 1988.

Rosenfeld, J., Bereavement and Grieving After Spontaneous Abortion, *American Family Physician, 43*:5, pp. 1679-1684, May 1991.

Rothschild, B., *The Body Remembers: The Psychophysiology of Trauma and Trauma Treatment*, W. W. Norton, New York, October 2000.

Ryan, R. S., *No Child in My Life*, Stillpoint, Walpole, New Hampshire, 1993.

Ryan, R. S., *L'insoutenable absence: Comment peut-on survivre à la mort de son enfant!*, Les Éditions de l'homme, Montréal, 1995.

Sabourin, G., *Le présent d'Escomelle*, Les productions Escomelle, Montréal, Québec, Canada, 1996.

Savage, J., *Mourning Unlived Lives*, Chiron, Illinois, 1989.

Saynor, J. K., *Genesis: A Personal Guide Through Grief*, W. L. Smith & Associates Limited, Ajax, Ontario, 1991.

Schiff, H. S., *The Bereaved Parent*, Crown, New York, 1977.

Schoeneck, T. S., *Hope for Bereaved: Understanding, Coping and Growing Through Grief*, Hope for Bereaved, Inc., Syracuse, New York, 1995.

Schreiner, R., Gresham, E., and Green, M., Physicians' Responsibility to Parents After the Death of an Infant, *American Journal of Diseases of Childhood, 133*, pp. 723-726, 1979.

Seasons of the Heart, London Interfaith Counselling Centre, London, Ontario, 1998.

Seibel, M., and Graves, W. L., The Psychological Implications of Spontaneous Abortion, *Journal of Reproductive Medicine, 25*:4, pp. 161-165, October 1980.

Seitz, P. M., and Warrick. L. H., Perinatal Death: The Grieving Mother, *American Journal of Nursing, 74*, pp. 2028-2033, 1974.

Semchyshyn, S., and Colman, C., *How to Prevent Miscarriage and Other Crises of Pregnancy: A Leading High-Risk Pregnancy Doctor's Prescription for Carrying Your Baby to Term*, Macmillan, New York, 1989.

Shneidman, E. S., *Deaths of Man*, Quadrangle, New York, 1973.

Shorr, M., and Speed, M. N., Delinquency as a Manifestation of the Mourning Process, *Psychiatric Quarterly, 37*, pp. 540-558, 1963.

Simos, B. G., Grief Therapy to Facilitate Health Restitution, *Social Casework*, pp. 337-342, 1977.

Simos, B. G., *A Time to Grieve*, Family Service Association, New York, 1979.

Skolnick, V., The Addictions as Pathological Mourning: An Attempt at Restitution of Early Losses, *American Journal of Psychotherapy, 33*, pp. 281-290, 1979.

Small, M., Engler, A. J., and Rushton, C. H., Saying Goodbye in the Intensive Care Unit: Helping Caregivers Grieve, *Pediatric Nursing, 17*:1, 1991.

Stack, J. M., Spontaneous Abortion and Grieving, *American Family Physician, 21*:5, pp. 99-102, 1980.

Stack, J. M., Grief Reactions and Depression in Family Practice: Differential Diagnosis and Treatment, *Journal of Family Practice, 14*, pp. 271-275, 1982.

Staudacher, C., *Men & Grief,* New Harbinger, Oakland, California, 1991.

Stevenson, R. G., Professional Burnout in Medicine and the Helping Professions, in *Loss, Grief, and Care,* A. H. Kutscher (ed.), *3*:1/2, pp. 33-38, 1988.

Stevenson, R. G., and Stevenson, E. P., *Teaching Students About Death,* The Charles Press, Philadelphia, Pennsylvania, 1996.

Stinson, K. M., Lasker, J. N., and Lohmann, J., Parents' Grief Following Pregnancy Loss: A Comparison of Mothers and Fathers, *Family Relations, 41*:2, pp. 218-223, 1992.

Stroebe, W., and Stroebe, M., *Bereavement and Health: The Psychological and Physical Consequences of Partner Loss,* Cambridge University Press, Cambridge, 1987.

Sunderland, R. H., *Helping Children Cope With Grief, A Teacher's Guide* (2nd Edition), Service Corporation International, 1995.

Tatelbaum, J., *The Courage to Grieve: Creative Living, Recovery, & Growth Through Grief,* Harper & Row, New York, 1980.

Taylor, P. B., and Gideon, M. D., Crisis Counseling Following the Death of a Baby, *Journal of Reproductive Medicine, 24*:5, pp. 208-211, 1980.

Taylor, R., *Exploring Creativity, Spirituality, Aliveness,* Third Age Outreach, St. Joseph's Health Centre, London, Ontario, Canada, 1999.

Theut, S. K., Moss, J., Zaslow, M. J., Rabinovich, B. A., Levin, L., and Bartko, J., Perinatal Loss and Maternal Attitudes Toward the Subsequent Child, *Infant Mental Health Journal, 13*:2, pp. 157-166, 1992.

Theut, S. K., Pederson, F. A., Zaslow, M. J., and Rabinovich, B. A., Pregnancy Subsequent to Perinatal Loss: Parental Anxiety and Depression, *Journal of the American Academy of Child and Adolescent Psychiatry, 27*:2, pp. 289-292, 1988.

Toedter, L., Lasker, J. N., and Alhadeff, J. M., The Perinatal Grief Scale: Development and Initial Validation, *American Journal of Orthopsychiatry, 58*:3, pp. 435-449, 1988.

Trouy, M. B., and Ward-Larson, C., Sibling Grief, *Neonatal Network, 5*:4, pp. 35-40, 1987.

Turco, R., The Treatment of Unresolved Grief Following Loss of an Infant, *Journal of Obstetrics and Gynecology, 141,* pp. 503-507, 1981.

Vachon, M. L. S., Unresolved Grief in Persons with Cancer Referred for Psychotherapy, *Psychiatric Clinics of North America, 10,* pp. 467-486, 1987.

Vander Meyden, C. D., *When Joy Withers Away,* de Ruyter-Nelson, Saint Paul, Minnesota, 1994.

Vedeka-Sherman, L., Coping With the Death of a Child: A Study Over Time, *American Journal of Orthopsychiatry, 52,* pp. 688-698, 1982.

Vogelsand, J., A Psychological and Faith Approach to Grief Counseling, *Journal of Pastoral Care, 37,* pp. 22-27, 1983.

Walton, C., *Twelve Faces of Grief—A Grief Recovery Handbook for Group or Personal Use,* Abbey Press, St. Meinrad, Indiana, 1998.

Ward, B., *Healing Grief, A Guide to Loss and Recovery,* Random House, London, England, 1993.

Watson, J., and Taylor, R. L. (eds.), *They Shall Not Hurt: Human Suffering and Human Caring,* Colorado Associated University Press, Boulder, Colorado, 1989.

Weinbach, R. W., Sudden Death and Secret Survivors: Helping Those Who Grieve Alone, *Social Work, 34,* pp. 57-60, 1989.

Weinfeld, I., *And They Say There Are No More Heroes: For All Caregivers Working in Intensive Care Nursing Situations and Facing Infant Death,* Centering Corporation, Omaha, Nebraska, 1987.

Wheat, R., *Miscarriage: A Man's Book,* Centering Corporation, Omaha, Nebraska, 1995.

Whispers from the Heart: A Collection of Poems and Thoughts Lovingly Written and Dedicated to All Our Babies, Circle of Compassion . . . SHARE Celebrates 20 Years, St. Louis, Missouri, October 10-12, 1997.

Williams, R., *Healing Your Grief* (Rev. Edition), Resurrection Press, Mineola, New York, 1995.

Wintz, J., *Making-Sense-Out-of-Suffering Therapy,* Abbey Press, St. Meinrad, Indiana, 1996.

Wolfelt, A. D., *A Child's View of Grief* (a guide for caring adults), Service Corporation International, 1990.

Wolff, J., Neilsen, P., and Schiller, P., The Emotional Reaction to a Stillbirth, *American Journal of Obstetrics and Gynecology, 101,* pp. 73-75, 1970.

Wong, M. M., *The National Directory of Bereavement Support Groups and Services,* ADM, Forest Hills, New York, 1996.

Zambri, B., *Morning Light: Miscarriage, Stillbirth and Early Infant Death from a Catholic Perspective,* Morning Light Ministry, Mississauga, Ontario, Canada, 1998.

Zeanah, C. H., Adaptation Following Perinatal Loss: A Critical Review, *Journal of the Academy of Child and Adolescent Psychiatry, 28,* pp. 467-480, 1989.

Zimmerman, M., et al., Past Loss as a Symptom Formation Factor in Depression, *Journal of Affective Disorders, 14,* pp. 235-237, 1988.

Zisook, S. (ed.), *Biopsychosocial Aspects of Grief and Bereavement,* American Psychiatric Association, Washington, D.C., 1987.

Index

Abiding Hearts, 187
Abortion
  breast cancer, 193
  casual attitude regarding, 113
  coercion, 124–128, 193, 195–196
  defining terms, 98
  on demand, 127
  elective, 112–115
  fathers of aborted babies, 115–118
  genetic reasons for, 113, 118–119
  information on, lack of, 128–129
  pain associated with, complicated,
    113–114
  preventive aspects, 123–129
  scheduling issues, 118
  sex education, 123
  statistics on, 123
  unresolved grief and multiple instances,
    115
  value system, violation of womens',
    128
  See also individual subject headings
"Abortion: An Issue to Grieve?," 48
Acknowledgment/accepting reality of the
  loss
  caregiver, caring for the, 159–160,
    170–171
  counseling, grief, 57
  Healing Process Model©, 37–39
  naming the deceased child, 42, 43, 45,
    117, 135
  tasks of mourning, 20–21
Active grieving, 68

Adoption, giving up a child for, 111–112
Adoption Resource Exchange of North
  America (ARENA), 189
Adrenocorticotropic hormone (ACTH),
  16
Affective symptoms of grief, 175–176
Agitation as a symptom of grief, 176
Alcohol use/abuse, 10, 22
Allergies, 13–14
Alliance of Grandparents, 186
"Allison Clare's Poem" (Maxwell), 179
Ambivalence during pregnancy, 78,
  85–86
American Academy of Pediatrics, 98, 123
American College of Obstetricians and
  Gynecologists, 98
American Journal of Psychiatry, 4
Amniocentesis, 44, 89–91
Anencephaly Support Foundation, 187
Angels in Heaven Ministries, 191
Angel statue memorial in Salt Lake City
  (UT), 28
Anger/hostility
  caregiver, caring for the, 165–166, 172
  counseling, grief, 62–63
  "Life After the Death of a Child,"
    47–48
  mothering instinct, 83–84
  overview, 175
  sudden death experiences, 93
  unexpressed, 78
  writing as a form of emotional
    catharsis/healing, 106